D1452070

# POLITICS AND CRISIS
# IN FOURTEENTH-CENTURY
# ENGLAND

# POLITICS AND CRISIS
# IN FOURTEENTH-CENTURY
# ENGLAND

Edited by
JOHN TAYLOR
and WENDY CHILDS

ALAN SUTTON

First published in the United Kingdom in 1990 by
Alan Sutton Publishing Limited, Brunswick Road, Gloucester

First published in the United States of America in 1990 by
Alan Sutton Publishing Inc., Wolfeboro falls, NH 03896-0848.

British Library Cataloguing in Publication Data

Childs, Wendy R.
    Politics and crisis in fourteenth-century England.
    1.   England, 1327–1377
    I. Title   II. Taylor, John
    942.03'7
    ISBN 0-86299-650-3

Library of Congress Cataloging in Publication Data applied for

*Jacket picture:* 'La traison et mort du Richard II, roy d'Angleterre' – Jean
Creton *(British Library)*

Typesetting and origination by
Alan Sutton Publishing Limited.
Printed in Great Britain

# Acknowledgement

The publication of this work has been assisted by a grant from the Twenty-Seven Foundation.

# Contents

# Abbreviations

Unless otherwise stated, the place of publication of cited works is London.

| | |
|---|---|
| BIHR | *Bulletin of the Institute of Historical Research* |
| BL | British Library, London |
| BRUC | A.B. Emden, *A Biographical Register of the University of Cambridge to 1500* (Cambridge, 1963) |
| BRUO | A.B. Emden, *A Biographical Register of the University of Oxford to 1540* (4 vols., Oxford, 1957–74) |
| CCR | *Calendar of Close Rolls* |
| CFR | *Calendar of Fine Rolls* |
| CPL | *Calendar of Papal Letters* |
| CPR | *Calendar of Patent Rolls* |
| DNB | *Dictionary of National Biography* |
| EcHR | *Economic History Review* |
| EETS | Early English Text Society |
| EHR | *English Historical Review* |
| HBC | *The Handbook of British Chronology*, ed. E.B. Fryde. D.E. Greenway, S. Porter, I. Roy (Royal Historical Society, 3rd ed. 1986) |
| PBA | *Proceedings of the British Academy* |
| PRO | Public Record Office |
| RC | Record Commission |
| Rot. Parl. | *Rotuli Parliamentorum* (7 vols., RC, 1783–1832) |
| RS | Rolls Series |
| SR | *Statutes of the Realm* (11 vols., RC, 1810–28) |
| TRHS | *Transactions of the Royal Historical Society* |
| VCH | *Victoria History of the Counties of England* |

# Introduction

The present volume has developed out of papers read to a conference of fourteenth century historians held at Leeds on 8 March, 1986. The volume comprises revised versions of papers which were delivered to that conference together with two or three additional items. It is hoped that this volume, which has been assisted by a grant towards publication from the Twenty Seven Foundation, gratefully acknowledged by the editors, may be seen as a useful fourteenth century addition to the collections of essays on the fifteenth century already published by Alan Sutton Ltd.

The theme of the present volume, *Politics and Crisis*, may seem a somewhat traditional approach to the history of fourteenth-century England. The medieval attempt to construct the secular state no longer engages the attention of modern historians to quite the same extent as once it did. Nonetheless, 'political history' continues to have some considerable relevance to an understanding of medieval history. In particular the manner in which medieval government was conducted, and the assumptions underlying the actions of kings and magnates remain one important element in the history of fourteenth-century England. Again, as these papers demonstrate, political history must be seen to include an economic, cultural, as well as a foreign dimension.

In endeavouring to understand the political character of fourteenth-century England we are obliged to strip away many of the assumptions of older historians. Unlike Stubbs we no longer see the England of the fourteenth century as a unified nation, conscious of its own identity, and capable of a common course of action. We no longer identify the Lancastrians with 'constitutional progress', first as a party, and then after 1399 as a dynasty. Even the more recent orthodoxies of Tout and Davies which saw the reign of Edward II as a struggle between king and magnates, the one seeking to govern through his household, and the others looking to the great offices of state, have, as Professor Prestwich indicates, been overthrown. Edward II's reign now appears as one in which 'there were probably as many "baronial policies" as barons', and where there were 'as many points of view as Ordainers'.

In writing of the political conflicts of the fourteenth century we can perhaps say what they were *not* about. They were *not* about political parties and political principles in any modern sense. The magnates with their retinues who constituted the power groupings of the time came together in temporary alliances, and possessed little, if anything, by way of a coherent political outlook. What the magnates desired primarily was to remove such hated royal favourites and servants, as Gaveston, the Despensers and Michael de la Pole. In the ensuing conflicts the failings of kings, as contemporaries perceived those failings, was one important element. The magnates were also concerned with matters of foreign policy, and at home with the distribution of royal patronage. In certain of the reigns, notably that of Richard II, we appear to have a struggle over patronage between the ins and outs, somewhat similar to the eighteenth-century scene as described by Namier. Above all, private interests dominated the political arena, and in any balanced view account must be taken of the fact that 'what really mattered in politics, it seems, were questions of private feud, rather than of public policy'.

Nigel Saul's important paper reinforces this point at the local level. Much of the conflict in the local community turned on private feuds. But the de-stabilizing effect of unrestrained self-help was kept in check by a complex network of cross-ties and a 'willingness to involve the apparatus of law'. What the gentry in this period were concerned with primarily was the preservation and extension of property rights, but they also needed stability to maintain the enjoyment of these. What was true of the gentry was true also of the magnates. They too were concerned with the preservation of property rights, while the rivalry of great families such as Lancaster and Pembroke determined much of the 'politics' of the time. As at the local level the gentry sought 'good lordship' to protect their property interests, so in the kingdom as a whole the great subjects sought effective lordship from the Crown.

However, the understanding of what was effective and good lordship from the Crown included not simply its protection of property rights (the need for which became acute in the last years of Edward II's reign when the Despensers held sway), but also perceptions of a just and acceptable form of government which might fairly be termed 'constitutional'. Government should not be arbitrary but should function through due processes established by precedents and by some specific concessions by the Crown. Particularly clear and important to contemporaries was the need for the king to take good counsel and advice and to ask for consent to certain actions. The interpretation of these terms changed with time, adapting to political and administrative developments, and also varied from person to person. It was quite possible, therefore, for opposition to a king to coalesce and disintegrate in a series of apparently inconsistent groups, determined partly by personal feuds and antipathies and partly by the lengths to which individuals would allow a king to go before becoming seriously concerned about the dangers of arbitrary government.

Many of the constitutional ideas and aspirations of the early fourteenth-century baronage are shown in the Ordinances of 1311, and Professor Prestwich provides the first full analysis of these for over fifty years. The text has indeed been 'the most neglected major constitutional document of the medieval period.' It was a document produced by the political crisis of Edward II's early years, in which his relationship with Gaveston played a great part, and contemporary writers emphasized the personal clauses in it; but its importance goes far beyond this. The emphasis placed by Tout and Conway Davies on its limitation of household government is now rejected, but it remains a document of constitutional interest. Professor Prestwich draws out two points in particular. First, the Ordinances contain an attempt to find solutions to many problems going well back into Edward I's reign. The major problems of general taxation and army recruitment without consent had been settled, but the matter of prise had not, nor had a number of other administrative and financial points which reformers now took the opportunity to deal with. Professor Prestwich demonstrates clearly that almost all clauses, even the personal ones, had their roots in the reign of Edward I. Secondly the method which the barons chose to provide for permanent reform is innovative in its emphasis on their consent in parliament, and perhaps even more in its specific list of matters on which the king was to seek consent, matters which until then had been clearly within the king's prerogative. The programme proved unworkable, because of the king's total unwillingness to accept such curbs, as well as his hatred of those of its supporters who had murdered Gaveston; nonetheless it strongly coloured politics until 1322 when it was revoked in the Statute of York. This rejection of the Ordinances, a reform programme carefully drawn up with the consensus of barons and prelates and viewed favourably by the Pope, undoubtedly helped to justify the accusation made against Edward at his deposition that he was incorrigible and without hope of amendment. Although his repeated reliance on favourites may have been the prime thought in the minds of those who framed the accusation, his repeated unwillingness over eleven years to maintain the Ordinances was a contributory element.

A number of clauses in the Ordinances refer to financial matters, to the Exchequer procedures, the customs revenue, and the king's Italian bankers. Financial problems were often the cause of discontent against medieval kings, and Edward II inherited a debt of £200,000 and unpopular financial practices from his father. However, in the last years of his reign it was not lack of money which was the problem, but his wealth. In the most astonishing transformation by any medieval king, in twenty years Edward II paid off all but £60,000 of the debt and had some £60,000 in cash in hand. His wealth was well known to his contemporaries, but not commended. This was largely due to the means of acquisition (especially the confiscations from the Contrariants, and the pressing of small debts) but may also reflect the fear of possible arbitrary rule of a king with no financial worries. Dr Childs' paper draws together the strands of recent work which has illuminated Edward's financial position, and examines particularly the importance of the customs revenue and the strength and characteristics of the trade from which it was drawn. Without this inheritance from his father Edward's wealth would have been far less. Through the customs revenue he had a large regular income which did not require consent, as did parliamentary subsidies, and which would have allowed him to come very close to 'living of his own'. Yet Edward squandered this advantage, pushing every possible source for cash, and so provoked another of the accusations against him that in his greed he had stripped his realm.

The constant conflicts of Edward's reign culminated in his deposition. The revocation of the Ordinances, and Edward's wealth, which are discussed in this volume, together with the crushing of all opposition after the battle of Boroughbridge allowed him from 1322 to enjoy peace without the overt clashes of earlier years. However, the peace was false, as the long-term distrust of the king and his favourites was exacerbated by the hatred and fear built up in these years. These led directly to the last political crisis of the reign and went far to reconcile most of England to Isabella's coup, although some men were uneasy at the deposition of a king. The English political classes had a good knowledge of their history and the final conflict of Edward's reign was a lesson never forgotten. An awareness of it runs through the reign of Richard II from the beginning. Clauses from the Ordinances were quoted in petitions in the very first parliament in 1377; chroniclers described Richard's opponents as mentioning Edward's deposition as early as 1386; Richard raised the matter in the questions to the judges, and in a royally sponsored petition in the parliament of 1391; he also kept the subject alive by his constant efforts to have Edward II canonized. Although, as Dr Barron argues, Richard's unpopularity was less than Edward's, the precedent and the lively awareness of Edward's deposition made it easier to contemplate taking the final step against him.

The middle years of the fourteenth century saw no political crisis comparable to those witnessed during the times of Edward II and Richard II. The reign of Edward III, which was the longest in English medieval history, constituted a period of relative political harmony at home. However, as Dr Helen Jewell demonstrates, these years were by no means devoid of crisis. The turbulence of the times is reflected in the different versions of Langland's great poem. Thus the A text of *Piers Plowman*, which was composed during the 1360s, reflects the effects of plague and subsequent economic legislation. What we find at this time are changes and shifts in economic status which threatened the traditional and conservative view of society held by Langland. Conditions such as the leasing of demesne lands, rising rents and wages, helped to prepare the ground for the rising of 1381. More particularly the decade of the 1370s, the decade of the B text, is notable for the declining political fortunes of Edward III. The lack of effective political leadership, and the influence of a corrupt camarilla at the court of the ageing king, find echoes in this version of the poem. The frustration felt with political government in the 1370s also found expression in one of the best known parliaments of the Middle Ages, namely the Good Parliament of 1376. For reasons which are explored in the article on this assembly the Good Parliament is the best documented parliament of medieval England. Not only do its sources illustrate the high level of contemporary reporting, but they reveal also something of the character of 'public opinion' at the time. Unfortunately as far as parliamentary reporting was concerned, the Good Parliament found few successors in the parliaments of the fifteenth century.

The long standing involvement with France was one major influence on the politics of the last quarter of the century. The parliament of 1376, for example, was held against the background of a deteriorating war with France. This was even more particularly the case with the Wonderful Parliament of 1386 which met under an actual threat of invasion from the French. Mr Sherborne looks specifically at the great invasion scare of this time. As he indicates, the preparations on both sides were considerable. The English had envisaged a possible combined operation by the French and the Scots, but in the event the Scottish forces never opened up an effective second front. Fears of an immediate attack from the north faded after Richard II led his expedition to Scotland in August 1385. The Scots concluded a one year truce with the English in June 1386. Despite this, preparations for the French invasion went ahead. As Dr Palmer has written, 'the invasion force of 1386 represented the most deadly threat to England throughout the entire Middle Ages'.[1] Nonetheless the plans for invasion were abandoned in November 1386. The reasons for this decision by the French have been much discussed. The decision may have been taken on account of adverse weather conditions, or it may have been due to opposition on the part of the individual commanders such as the Duke of Berry. The mounting cost of the expedition, however, may have been the deciding factor. The English response to the invasion threat, which included among other measures the strengthening of the coastal defences, and the levying of troops including the despatch to London of contingents of archers from various parts of the country, was the subject of outspoken criticism in the parliament which met on 1 October 1386. In this parliament the Commons judged that money ear-marked to be spent on protecting the seas, had not in fact been spent on that objective. This charge formed the basis of one important accusation against Michael de la Pole, the chancellor, whose impeachment forms the most dramatic episode in the Wonderful Parliament. As regards the substance of the charge, after a detailed examination of the Receipt and Issue Rolls, Mr Sherborne concludes that money designed for the war effort had gone not to protect the seas as had been promised, but had almost certainly been used in repayment of loans already advanced.

The influence of the French war on the domestic situation in England is also brought out in Dr Tuck's paper which deals with Richard's negotiations for peace with France extending from 1389 to 1394. Dr Tuck stresses the difficulties inherent in concluding a final peace with France, and the financial reasons which impelled Richard to seek such a policy. In these negotiations one crucial question was whether Richard should perform liege homage for the duchy as the French insisted, or perform simple homage only as the English initially argued. Although Richard was prepared to make substantial concessions in this area, the English parliament's refusal to accept the notion of liege homage was one important obstacle on which the negotiations finally foundered. In the course of the negotiations Richard was prepared also to abandon the traditional position that parts at least of the territory of Aquitaine should be held by the English king in full sovereignty. The French for their part advanced the proposition (not in itself novel) that Aquitaine should be separated from the English crown, and granted in perpetuity to the House of Lancaster. This proposal came to nothing, not least because of the hostility of the Gascons themselves. In the event the draft articles of 1393 were never embodied in a full treaty. Instead the two sides agreed to a twenty-eight years truce in 1396.

Financial considerations had inclined Richard to this peace policy. Although at the beginning of Richard's reign the English still held certain fortresses such as Calais, Cherbourg and Brest, the cost of maintaining these garrisons was proving to be prohibitive. In addition there was the cost of maintaining the defence of the north against the Scots. The 1380s was a decade notable for its lack of military victories, yet it has been calculated that during a part, at least, of these years more than half the king's revenue was spent on the defence of his garrisons in France and the north. In this connection Dr Tuck examines the sources of revenue available to augment the meagre amounts that the Commons granted the king, while at the same time considering the financial difficulties involved in persuading the magnates to involve their retinues in the king's wars.

Whatever judgement is passed on Richard's diplomacy during the negotiations with France the difficulties inherent in achieving a solution, which was satisfactory to all parties, were considerable. 'The problem of Aquitaine was perhaps insoluble'. The fact is, however, that the twenty-eight years truce which concluded the period of negotiations failed to strengthen Richard's position at home. If the truce was in the financial interests of the king, at the same time it was unpopular in England, and led to the suspicion that Richard intended to enlist the support of the French against his own subjects. The negotiations for the marriage of Richard and the daughter of the French king, which were concluded in March, 1396, increased that suspicion. On all fronts, therefore, Richard's negotiations with France helped to heighten the feeling of insecurity in England which led to the events of 1397-9.

Dr Caroline Barron's article takes us to the final crisis of Richard II's reign. Bolingbroke's return in 1399 was facilitated by the political background in Europe and, in particular, by the diplomatic support which he received from Louis, Duke of Orleans, brother of the French king. After the death of Gaunt an alliance of mutual friendship and defence was concluded between Bolingbroke and Louis in Paris on 17 June 1399. When Bolingbroke set out for England Louis was in control of the French government, and no obstacle appears to have been placed in the way of Bolingbroke's preparations.

In England the crisis of 1399 marked the culmination of a reign which had witnessed intense political conflict interspersed with periods of uneasy political truce. How we account for Richard's policies during his reign has long been the subject of debate. It is just possible that the king nurtured a theory of royal despotism which he endeavoured to put into effect during these final years. A debate on regality runs throughout the literature of the time. What appears more certain, however, is that during the 1390s tension remained high between the king and the nobility. All parties were concerned with building up their military forces and increasing their power in the localities. The crisis came with Richard's coup in 1397. The main episodes of the two final years (1397–9) are well enough known, but are difficult to interpret on account of the fact that much turns on the character and intentions of Richard.

As regards the events of the summer of 1399 Dr Barron suggests that Richard had by no means exhausted his reserves of support at that time. His problem was how to mobilize what support he had while he was absent in Ireland. In looking at the final weeks of the reign Dr Barron concludes that irresolution on the part of the king is one explanation for his downfall. She also questions some well known assumptions concerning Richard's deposition, namely that his government was generally un-popular, and that there was from the start wide spread enthusiasm for Bolingbroke's 'challenge' to the Crown. Although most of the chronicles of the Lancastrian revolution written after the deposition give a Lancas-trian version of events, and not surprisingly suggest that Richard's government was unpopular, more contemporary accounts such as the short *Kirkstall Chronicle* and the *Dieulacres Chronicle* do not entirely bear out the suggestion that Richard's government had lost all support even at that late hour. Regarding Richard's failure to hold the country, Dr Barron suggests that Richard's fatal error lay in his delay in Ireland, 'it was his absence, not his unpopularity, which led men to desert him.' The reasons for Richard's absence of some three weeks after Bolingbroke's landing are still not entirely clear. On 12 July Richard Penry, valet to William Bagot, one of Richard's infamous chamber knights, was despatched to Ireland, almost certainly with news of events in England, and it seems certain that Richard must have known about the invasion by 17 July at the latest. Nonetheless, Richard does not appear to have left Ireland until about a week later. This delay may have been due to administrative difficulties. More likely it was due to Richard's own procrastination. Either way, in military terms, the absence was crucial. As Richard had taken the cream of the military strength of Chester with him to Ireland it meant that, as Dr R.R. Davies has written, 'Bolingbroke was never forced to face the reliable corps of Richard's army on its home ground'.[2] In the case of London, Richard's absence was, as Dr Barron notes, especially important. In London, despite past differences, the mayor and aldermen remained loyal to Richard for some time. Here again it was Richard's absence and his failure to rally his forces on the spot which led ultimately to London's switch of support to Bolingbroke.

WRC
JT
University of Leeds

## Notes

1   J.J.N. Palmer, *England, France and Christendom 1379–99*, (1972) p.74.
2   R.R. Davies, 'Richard II and the Principality of Chester', *The Reign of Richard II. Essays in Honour of May McKisack* (1971), p.278.

1

# The Ordinances of 1311 and the Politics of the Early Fourteenth Century

Michael Prestwich
*University of Durham*

Interpretation of the reign of Edward II has been transformed in recent years. The old orthodoxies were centred on what was seen as a constitutional struggle, with the king seeking to govern through his household, and the barons looking to the great offices of state as an alternative method of ruling the country. Such views have largely been overturned. The 'Middle Party', for long seen as the most constructive force in early fourteenth-century politics, has been shown to have as much substance as the emperor's clothes. The names of Tout and Davies have been replaced in the modern historiography of the period by those of J.R. Maddicott and J.R.S. Phillips.[1]

Edward II's reign now appears as one in which 'there were probably as many "baronial policies" as barons', and where there were 'as many points of view as Ordainers'.[2] What really mattered in politics, it seems, were questions of private feud, rather than of public policy. In the complex negotiations that took place after the death of Piers Gaveston in 1312, the crucial elements included the feud between John Charlton and Gruffudd de la Pole in the Welsh Marches, and the rivalry between the Earls of Lancaster and Pembroke over possession of the manor of Thorpe Waterville. Maddicott argues convincingly that this dispute suggests that Lancaster 'wanted territorial gains as much as his overt political objective, the Ordinances'.[3] Another example of personal enmity which had major political consequences, is the younger Despenser's hostility to the Mortimers, which went back to the death of his grandfather at the battle of Evesham.[4] Lancaster's feud with Earl Warenne was complicated by the purely personal factors of their respective unsatisfactory marriages.[5] Such political groupings as there were during this period lacked real cohesion and had to be cemented by sanctions of different types. The Boulogne agreement of 1308 was to be enforced by means of threats of excommunication, while breach of later arrangements such as the indenture between

Badlesmere and Pembroke on the one side, and Roger Damory on the other, involved heavy financial penalties, in this case of £10,000.[6] This hardly suggests that men were acting according to deeply felt political convictions.

In many ways, this type of interpretation is a very old one, for the author of the contemporary *Vita Edwardi Secundi* pointed the way to it. He noted 'how often and abruptly great men change their sides . . . the love of magnates is as a game of dice, and the desires of the rich like feathers'. He suggested that Lancaster lost his reputation and name for constancy when he received a sum of money, allegedly from the Scots, abandoning his principles in return for financial gain.[7] Such explanations are very tempting, for it is often much easier to disentangle personal rivalries and base motives than it is to find satisfactory explanations in terms of broader political principles. It also becomes unnecessary to analyse in detail the one major attempt at reform in this period, the Ordinances of 1311. The author of the *Vita Edwardi Secundi* was the first of many historians who have clearly found the Ordinances tedious. He merely gave details of the clause requiring the exile of the king's favourite Piers Gaveston, and directed his readers elsewhere for the rest of the text.[8] Such treatment of a lengthy document is pardonable in a chronicler, but less so in the case of modern historians.

The text of the Ordinances of 1311 is surely the most neglected major constitutional document of the medieval period. There have been no centenary celebrations of 1311 as there have been of 1215, no books on the text, and surprisingly few articles. Perhaps Stubbs is to blame. He was clearly disappointed by the Ordinances, for 'the leaders of opposition were behind rather than before their time'. Their particular sin, in Stubbs' view, was a failure to allow for the participation of the Commons in parliament, and without that, 'no constitutional settlement could be permanent'.[9] It is easy to laugh at such anachronistic views, but the absence of obviously 'radical' or 'progressive' views in the programme put forward by the Ordainers probably does help to explain something of the neglect of the document. For Tout and Davies, however, the Ordinances were of central importance, for the document demonstrated the way in which the role of the household in royal government was attacked. Tout considered that the magnates were politically frustrated 'by reason of the organized household system, whose ministers alone possessed the ear of the king'.[10] For Davies, who analysed the Ordinances in some detail, the restraint under which the king was placed by the Ordainers meant that, if fully put into effect, 'he could no longer have played off the household against the administrative departments'.[11] A dissenting voice came from Wilkinson, who protested that 'there was nothing in the antecedents of the Ordinances of 1311 to suggest that the barons were hostile to the general position of the household officials in the administration of the king'.[12] Recent interpretations of the reign, which have discarded Tout's framework, have placed the Ordinances in a different perspective. Maddicott, for example, stressed the importance of opposition to prises, or seizures, of foodstuffs, and the clause demanding the resumption of grants made by the king after March 1310.[13] Harriss argued that as the crisis of 1310–11 proceeded, increasingly 'fiscal and administrative reform took second place to personal and political demands'.[14] These personal demands were for the expulsion of specific individuals, above all Piers Gaveston, from the realm.

There are many questions which need to be asked in reassessing the Ordinances of 1311. The extent to which the crisis resulted from long-term problems, going back to Edward I's reign, and how far they simply reflected discontent at Edward II's mismanagement of affairs is important. The nature of the solution to the difficulties of the day provided by the Ordinances needs to be examined, particularly in relation to the use made of parliaments. Study of individual clauses can reveal something of the origin of specific remedies to particular abuses, and there is some new evidence to be considered. Until recently, it was thought that no drafts or alternative versions of the Ordinances existed, but the recent discovery in the archives of Durham Cathedral Priory of what appears to be a draft version of the Ordinances provides some new evidence about the way in which the text developed.

To understand the Ordinances, it is necessary to look back to the 1290s. The burdens placed on the country by Edward I as a result of his wars in Wales, Scotland, Gascony and Flanders, in the form of direct and indirect taxation, as well as military recruitment and prises, caused widespread discontent. Major crisis erupted in 1297. The lay opposition was headed by the Earls of Hereford and Norfolk, the ecclesiastical by Archbishop Winchelsey. In the autumn of that year, a solution of sorts was cobbled together with the issue of the *Confirmatio Cartarum*, but criticism of the king was not stilled. The question of whether he would accept a revision of the boundaries of the Royal Forest became a test of Edward's good faith. It was a test he failed, to the extent that he was unable to mount a planned expedition to Scotland in 1299. In 1300 considerable concessions made in the *Articuli super Cartas* again failed to resolve matters completely, and in the next year Edward finally gave in over the question of the Forest, such was his desperate need for a grant of taxation. In 1305, however, he was able to obtain papal absolution from his promises. Of his major opponents from 1297, Hereford died in 1298, Norfolk was effectively neutralized as a result of his financial problems, and died in 1306, while Winchelsey was forced into exile. Edward was even in a strong enough position to quarrel bitterly in his final years with one of his long-standing supporters,

Anthony Bek, Bishop of Durham, without loss of authority. It may be doubted whether the king was 'inwardly cherished with the scent of satisfaction amidst the flowers of hoped-for peace', as he, or rather one of his clerks, put it in 1306, but the end of the reign was not marked by any renewal of the arguments of the 1290s.[15]

The honeymoon period at the start of the new reign of Edward II did not last long. There were clear signs of trouble by January 1308, and the drafting of a new clause, added to the coronation oath, failed to ease matters. The king's favourite, Piers Gaveston, who had provocatively been made Earl of Cornwall in the previous year, was exiled. In 1309, the price paid for his return was the redress of grievances in the Statute of Stamford. The concessions were not adhered to, and in 1310 Edward II was compelled, largely by financial pressure, to agree to the appointment of the Ordainers. Six preliminary Ordinances were issued in March 1310, but the main text of the reforms, forty-one articles in all, took a long time to prepare, and was not issued until Michaelmas 1311.

A comparison of the issues of 1311 with those of 1297 suggests that there was little continuity between the problems faced by Edward II, and those which had confronted his father. The clergy had been incensed in 1297 when they were, in effect, outlawed following their refusal to grant a tax, but that was no longer an issue in the early fourteenth century. The papal prohibition on the payment of taxes by the clergy to the lay power, set out in the bull Clericis Laicos of 1296, had been replaced by a policy whereby the papacy imposed income taxes on the clergy, and shared the proceeds with the Crown. The laity had been angered by the form of military summons used in 1297, and the demand that all who held at least twenty pounds worth of land should serve. This issue had been effectively resolved in Edward I's later years, with the abandonment of innovatory forms of summons, and the question of the nature of military service was not included in the clauses of the Ordinances. This was perhaps a mistake, for in 1316 Edward II attempted summonses very similar to those of 1297, but that was not to be expected in 1311.[16] In 1297, the question of how grants of taxation should be made was of major importance, above all with Edward I's attempt to levy an eighth without the usual full consent. By the time of the Ordinances, there was no question of similar unconstitutional methods of raising money. The forty shilling duty on wool exports, a matter of much complaint in 1297, was abolished in the autumn of that year. It was only the matter of prises, compulsory purchase of foodstuffs by the Crown, that featured clearly both in 1297 and in 1311. Although Edward I had conceded in the Confirmatio Cartarum of 1297 that in future he would obtain consent for prises, this had not been done with the sole exception of 1301, and by the time that the Ordinances were drafted, there were even fears that the level of prises might provoke popular uprisings.

If there was little direct continuity between the issues of 1297 and those of 1311, there was equally little continuity of personnel as far as leadership of oppostion to the Crown went. The earls who had protested with such effect at Edward I's policies were both dead by the time his son succeeded, and Archbishop Winchelsey was a spent force. John Lovel and Robert FitzRoger, who accompanied Roger Bigod, Earl of Norfolk, when he appeared at the Exchequer in 1297 to protest at the Crown's policies, were both involved in the crisis of the Ordinances. Others among Edward II's opponents had grievances against that feeble king's redoubtable father.[17] Yet what is most striking about the composition of the Ordainers, and the politics of Edward II's early years on the throne, is the way in which men who had been loyal to Edward I turned against his son. Those who protested early in 1308 in the Boulogne Declaration at the current state of affairs were all former councillors of Edward I, and the Earls of Lincoln, Pembroke and Richmond, along with Robert Clifford, firm supporters of the old king, were all selected to act as Ordainers.[18] All this suggests that a lack of continuity between 1297 and 1311 was more striking than the connections between the two crises.

A closer examination of the Ordinances of 1311 shows, however, that many clauses did have their origins in Edward I's reign, and that in many cases they relate to events of the year of crisis, 1297, as well as to policies adopted in the last decade of the reign. The *Confirmatio Cartarum* of 1297 was a hastily drafted document, put together in an urgent attempt to defuse the domestic crisis in the aftermath of the news that English troops had been roundly defeated at Stirling Bridge in Scotland, and it is very clear that it did not in any sense provide a comprehensive solution to all the problems of the day.

The central question in the 1290s had been war, and the difficulties of organizing and collecting together men, money and materials in sufficient quantity. The *Confirmatio Cartarum* dealt with recruitment, supplies and taxation, but did not tackle the fundamental issue of consent to war itself, even though there can be no doubt that Edward I had sailed for Flanders without the agreement of his baronage. Military strategy had, admittedly, been discussed at the Salisbury Parliament early in 1297, but Edward had not accepted the views put to him, and in the Remonstrances later in the year the earls advised the king against his planned campaign.[19] In the Ordinances, in contrast to the *Confirmatio Cartarum*, the problem was tackled head on in clause 9: the king was not to make war or leave the realm without the consent of the baronage in parliament.[20] This certainly had specific reference to the Scottish campaign of 1310, but it is hard to believe that memories of 1297 did not lie behind it. There may also have been recollections of the way in which Edward had tacitly conceded this issue, when in 1298 he did obtain approval in a council at York for the forthcoming Falkirk campaign.[21]

There was no need in the Ordinances for the inclusion of clauses re-emphasizing the principle that direct taxation should not be imposed

without consent. Edward I had not attempted to repeat his unconstitutional tax of an eighth which he tried to levy in 1297. He had even taken
care in 1306 to obtain consent for the collection of a tax on the occasion
of the knighting of his eldest son, a tax to which he was entitled under
feudal law.[22] It would be wrong to criticize the Ordinances because there
was no demand for consent by representatives to the grant of taxes, for the
principle was sufficiently well established to need no reinforcement.

Direct taxation was only one element of royal finance, however, and
the Ordinances contain much on other aspects of the financial system,
which reflects the arguments and practices of Edward I's later years. One
very important idea expressed in three clauses, 4, 8 and 10, was that the
king should live of his own. B.P. Wolffe suggested that this was 'the
earliest actual use of the phrase'. He stressed, however, that it was linked
with the Crown's use of prises, and that there was no assumed distinction
between 'ordinary' and 'extraordinary' royal income.[23] The broad context
of clauses 4 and 8 was that of customs revenue and other royal income, and
the financing of the royal household: the suggestion was that as insufficient
income was directed towards the household through the Exchequer, so the
king had been forced to resort to prises, and was not able to live off his
own. This latter concept, however, was not as new as Wolffe supposed. In
1298, when Edward I informed the clergy that he did not want to ask them
for a tax, he stated that he intended to finance the Scottish campaign that
year 'of his own'. In French this was reported as *del vostre demeyne chevir*,
but in Latin the king's intention was expressed as being *quod de suo proprio
in hac guerra sua contra Scotos se et suos in quantum se extenderit sustinebit*.[24]
The Ordainers, therefore, had picked up an idea initially expressed by
Edward I, and were using it in a slightly different context to try to re-order
part of the financial system.

The central idea expressed in clauses 4 and 8 was that all the revenues of
the land should be paid into the Exchequer. If carried through, such a
policy would have destroyed the financial independence of the household,
and in particular of the department of the wardrobe. This concept lay at
the heart of the interpretations of older scholars which saw the Ordinances
as an attack on the household system of government which was so striking
a feature of Edward I's rule. There had been nothing of this in 1297, but
the arguments put forward by the Ordainers in 1311 had their roots in
administrative measures put forward in Edward I's last years. In 1304 the
treasurer and barons of the Exchequer had announced that in future no
one was to pay money to the wardrobe, save when this was specifically
authorized by means of a royal writ. All normal payments were to be made
to the Exchequer. The following year saw a scheme conceived whereby
the household was to be supplied by means of regular payments in cash
from the Exchequer: there would be no need for it to receive money from

outside sources. These plans did not work, because of the pressures of war and the financial difficulties of the day: the Crown was sinking deeper and deeper into debt.[25] What they demonstrate, however, is that the plans put forward by the Ordainers were not necessarily all being pressed on an unwilling administration by the Crown's opponents. At least some of the policies advocated were ones which many officials undoubtedly felt were the right ones.

The draft version of the Ordinances preserved at Durham carried the matter of Exchequer control over wardrobe finance still further. In clause 11, a committee was proposed which would oversee royal receipts, and it was laid down that the officials of the wardrobe should account annually at the Exchequer. No allowances should be made on their accounts without proper documentation being provided. The principle of annual accounting by the wardrobe at the Exchequer was certainly one with which the government would have agreed: it was of long standing, but had broken down in the 1290s. Indeed, no wardrobe accounts for the period from 1298 to 1307 were ever enrolled on the Exchequer Pipe Rolls. This clause was not included in the final version of the Ordinances, though the principle of annual household accounting would feature later in the Exchequer reforms of 1324. It is unlikely that the clause was dropped as a result of royal opposition: what happened was that in the Ordinances proper, the same committee of a bishop, two earls and three barons was given a different task. It was to hear complaints brought against royal officials in parliament. It seems that the question of financial control by the Exchequer, so central to Tout and Davies' interpretation of the Ordinances, was in fact of secondary importance in 1311.[26]

Although they demanded that all revenues be paid in to the Exchequer, the Ordainers did not give their full approval to that department's practices. Clause 24 complained about the way in which men were hounded to pay debts which they had in fact already paid. For Davies, this was hardly worth comment: 'a matter which concerned merely the efficiency of administration and as far as can be seen no ulterior motive can be assigned to this Ordinance.'[27] This, however, is a matter which can be traced back to Edward I's day, and to 1297. In March of that year commissions had been set up to levy all debts due to the Crown, and in July they were reinforced.[28] The debt collection could be used as a personal and as a political weapon. On a personal level, in 1304 Edward I punished Marmaduke Thweng for abducting William Latimer the Younger's mistress, and leaving royal service, by asking the Exchequer to collect all debts he owed *santz faire a lui nule manere de grace ou de suffrance*. More political was the way in which the threat of collecting debts had been used in 1295 to compel a group of magnates to go to fight in Gascony. In 1303 Edward I wrote to the Exchequer to tell the officials that

John de Ferrers, one of his opponents in 1297, was now in better favour than in the past, and that he was accordingly to have his debts looked into, to have any distraints released, and respite of payment allowed.[29] Such cases naturally involved argument as to whether long-standing debts were still due, or had been paid off. Politics as well as maladministration almost certainly lay behind this clause in the Ordinances, and it is very probably the kind of matter which was in the minds of those who complained in 1301 that the treasurer, Walter Langton, had been subverting the ancient customs of the Exchequer.[30]

Another clause, 25, dealing with Exchequer procedure also looked back to Edward I's reign. The question of the hearing of private pleas in the Exchequer, especially those concerning merchants – the Italians were probably particularly in mind – was one which had been raised as early as 1284, with the Statute of Rhuddlan. In 1297 it had not been brought up by the king's opponents, but by Edward I himself, who in a memorandum of 2 July effectively forbad the hearing of such cases, as well as forbidding the use of private lawyers in the Court of the Exchequer.[31] The support given to the Ordinances by men formerly loyal to Edward I is less surprising since some clauses at least reflected government thinking from his reign.

The treatment of customs duties by the Ordainers, on the other hand, was counter to the system that had been operated by Edward I. When customs duties on the export of wool and hides were introduced in 1275, it was intended that they should be used to repay Italian merchants for their loans to the Crown, rather than being paid into the Exchequer.[32] The New Custom, established in 1303, had been negotiated with the alien merchants, and provided an important prop to the shaky financial edifice of the time. It was one element of Edward I's machine which was annulled by the Ordainers. The reasons produced for this were not constitutional, but economic: the additional duties harmed trade, and put up prices. There was also resentment at the favours granted by Edward I to foreign merchants in return for the New Custom, which had no baronial authorization.[33]

The Chancery did not receive the same sort of attention in the Ordinances as the Exchequer. In the treatment of the privy seal, however, Tout saw an attempt to enhance the authority of the Chancery, just as he considered that the financial measures were designed to increase the Exchequer's power.[34] Some of the measures concerning the privy seal did no more than reinforce what had been said in the *Articuli super Cartas* of 1300, and in the Articles of 1309. Privy seal writs were, according to clause 33, not to be used to interfere with the process of the common law. This type of abuse is demonstrated by privy seal letters of 1310 ordering cases brought by a royal official, and by the Friars Preacher of London to be heard at the Exchequer.[35] Tout considered, however, that a real advance was made by the Ordainers, when they laid down in clause 14 that there should be a suitable clerk appointed to keep the privy seal. He saw this as 'in effect the institution of a new office'.[36] Wilkinson, in contrast, argued that all the Ordainers intended was 'an enumeration of the existing officials whom the barons wish to be elected with their consent'.[37] Up to this time, the privy seal had been in the charge of the controller of the wardrobe: the Ordainers now listed the controller separately from the keeper of the privy seal, and the question is whether this was intended as a major change in administrative practice, or simply as a means of preventing the king from entrusting the privy seal to an unauthorized official. The draft version of the Ordinances preserved at Durham merely specified 'un chief clerk covenable por garder son seal', omitting to make it clear that this was the privy seal.[38] If the Ordainers really intended to create a new and separate office for the privy seal, they went about it in a most oblique manner, and Wilkinson's arguments are surely the more persuasive.[39] The mention of the keeper of the privy seal in clause 14 of the Ordinances does not mean that some new problem had arisen under Edward II, or that any radical restructuring of the administration was envisaged as a means of resolving it.

There is, in fact, remarkably little in the Ordinances which cannot be related to the situation in Edward I's day. The demand in clause 30, that there should be no changes in the currency without baronial consent, may have resulted in part from suspicions that Edward II was manipulating the coinage. In fact, no changes to the weight or purity of coins were made by Edward II, and the clause most probably refers to the recoining of pollards and crockards at the turn of the century by Edward I.[40] Lavish grants of pardon to criminals, and the misuse of writs of protection issued to men going on campaign, raised in clauses 28 and 37, were matters which went back to the 1290s.[41] Clause 33 complained about the Statute of Acton Burnell of 1283: it should henceforth only apply between merchants, and not be applicable to landowners. Edward II had not introduced any changes to the law in this regard, though the issue may have been highlighted by the proceedings against Edward I's treasurer, Walter Langton, who had used statute merchant unscrupulously in his greed to acquire landed estates.[42] Complaints about the jurisdiction of the royal household had featured in the *Articuli super Cartas* of 1300, and there is no evidence that abuses had increased under Edward II, although this matter featured in clauses 26 and 27 of the Ordinances.[43] While the Ordainers were not concerned to continue the assault on the boundaries of the Royal Forest that had been a major preoccupation in Edward I's last years, clause 19 which dealt with the provision of adequate means of bringing action against oppressive Forest officials strongly echoed worries from the old

king's reign. Even when the clauses dealing with the specific individuals
are turned to, the issues had all come up in Edward I's last years on the
throne. It was Edward I who had permitted the grant of the custody of
Bamburgh Castle to Isabella de Vescy. It was under Edward I that the
Frescobaldi became royal bankers. Even the attack on Piers Gaveston was
presaged by the way in which the old king drove his son's unfortunate
favourite into exile.[44]

There were certainly no demands under Edward I for limits to be placed
on royal patronage, such as were made in the Ordinances with the
requirement that all grants made since the appointment of the Ordainers
should be revoked. Edward I had been immensely careful not to deplete
the stock of royal estates, and had indeed engaged in distinctly questionable means of increasing that stock. The chronicler Pierre Langtoft had
criticized him for his lack of generosity in granting out conquered lands in
Wales and Scotland.[45] In attacking Edward II's profligacy, the Ordinances
can be seen as looking back to the stricter policies of Edward I.

To a very considerable extent the Ordinances restated familiar questions which had been debated under Edward I. Most of the grievances
which were tackled were not new in Edward II's reign, but had featured in
such documents as the *Articuli super Cartas* of 1300. In some cases what
was attempted in 1311 was to revert to the practices and objectives of the
Crown prior to 1307. Even as regards financial administration, some of the
measures proposed by the Ordainers reflected the thinking of Edward I's
officials. What, however, of the means to enforce the Ordinances? Here
there was clear innovation. The technique of trying to control the king by
imposing a council on him, as had been attempted in 1258, was not tried
again: it was perhaps too revolutionary a step for a fairly traditionally-
minded body of men. Clearly, however, something more was needed than
the formula of 1297, when the king's opponents had simply relied upon a
confirmation of the Charters, with additional concessions, providing for
consent to taxes and prises by the ill-defined 'common assent of the realm'.
The only form of enforcement then envisaged had been that of excommunication. Now, in 1311, it was laid down that on a wide range of
questions consent was to be given by the baronage in parliament, and that
complaints against royal officials could be brought before a commission in
parliament. Parliament had not been mentioned in the settlement of the
crisis of 1297, and parliamentary consent was the new element in the
control of government provided by the Ordainers.

The position of parliament in the Ordinances has been the subject of
some misunderstanding. According to G.O. Sayles, 'the barons insisted
that their advice must predominate in the king's council, especially in
time of parliament. Therefore parliament was to meet once a year, if
necessary twice'.[46] In fact, clause 29 of the Ordinances made it quite clear

that the reason why frequent meetings of parliament were needed was so that legal cases might be brought to a proper conclusion, and so that men could bring forward complaints about the activities of royal officials. There was no suggestion that biennial meetings were needed so as to ensure that baronial advice prevailed. This grievance about how often parliament should meet was another which dated back to Edward I's days. The pressures of affairs in the second half of the reign meant that meetings were far from regular. In particular, there was a long spell with no parliaments between 1302 and 1305.[47] Sayles then suggested that the Ordainers 'were determined to underline unmistakably the ancient rule that the king must take counsel with the barons on important issues'. He saw little new in this, save for a new emphasis on the importance of the barons in parliament at the expense of the king's professional administrators.[48]

The demands for consent by the barons in parliament were hardly as traditional as Sayles suggested. Many issues were covered. They comprised the king's making war, and his leaving the realm; the granting out of castles, towns and lands; the appointment of the chancellor, chief justices and important officials of the Exchequer and household; changes to the currency. The clause directed against Henry de Beaumont, Isabella de Vescy's brother, even implied baronial control of the membership of the royal council.[49] These were not matters covered by some ancient rule requiring baronial agreement. No such rule existed, and these matters were surely what in the Statute of York, in 1322, would be considered as aspects of royal power, and of the estate of the Crown.[50] When in 1301 Edward I had been urged in parliament to agree that his chief officials should be appointed by common counsel of the realm, he responded very firmly indeed, pointing out that the barons had the right to appoint whoever they wanted to posts in their households, and argued that he should have similar freedom with regard to his own officials.[51] The making of grants was clearly a matter of royal prerogative: there were no rules as to who should witness charters. Control of the coinage was not a matter on which English kings accepted dictation, though it is interesting that in 1303–4 in France the bishops declared that the king should not alter the currency without obtaining episcopal and baronial approval. The policy of the Ordainers fitted into a general European trend.[52] As for the important question of the king's right to make war, while Edward I had often consulted his subjects, as at Devizes on the eve of the second Welsh war, or at York prior to the Falkirk campaign, this consultation rarely took place in parliament, and there is nothing to suggest that there was any compulsion on the king to obtain consent. It was not, for example, necessary to obtain the agreement of the magnates prior to issuing a feudal summons. Consent was not a part of the theories of the just war. It was, of course, sensible political practice to engage in some form of consultation, but that is a long way from a formal requirement as set out in the Ordinances, to consult the baronage in parliament.[53]

The form of consent specified by the Ordainers in 1311 was very limited in character, in that it was confined to the baronage in parliament. No mention was made of the role of the prelates, or of the representatives of shire and borough. Yet it was surely not intended to change the existing pattern of consent. No attempt was made to provide a list of all matters for which consent was needed. Where the practice was well established, as was the case with taxation, there was no need to make the point again, and there was no suggestion of denying representatives their role. In 1312 the magnates made it quite plain that they alone could not concede a tax, but they promised to do all they could 'when they will have their peers more fully with them, and the community'.[54]

What was done in the Ordinances was to define a new range of business for which consent was needed. That consent was to be of a limited baronial character. It is striking that the Ordainers did not use the terminology of community, which had been so dominant in the thirteenth century.[55] In 1258 the baronial cause had been largely synonymous with that of the community of the realm, and in 1297 the earls had no apparent qualms about speaking on behalf of the community. The term, however, increasingly implied the participation of the representatives of shire and boroughs. No representative had been summoned to the parliament of February 1310, and the grant by the king authorizing the selection of the Ordainers had been addressed to the prelates, earls and barons, with no mention of the community. The Ordainers were not representative of the community in the widest sense, and it can be argued that the absence of any mention of representatives in the Ordinances reflected an awareness on behalf of the magnates that they could no longer claim to speak on their behalf. The 'baronial' character of the Ordinances is undeniable, but it is a character which reflects the way in which the Ordainers were given their commission at least as much as it does their own oligarchic conceptions.

No doubt the Ordainers thought that baronial approval was the most important form of consent – it is interesting that in clause 11 they objected to the absence of baronial agreement to the New Custom of 1303 – but it should not follow that they considered that only the barons had the right to provide consent. They did not intend to change existing customs and conventions regarding consent. What they did was to add a new range of matters relating to royal power, for which no consent had been required in the past. These were now to be subject to baronial scrutiny in parliament.

This meant that parliament was given a clear and exclusive role in the Ordinances, in a way that had not been the case in the past. In 1297 there had been no mention of parliament, either in the demands made by the earls in the Remonstrances and the *De Tallagio*, or in the agreement made with the Crown, the *Confirmatio Cartarum*. Great affairs of state could be discussed under Edward I in non-parliamentary assemblies as much as in parliaments. It was in the Ordinances that for the first time it was specified that parliamentary consent was required for a range of important matters.

Discovery of the new draft version of the Ordinances shows something of the way in which the document was developed. The draft does not include the first six clauses, which were issued initially as a preliminary measure in March 1310. The order of the clauses that do feature in it is different from that of the final version. There are blocks, such as clauses 13 to 17, or 31 to 37, which are broadly identical with the final version, and this suggests the way that various sections of the Ordinances were drawn up, but there is no particular logic in the way in which the final text was assembled. In some cases, as in clauses 9 and 19, it is clear that the initial version was considered inadequate, and that amplification was required. It was also necessary to tone down the draft somewhat: the Durham draft version makes much of the treasonable character of Piers Gaveston's activities. The transformation of clause 11 of the draft into clause 40 of the Ordinances, providing for the commission to hear complaints in parliament against royal officials, shows the way in which ideas changed during the time that the Ordainers were working on the document. Such developments are not surprising, but the differences between the draft and the final document do help to demonstrate the care that was taken in preparing the Ordinances.[56]

The draft version of the Ordinances unfortunately does not help to show who was consulted in drawing up the text, or assist in the task of attributing authorship to it. To a considerable extent the document summed up and brought together questions that had been raised earlier, notably in the *Articuli super Cartas* of 1300, and the articles drafted at the Westminster Parliament of April 1309, which were answered at Stamford in the following July. In both those cases, it is very likely that consultation took place between knights and magnates.[57] There is, however, no evidence to support the view that the opinion of the knights was sought in 1310–11. While 'it is inherently unlikely that the magnates failed to see the value of the "middle-class" support which the knights could provide in the shires',[58] it may be that the Ordainers considered that knightly views were sufficiently well-known as not to need any elucidation. The relative lack of concern with reform at the local level suggests that there was little consultation at this level.[59] The author of the *Vita Edwardi Secundi* suggested that the Earl of Warwick played the decisive role in the drafting process.[60] Lancaster has also been seen as possibly playing a major part, though it is dangerous to assume that because he defended the Ordinances staunchly later, he had necessarily done much of the work involved in drawing them up. His later contributions to the political debates of Edward II's reign do not show any close similarities to the Ordinances in style or content.[61] The other candidate who has been suggested is Archbishop Winchelsey. Clause 12, which deals with men who maliciously obtained writs to prevent the hearing of cases by ecclesiastical courts, was not included in the Durham draft version of the Ordinances. Had Winchelsey taken a leading role in the debates, then it is surely likely that this clause, which suggests a direct link between the Ordinances and the clerical *gravamina* of this period, would have featured from the outset. The scant signs of clerical involvement argue against Winchelsey's authorship.[62]

What a study of the document itself suggests is that the Ordinances was drawn up by men with a considerable practical expertise in public affairs, who fully understood the workings of the royal administration, and who had a good knowledge of the way in which the legal system operated. Through their stewards and other officials, magnates such as the Earl of Warwick had such expertise readily available to them. It also seems very possible that assistance was provided by some royal officials, sympathetic to the point of view of the Ordainers. It is almost certainly wrong to try to suggest a single author. Many of the clauses of the Ordinances represented what had become a consensus view. Some had their origins in policies adopted by Edward I, and discarded by his son; others strongly echoed the views expressed by those opposed to the old king. The way in which the Ordinances was dominated by past events meant that not all of the problems of the present were properly addressed. It very rapidly became clear that all the changes that were needed to Edward II's regime had not been set out. Additional instructions were drawn up, a few of which reinforced points made in the Ordinances, but most of which specified the numerous individuals who were to be expelled from the royal household.[63]

The Ordinances dominated political thinking from the time of their publication in 1311 until 1322, when the Statute of York saw the work of the Ordainers repealed.[64] No regime proved capable of carrying out the programme. What was desirable in the Ordinances was impractical, and what was practical was undesirable. In part, the Ordinances proved unworkable because the administrative mechanisms proposed, notably the payment of all the revenues of the land through the Exchequer, could not be put into effect at a time when the government was placed under very considerable strain. There was no proper mechanism suggested for the day-to-day supervision of government, and the concept of baronial parliamentary consent for many matters was difficult to put into effect. In some cases, particularly as regards war, there was not enough time for due consultation with the baronage in parliament to take place. Above all, the Ordinances failed because it was impossible to impose terms on an unwilling king: and Edward could never accept a document which demanded the expulsion from the realm of his favourite. As the final outcome of the reign showed, it was only by deposition that royal power could be effectively curbed.

In many ways, the Ordinances mark the end of a chapter, rather than the beginning. The document is very different in character from the *Confirmatio Cartarum* of 1297, but to a considerable extent it looked back to the crises of Edward I's last ten years on the throne. The problems it addressed were more the result of the strong government of Edward I, than the weak rule of his son, with the obvious exception of the role of Piers Gaveston. On many matters a consensus had developed. There was no sharp divergence between the way in which Edward I's officials aimed to run the financial system, with Exchequer control and proper annual accounting, and the objectives of the Ordainers. The measures dealing with the activities of Forest officials and other royal servants were very much in accord with the approach adopted by Edward I. Even the notion of a commission which would receive complaints against royal officials was little more than establishing as a permanent institution the kind of system that Edward I had set up in 1289 to deal with the complaints against his justices and other ministers. Tout and Davies saw a fundamental division of opinion over the role of the household in government, and saw the Ordinances as a firm attempt to reassert the dominance of the great offices of state, the Exchequer and the Chancery, over the household departments. In practice, there is no evidence that such a division existed. The problem was that the practical exigencies of the day, particularly those imposed by war, meant that there was no real alternative to extensive use of the household in royal administration. It was perhaps because there was so little disagreement over fundamental principles that politics became less concerned with major constitutional issues, and that what mattered increasingly were the personal rivalries and disputes so rightly stressed in recent work on this period. Yet the Ordinances did have their importance in the full recognition accorded to parliament. The absence of any reference to the role of representatives should not obscure recognition of the fact that parliamentary consent was specified as being needed for a wide range of matters that had hitherto been the king's alone to decide. The imprecise thirteenth-century terminology of consent by the community of the realm was replaced by a new clear definition. The aristocratic dominance implied by consent of the barons in parliament may not seem attractive, but it did reflect the reality of early fourteenth-century politics.

## Notes

1   See in particular T.F. Tout, *The Place of the Reign of Edward II in English History* (Manchester, 1914); J.C. Davies, *The Baronial Opposition to Edward II* (1918); J.R. Maddicott, *Thomas of Lancaster 1307–1322* (Oxford, 1970); J.R.S. Phillips, *Aymer de Valence, Earl of Pembroke 1307–1324* (Oxford, 1972).

2   Maddicott, *Thomas of Lancaster*, p.325; Phillips, *Aymer de Valence*, pp.30–1.

3   Maddicott, *Thomas of Lancaster*, p.156.

4   *Vita Edwardi Secundi*, ed. N. Denholm-Young (1957), p.109.

5   Maddicott, *Thomas of Lancaster*, p.197.

6   Phillips, *Aymer de Valence*, pp.316–8.

7   *Vita Edwardi Secundi*, pp.7–8, 97.

8   *Vita Edwardi Secundi*, pp.18–20.

9   W. Stubbs, *Constitutional History of England* (4th ed., Oxford, 1906), II. 346.

10  Tout, *Place of the Reign of Edward II*, p.92.

11  Davies, *Baronial Opposition to Edward II*, p.372.

12  B. Wilkinson, *Studies in the Constitutional History of the Thirteenth and Fourteenth Centuries* (Manchester, 1937), p.229.

13  Maddicott, *Thomas of Lancaster*, pp.106–8, 178.

14  G.L. Harriss, *King, Parliament and Public Finance in Medieval England to 1369* (Oxford, 1975), p.168.

15  For a full account of Edward I's later years, see M.C. Prestwich, *Edward I* (1988), pp.400–35, 517–55. The quotation is given on p.517.

16  M.C. Prestwich, 'Cavalry Service in Early Fourteenth Century England', *War and Government in the Middle Ages*, ed. J. Gillingham and J.C. Holt (Woodbridge, 1984), p.154.

17  M.C. Prestwich, *War, Politics and Finance under Edward I* (1972), p.276.

18  Phillips, *Aymer de Valence*, p.316, prints the Boulogne Declaration.

19  Prestwich, *Edward I*, p.416; *Documents illustrating the Crisis of 1297–98 in England*, ed. M.C. Prestwich, Camden Soc. 4th series, XXIV, (1980), pp.116–7.

20  The Ordinances are printed in *SR*, I. 157–67; the document is also given in *Rot. Parl.* I. 281–6.

21  *The Chronicle of Pierre de Langtoft*, ed. T. Wright (RS, 1868), II. 313.

22  This tax took the same form as the usual lay taxes, rather than being assessed in a feudal manner, on the knights' fees. Although consent was given by representatives, they were not authorized to act in the normal way, and the assembly of 1306 did not meet the normal criteria of a parliament. See Prestwich, *Edward I*, pp.455–6.

23  B.P. Wolffe, *The Royal Demesne in English History* (1971), pp.47–8.

24  *Councils and Synods, II, 1205–1313*, ed. F.M. Powicke and C.R. Cheney (Oxford, 1964), II. 1191, 1197.

25  M.C. Prestwich, 'Exchequer and Wardrobe in the Later Years of Edward I', *BIHR*, XLVI (1973), 1–9.

26  M.C. Prestwich, 'A New Version of the Ordinances of 1311', *BIHR*, LVII (1984), 190–1.

27  Davies, *Baronial Opposition*, p.376.

28  *Documents illustrating the crisis of 1297–8*, pp.48–50, 102.

29  PRO E368/74, m.39; E101/77, m.13; E159/78, m.7; *Book of Prests of the King's Wardrobe for 1294–5*, ed. E.B. Fryde (Oxford, 1962), p.xlviii.

30  *Langtoft*, II. 328.

31  *Documents illustrating the crisis of 1297–8*, p.101.

32  R.W. Kaeuper, *Bankers to the Crown: the Riccardi of Lucca and Edward I* (Princeton, 1973), pp.149–51.

33  Ordinances, clause 11.
34  T.F. Tout, *Chapters in the Administrative History of Medieval England*, II (Manchester, 1920), 282–92.
35  *Rot. Parl.* I. 444; Davies, *Baronial Opposition*, pp.550–1.
36  Tout, *Chapters in Administrative History*, II. 285.
37  Wilkinson, *Studies in Constitutional History*, p.239.
38  Prestwich, 'A New Version of the Ordinances of 1311', p.194.
39  The question of the privy seal is considered in detail by J.H. Trueman, 'The Privy Seal and the English Ordinances of 1311', *Speculum*, XXXI (1956), 611–25. Trueman examined privy seal warrants for pardons and protections, which show a sharp decline in such warrants after the issue of the Ordinances. This, however, merely reflects the criticism of such grants made in the Ordinances, not policy towards the privy seal as such.
40  M. Mate, 'Monetary Policies in England 1272–1307', *British Numismatic Journal*, XLI (1972), 66–70, discusses the recoinage of 1300. *CCR 1307–13*, p.225, shows that there were false rumours about in 1309 of a change in the currency.
41  R.W. Kaeuper, *War, Justice and Public Order: England and France in the Later Middle Ages* (Oxford, 1988), pp.126–7; Prestwich, *War, Politics and Finance*, p.237.
42  A. Beardwood, 'The Trial of Walter Langton, Bishop of Lichfield, 1307–1312', *Transactions of the American Philosophical Society*, n.s. LIV (1964), 16, 21–2, 27–31.
43  Household jurisdiction is discussed in Prestwich, *Edward I*, pp.165–8.
44  Ordinances, clause 19; C.R. Young, *The Royal Forests of Medieval England* (Leicester, 1979), p.141; M.C. Prestwich, 'Isabella de Vescy and the Custody of Bamburgh Castle', *BIHR*, XLIV (1971), 148–52.
45  *The Chronicle of Pierre de Langtoft*, II. 216, 328. See also M.C. Prestwich, 'Colonial Scotland: the English in Scotland under Edward I', *Scotland and England 1286–1815*, ed. R.A. Mason (Edinburgh, 1987), pp.7–12.
46  G.O. Sayles, *The King's Parliament of England* (1975), p.97.
47  The dates of parliaments in this period are best set out in *HBC*, pp.545–52.
48  Sayles, *King's Parliament of England*, pp.98–9.
49  Ordinances, clauses 7, 9, 14, 22, 30.
50  *SR*, I. 189–90. The precise implications of the Statute of York have, of course, been the subject of intense debate.
51  *Willelmi Rishanger, Chronica et Annales*, ed. H.T. Riley (RS, 1865), p.460.
52  P. Spufford, 'Assemblies of Estates, Taxation and Control of Coinage in Medieval Europe', *Studies Presented to the International Commission for the History of Representative and Parliamentary Institutions* (Vienna, 1965), pp.121–3.
53  It is interesting to note that even as late as 1914 parliament did not formally approve the declaration of war until after the event: A.J.P. Taylor, *English History 1914–1945* (Oxford, 1965), p.2.
54  *Chronicles of the Reigns of Edward I and II*, ed. W. Stubbs (RS, 1882), I. 211.
55  Prestwich, 'Parliament and the Community of the Realm in Fourteenth Century England', pp.5–20.
56  Prestwich, 'A New Version of the Ordinances of 1311', pp.189–203.
57  Maddicott, *Thomas of Lancaster*, pp.97–102. The contents of the *Articuli super Cartas*, notably with the demand for local election of sheriffs, strongly suggests substantial knightly involvement. See Prestwich, *Edward I*, pp.522–4.
58  Maddicott, *Thomas of Lancaster*, p.119.
59  Kaeuper, *War, Justice and Public Order*, p.287.
60  *Vita Edwardi Secundi*, pp.11, 62–3.
61  Lancaster's possible role is discussed by Maddicott, *Thomas of Lancaster*, pp.119–20. See also the comments of J.A. Tuck, *Crown and Nobility 1272–1461* (1985), pp.64–5.
62  J.H. Denton, *Robert Winchelsey and the Crown, 1294–1313* (Cambridge, 1980), p.264.

63 The additional ordinances are printed in *Chronicles of the Reigns of Edward I and II*, I. 198–202.

64 Although the Ordinances was repealed in 1322, six clauses as 'good points' were retained: M.C. Buck, *Politics, Finance and the Church in the reign of Edward II* (Cambridge, 1983), p.139, n.67; *Rot. Parl.* I. 456–7. The clauses of the Ordinances concerning the statute of Acton Burnell, and malicious appeals, were the most significant of those re-enacted.

# 2

# Finance and Trade under Edward II

Wendy Childs
*University of Leeds*

Finance was generally a problem for later medieval kings trying to 'live of their own', but finance seems, superficially, to be the one successful feature of Edward II's reign. The start of the reign, it is true, looked particularly unpromising. Edward I left debts amounting to £200,000 and chaos in the auditing procedures of the Exchequer;[1] he left an expensive war, and a baronage sensitive to, and critical of, royal manipulation of finance through maltotes, prise, and purveyance. In 1311 the preamble to the Ordinances and clause 10 referred to the oppression of the people who, it was feared, were near to rebellion. The period 1305–10 saw marked inflation, and food prices were again so high in 1315, even before the famine years, that the government unsuccessfully issued a price-fixing Ordinance.[2] The great famine of 1315–17 and the murrain of 1322 caused further great hardship. Yet after 1322 contemporary chroniclers of quite different views referred to Edward II's great riches.

The writer of the *Flores Historiarum* under the year 1323 noted that in a short time Edward had heaped up countless treasure, far more than any of his predecessors. The *Vita Edwardi Secundi* notes the astonishment of the people that Edward did not pay his footsoldiers in 1325, because 'the king had plenty of treasure. Many of his forbears amassed money; he alone has exceeded them all.' The long continuation of the *Brut*, written shortly after Edward's death, also recorded that he was 'the richest king that ever was in England, after William Bastard of Normandy, that conquered England'. Sir Thomas Grey, writing his *Scalacronica* in the 1350s and possibly using a copy of the *Brut* continuation, also noted that Edward acted 'so as to become rich'.[3] The work of modern historians has confirmed his success. Before the end of his reign he had paid off about £140,000 of his father's debts.[4] Although he still seems to have been somewhat short of money in 1321, he had about £27,500 in hand by 1323, over £69,000 in 1325 despite the expenditure on the Gascon war, and in 1326, although he took £29,000 with him when he fled, some £58,000 remained in London.[5] Certain particular circumstances had contributed heavily to this success. Fines on the supporters of the rebels of 1321–2 were potentially worth £15,000.[6] The confiscated lands of the Contrariants kept in royal hands brought in about £12,000 a year,[7] and the thirteen-year truce with the Scots cut war expenditure just as Edward received both the heaviest lay subsidy of his reign, assessed at £42,400, and a papal tenth for two years which probably brought him about £38,000.[8] Although Edward received no further subsidies, this was enough for him to finance the Gascon war. This war, short and unsuccessful although it was, cost him some £65,000,[9] but still left him with money in the Treasury. Edward was not, however, simply relying on windfalls. Mrs Fryde and Dr Buck have both emphasized the deliberate financial drive in the last years of Edward's reign. Whether the driving power was the king himself or the Despensers, civil servants were exhorted by royal writs to 'serve us so we become rich'. The pressure on the Exchequer possibly started as early as 1316 and was constant in the 1320s. There was a strong drive to collect all possible arrears, and to exploit all possible traditional rights and income, including lands, forests, and feudal dues which had caused so much trouble in previous reigns. The Crown also sought to bring all accounts up to date, and even to economize on the costs of Exchequer staff, although in the event more staff were needed to cope with the new work.[10]

Professor Prestwich recently pointed out that Edward I's fiscal policies were a financial failure but a great political success.[11] Edward II's case was quite the reverse; his great financial success was achieved at great political cost. The opportunity to confiscate the Contrariants' lands came only because Edward's political ineptitude and support of the Despensers drove some opponents to open rebellion by 1321. The subsequent savage treatment of the rebels and their families and the permanent forfeiture of their lands stirred up further hatred which largely contributed to Edward's lack of support in 1326. An additional £12,000 a year seems poor compensation for this. The exceptionally heavy subsidy of a tenth and a sixth in 1322 for the Scottish war was singled out in the short continuation of the French prose *Brut* as greatly distressing to the people of England,[12] and the financially helpful truce with Scotland was itself seen by many as politically shameful, especially as it followed Edward's ignominious flight from the Scots at Blackhow Moor near Rievaulx. While the internal reform of the Exchequer might have been seen by those who knew of it as useful, the reason for it, namely the desire to squeeze every last penny due to the king, was not approved. It is not surprising that contemporaries were aware of Edward's rising fortune since the collection of it touched many in the land, and provoked yet more hostility. Grievances were aired in parliament, probably as early as 1324, when a

Commons petition complained of Exchequer demands for debts going back to Henry III and beyond, many of which had been paid or pardoned so long ago that tallies and acquittances had been destroyed. In 1325 there were complaints at the unjust extention of Forest jurisdiction, and in 1327 in Edward III's first parliament yet further complaints were made about these exactions.[13] The amount which could be collected from these old traditional sources of income was limited, probably little more than £2,000 a year,[14] and (as with the Contrariants' lands) the amount brought to the Treasury was poor compensation for the political ill-will created.

The increasing hostility to financial exactions is seen not only in the parliamentary complaints but also in contemporary writings and in the final accusations against Edward at his deposition. The chroniclers record his wealth not to praise it but to criticize his methods, his advisors, and the officials most closely involved. The author of the *Flores Historiarum* was particularly critical of Edward. He wrote of extortion, unjust exactions, and tyranny after 1322; he emphasized the impoverishment of the counties from which Edward unjustly levied sums ranging from £500 to £900, which he termed 'spolia et extortiones diabolicas'; and in his account of the parliament of 1324 he wrote of money as the main bone of contention with parliament refusing with one voice the king's demands because of the great hardship the country was falling into. The more moderate author of the *Vita Edwardi Secundi* was also critical of the build up of treasure. He wrote that some blamed the Despensers for the king's meanness, and later referred to the avariciousness of Bishop Stapledon when Treasurer, but he also wrote of the king's own harshness and his determination to have his own way. The continuation of the *Brut* mentioned the greed and advice of the Despensers, and also criticized the greed of Robert Baldock, the Chancellor. The confiscation of the queen's lands, which probably brought Edward about £1,800 a year, was also widely criticized, especially as chroniclers greatly underestimated the amount of income allowed to her through the Exchequer. The accusations against Edward at his deposition referred mainly to his political and military failings, and to his use of evil counsel; but they did not spare Edward himself – his pride, his obstinacy, his cruelty, and his greed – and also included financial criticism. Apart from seizing Church temporalities and disinheriting his nobles, he had stripped his realm and ruined it and his people.[15] Although it can be argued that it was the windfalls and the extortions of the last years which made Edward really rich, he had a solid regular income which was probably enough for solvency in peacetime. If this was so, then his reckless drive for money was even more politically inept as being to a large extent unnecessary.

The foundations of solvency were laid by his father, who bequeathed not only financial problems to his son, but also enormous potential

financial strength. Building on the occasional experiments of his predecessors, he had found ways to tap regularly the growing prosperity of his
country. Taxes on lay moveables, grants of clerical tenths, customs duties,
and loans to anticipate these revenues and obtain immediate liquid funds
had completely changed the financial basis of the English Crown.
Edward II took full advantage of this bequest. He took seven lay subsidies
in twenty years; he received four clerical tenths and a number of smaller
sums granted by the English clergy; clerical tenths granted by the papacy
were collected in eight years; he continued to enjoy both the wool tax and
the tax on all alien trade instituted in 1303. These new resources were not
without their problems as taxes needed consent. The laity and clergy were
not always willing to make direct grants without conditions being met,
and they were clearly uneasy about the collection of indirect taxes without
wider consent than kings sometimes took. Nonetheless kings could now
tap far greater and more flexible resources of wealth than ever before and,
for the first time for well over a century, an unextravagant king could
probably 'live of his own'.[16] The most useful component in this new
revenue was undoubtedly the income from customs duties, which provided
large, regular sums, which could be used as security for loans, and which
needed no consent for annual collection after their initial establishment.
The work of several historians over the last two decades has made the
finances of Edward II and the place of customs duties in them much clearer
and the rest of this paper will look more closely at them and at the trade
from which they came.

Before 1275 the Crown had already drawn on trade income: local tolls
in royal towns and ports, the wine prise, King John's tax on trade in
1202–4 and 1210–11, and the taxes collected for Edward as Prince of
Wales from 1266; but the wool tax imposed from 1275 at the rate of 6s 8d
on a sack of wool, 300 woolfells or a last of hides became the first
long-lasting national system. It was simple, clear, and relatively easy to
run, especially with the growing administrative skills of the government in
the thirteenth century. With wool exports running at about 24,000 sacks a
year it added an immediate £8,000 a year to the regular royal income. The
boom in the wool trade after 1300 raised this revenue to £10,000, and
then at its peak, for a short time, to over £15,000. Edward II inherited a
buoyant wool trade which ran at an average export of about 36,000 sacks a
year until the great famine and murrain years between 1315 and 1322.
This provided him with some £12,000 a year.[17] The duty was obviously a
great success. In 1303 Edward I had further extended his customs income
by negotiating a tax with alien merchants on all their import and export
trade in return for freer trading conditions for them while they were in
England. They were to pay an extra 3s 4d on a sack of wool, new specific
duties on cloth, wax and wine, and a duty of 3d in the pound value of all

other goods. In 1304–5 when it was fully under way, this levy (excluding the wine duties) added over £6,000 to Edward's annual income, about two-thirds of that coming from the increased wool duty. Alien trade did not continue at that level for long, but Edward II still drew a useful income from it. In 1307–8 (again excluding the wine duty) it was worth over £4,000 and in 1308–9 and 1310–11 worth nearly £4,000. Alien wine duties are not clearly recorded, but in London alone in 1307–8 and 1308–9 aliens imported 5,481 and 7,291 tuns which would have paid duty of £548 and £729 respectively.[18] The income from customs duties naturally varied with trade fluctuations, but after the expenses of collection Edward II would have received an average of about £16,000 a year from these sources – a little down from the last years of Edward I's reign but still a very good sum.

A further advantage of the customs revenue, emphasized by Dr Kaeuper and Professor Prestwich, is its role as security for loans from Italian bankers. The role of the Italian merchants in the English economy has been debated: the early exaggerated view of their importance as mentors for the underdeveloped English economy was strongly criticized by the late Professor Postan, but more measured recent views have granted the Italians some positive influence in commerce and have accepted their important and beneficial role in Crown finance. They probably did not bring much capital in from abroad, but their disbursement of their English resources allowed the king immediate access to liquid funds. This was politically important in spreading the costs of campaigns much more smoothly over several years.[19] However, Italian bankers would not lend without good guarantees and some reasonable prospect of repayment: in 1298 they preferred guarantees from the Church rather than a king in financial difficulties and at other times in Edward I's later years some companies refused loans.[20] The customs income, however, usually provided sufficient security. It is almost certain that the system was set up in 1275 primarily to repay the Riccardi, who were closely involved at that stage, and who managed the customs until 1294. Of the £400,000 they lent to Edward I they recouped at least half from customs duties.[21] The new custom of 1303 may also have been partly stimulated by the need for security for the Frescobaldi, who also drew on the wool custom and the Gascon revenues: over 80 per cent of their repayment came from customs duties. The Frescobaldi lent some £155,000 to Edward I and Edward II (who continued his father's borrowing policies) between 1294 and 1311, most of it between 1304 and 1310. They had been repaid £125,000 by 1310, at least £103,325 of this coming from customs revenue.[22] Even after the expulsion of the Frescobaldi in 1311, Edward continued to borrow from the Italians. Antonio Pessagno raised loans for him, often drawn from other merchants rather than from Pessagno's own resources. His account for 1314 shows he had by then advanced £111,506 and had already been repaid about £103,000. Edward used a wider range of resources to repay Pessagno, but customs duties remained important and at least 30 per cent of repayments came from them.[23] Customs duties thus provided both the security the Italians wanted, and considerable sums of money for their repayment. Without this income Edward I and Edward II would have needed more direct taxation for their wars and would have run into more political trouble than they did.

Unfortunately for Edward II the income did not stay at the early high level throughout his reign, partly due to political factors and partly due to changes in trade. Edward's actions in the early years of his reign, and particularly his inordinate love for Piers Gaveston, brought increasing opposition. Baronial opponents in 1309 and in 1311 took the opportunity not only to amend Edward's own shortcomings, but also to put a stop to some of the unpopular practices he had inherited from his father, among them the collection of the tax on alien trade, which was blamed for the great increase in prices visible between 1305 and 1310. Already in 1309, in return for the end of Gaveston's period of exile, the king had accepted the Statute of Stamford which included the suspension of the alien duties from 20 August that year. The petition for the abolition of the duties claimed that due to them the people of England were paying one-third more for goods than they used to. The king and his advisors were not convinced by this argument and agreed only to suspension at the king's will to see what benefit might appear. The king would then take further advice once the effect of the suspension had been seen. On 2 August 1310 the suspension was lifted on the grounds that it was clear that king and people had in no way benefitted from lower prices.[24] The duty was collected again for just over fourteen months before abolition in October 1311. Clause 5 of the Ordinances reiterated, among other points, the complaint about high prices.[25] It claimed that the duties had resulted in fewer alien merchants bringing fewer goods; those who did come could stay longer under the terms of the *Carta Mercatoria* of 1303, and since they did not need to sell quickly and leave, prices had risen; moreover their freedom from restrictions contravened London's own charter. Further, the tax, although it had been negotiated with those who paid, had not received the assent of the baronage.

The inflation of the first years of Edward's reign, of which the petitioners were so aware, was certainly severe and without doubt was largely the result of the state of England's overseas trade, but prices were driven up by the influx of silver from the booming wool trade, possibly complemented by English mint prices, rather than the tax on aliens. Nonetheless, this may have looked a plausible reason to contemporaries and it would have received much support from Londoners perennially irritated at the overriding of their charter. The clause also illustrated the unease at the possibility of the Crown using taxes not subject to English consent. The relationship of consent to customs duties was not fully or formally clarified at this time. The older trade dues were accepted as part of the king's prerogative. The newer ones were introduced at a time when the general principle that those who paid tax must assent to it had become established, but whose assent was necessary for payments on trade was not clear. The wool custom of 1275 had in the event been accepted in parliament; Edward I's added taxes on wool, the maltotes, which had raised great controversy as being without consent, had been abandoned. Perhaps this was in the minds of the Ordainers, yet the custom of 1303 was different, in that it was not collected from English subjects and had been duly negotiated with the consent of representatives of the alien merchants who did pay. Nonetheless, the baronage clearly felt that this was inadequate since the effects of the tax (as they perceived them) touched and damaged English subjects. Not surprisingly the tax received no formal English consent at its re-imposition in 1322. Then Edward was riding high after the battle of Boroughbridge and the destruction of his enemies, and parliamentary agreement to the revocation of the Ordinances, by which the duties had been abolished, provided an implicit acceptance of the king's right to collect them. Thereafter they continued as an accepted part of royal revenue and were never given formal consent in later reigns. The later cloth custom, paid by English merchants as well as aliens, was similarly negotiated with those paying it and was without parliamentary consent.[26] The obvious practical difference between these and the subsidies, which produced much criticism if consent was not obtained, was the level of the duties, and perhaps the smaller customs duties were seen as less dangerous than the larger subsidies. Nonetheless the king's opponents in 1311 had not seen customs duties as automatically exempt from what they considered proper consent. Which of their objections to the 1303 duty was the strongest is impossible to assess and probably does not matter very much from the practical point of view. What is clear is that this was one of the most effective clauses in the Ordinances and stopped the collection of alien duties dead until the Ordinances were repealed with the Statute of York in 1322. It removed, as we have seen above, £4,000 or more from Edward's regular annual income.

Other clauses in the Ordinances were directed at the king's use of Italian bankers with loans secured against the customs. Clause 4, repeated in clause 8, insisted that customs duties and all other income should be collected by Englishmen and must be accounted for at the Exchequer; clause 5 provided that all aliens who had received customs duties or other income since 1307 should be arrested until they had fully accounted for what they had collected; clause 21 provided specifically for the arrest of the Frescobaldi if they did not account before the middle of October. The political advantage of using Italian bankers had become a political liability under Edward II. The system of borrowing does not in itself seem to have aroused much antagonism under Edward I but Edward II was himself unpopular and distrusted, and his increasingly lavish personal grants to members of the Frescobaldi company and their close association with Gaveston made them a clear target for Edward's opponents. The Ordinances were completely effective in removing the Frescobaldi from the English scene, and the narrative of the company's withdrawal and prosecution is clearly set out by Dr Kaeuper.[27] They certainly did not, however, deprive Edward of Italians as bankers: the Genoese merchant Antonio Pessagno advanced Edward some £145,000 between 1310 and 1319 and smaller sums were received from the Bellardi and Bardi companies. Nor did they entirely stop Italian involvement in the collection of customs duties: Pessagno held half the cocket seal for the wool custom in London, Great Yarmouth and Boston at various times between 1312 and 1314, and Bardi nominees were appointed surveyors of the collection of wool customs in Hull and London in 1316; but this was on a much smaller scale than the direct involvement of the Frescobaldi, and in all cases the Italians had to account through the Exchequer in accordance with the Ordinances.[28]

The decline in Edward's income from customs duties came not only from political action but also from trade changes. The wool exports continued at a high level until 1315 but from then until 1319 dropped to an average of some 24,456 sacks a year, which brought the duties (now after 1311 back to the flat rate of 6s 8d for all) down to just over £8,000 a year, about the level they had been in Edward I's first years. There was some recovery in trade in 1319–21 to an average of 30,700 sacks but then exports slumped to an average of well under 24,000 sacks a year for the rest of the reign. The income was still on average some £7,700, which was not far under that for the early years of Edward I's reign, but it was much less than the Crown had grown accustomed to over the previous twenty years. The reintroduction of alien duties helped but alien trade also declined in the last years of Edward's reign. When the tax on aliens was restored in 1322 the situation still looked reasonably healthy. In the first fourteen months alien trade, now including wine imports, was still worth some £4,270, but this dropped to about £3,800 in 1323–4, and declined steadily to about £2,600 by 1326–7. Since the most important part of the tax had always been the enhanced duty on wool, the decline is partly explicable by the decline in the wool trade, but it is clear that alien activity in the general trades and in wine was also falling.[29]

The drop in customs income has political significance and political repercussions as it helped push Edward and his advisors to the politically unwise expedient of over-exploitation of traditional revenues mentioned above. The first signs of Exchequer reform came in 1316 when the first severe drop in the wool trade had brought the customs income down to only £7,100.[30] This also came at exactly the time when the war with Scotland was at its most active and expensive, prompting parliament to agree to two subsidies in successive years despite the hardship caused by the famine years and prompting Edward to try to raise a subsidy in Gascony too. Continued lower customs yields also coincided with the further financial squeezes of the 1320s. However, despite the decline in trade, in the last years of Edward II, the wool tax and the reinstated alien duties together were still providing over £10,000 a year for the government. This was an important sum, although observably less that the £16,000 possible in the short trade boom at the beginning of the reign.

The exact position of the customs duties in the annual income of the Crown is difficult to assess precisely, since the Exchequer did not draw up annual balance sheets, and the accounts themselves include collection of arrears, desperate debts, and other factors complicating the picture of actual income. Nonetheless recent work has made the picture clearer and allows the great importance of the customs duties to appear. It was not only that the sums collected were large but that, even more importantly, they became part of the regular annual revenue of the Crown after 1275. They should therefore be considered alongside the Crown's traditional income. In the 1280s the income from the shires possibly came to between £13,000 and £14,000 a year, other traditional income was estimated in 1284 at about £4,000, and the customs brought in some £8,000. The figures have shortcomings but probably indicate the right order of magnitude and show customs duties to be some 30 per cent of the Crown's normal English income.[31] As the wool trade boomed, they probably came nearer to providing 50 per cent of normal income. The unusual estimate of revenue made by the Exchequer in 1324 shows the duties as still important in Edward's later years.[32] Then shire revenues were estimated at only £11,743, and all other traditional income together with customs at some £21,730. At that time the ancient and the restored new customs were still worth over £13,000 and so would have provided nearly 40 per cent of normal, regular, English income. The additional £12,652 from the confiscated Contrariant lands doubled the king's landed income, but even with this windfall taken into account, customs still made up nearly 30 per cent of his English income. Customs income was not only important in England: the estimate of 1324 also expected clear income from Ireland of £1,424, and from Gascony of £13,000, and in both countries customs duties also played a part. In Gascony the great custom on wine collected in Bordeaux was particularly important probably providing a third to a half of Gascon revenue: in 1308–9 it amounted to £31,191 18s 2d of Bordeaux money, or about £5,198 sterling, and as the wine trade was fairly buoyant for much of Edward's reign it probably remained high in normal years. It was, however, reduced by the decline in trade during bad vintages and during the Gascon war in 1325.[33]

Although it is better to consider customs revenue alongside traditional revenue a further illustration of the importance of the customs duties may come from a comparison of them with the sums received from extraordinary direct taxation. Overall in his reign Edward took seven lay subsidies which brought him some £266,044; he received clerical and papal grants totalling between £203,297 and £271,364; the customs revenue overall probably came to some £240,328.[34] Customs thus provided a third of non-traditional revenue.

It is important to emphasize again, however, that customs revenue had the advantage of being regular and not normally dependent on consent. Although Edward's liquid resources at the end of his reign could be argued to have come primarily from the Contrariants' lands and from unused papal tenths, these could not have been kept in hand so easily without the great addition to regular income provided by the Crown's income from trade.

Although the income was so important the customs system was still relatively unsophisticated and lacked much of the supervision which was there by the fifteenth century. Dr Baker criticized the government for failing to tighten the administration, and even suggested that the decline in the customs income was due to increasing fraud rather than declining trade.[35] Dr Buck confirmed that the customs system was not overhauled with the same energy shown in reforming the Exchequer for traditional revenues and undoubtedly the more distant and less busy areas were less well supervised – in the beginning the Riccardi themselves had not felt that the return from the south-western ports was worth much effort.[36] Nonetheless the government was quite aware of the importance of this income and did not neglect it. As Dr Baker himself showed, it was always ready to inquire into suspected offences and the main southern and eastern ports were closely watched. The customs particulars were used in the inquiry into evasions of the St Omer staple in 1320 to check the amount of wool exports against arrivals at St Omer.[37] The careful auditing of customs accounts was covered of course by the general Exchequer reform and once the Exchequer had a run of accounts and knew what to expect, inquiries were set up if income dropped off. Officials knew enough about trade to expect fluctuations, and some slumps might be easily ascribed by contemporaries to obvious agricultural or political problems at the time, but when the decline in the alien wine imports, visible in the last years of Edward II's reign, continued, the Exchequer instituted an inquiry. The ensuing report in 1330 indicated that wine imports to England were in fact higher than ever, but Gascon merchants were now taking their wines to Flanders and Northern France and the increasing amounts of wine were brought by English merchants and were untaxed.[38]

The great success of the customs duties was only possible because of the strength of English overseas trade, and this was important to the Crown not only for the direct taxes which could be imposed on it, but because of its contribution to the general prosperity of the realm. The livelihoods of many rent-payers and tax-payers who contributed to the king's treasury depended on production for export or production of manufactured goods from imported raw materials, or on the collection and distribution of these things. The customs returns to the Exchequer show where this strength lay. The documents are of course tax returns and not complete surveys of trade, so the picture remains incomplete, but nonetheless they provide many details about the pattern of England's international trade. Analyses of the wool, alien and wine trades are easily accessible and will not be repeated here, but some general points can usefully be emphasized.[39]

First, the figures given above show that the wool trade was crucial. In this the government found a busy branch of trade which would provide large sustainable taxes, which could be collected relatively simply, and which would not quickly price the commodity out of the market. When they were first taxed wool exports were already high at some 24,000 sacks a year provided by the fleeces of perhaps six million sheep from the flocks of both peasants and large lay and ecclesiastical landowners all over England. Although the precise meaning of their words is debated, its all pervading influence was recognized by the opponents to Edward I in 1297 when they spoke of wool being half the wealth of England. The wool attracted large numbers of European buyers, but export was likely to be through a few main ports which could conveniently provide the warehousing and accommodate the large amount of shipping necessary for profitable trade. The tax of 6s 8d a sack brought in large sums but was relatively light given the price of wool. The prices varied of course according to quality. Pegolotti, a Bardi agent whose manual included lists of English religious houses from which the company purchased wool, recorded the best 'collecta' wools at £7 to £9 the sack; a price-fixing list of 1337 listed the poorer export wools at under £4. It is thus somewhat misleading to write of average prices, but to estimate the level of taxation, if we take £5 10s to £6 10s as a possible level, then the tax of 6s 8d amounted to only 5 or 6 per cent of the buying price of wool.[40] It would be an even smaller percentage of the selling price in Flanders or in the growing market in Florence where transport costs would increase the selling price yet further. In any case there were no obvious alternatives to English wools in quality or volume at this time: Scottish and Low Country wools were of generally poorer quality, and as yet the Mesta had not raised the quality or volume of Spanish wool to compete with English wools.

Secondly, because of the enormous scale of the wool exports and the high profile of alien merchants, especially Italians, England's economy has been described as colonial and underdeveloped, but in its implications of a country impoverished and wholly dominated by a much more advanced economy the description is misleading. The analogy with some modern oil-producing countries is better but still somewhat misleading. English kings could rely on an economy much more varied and stronger than this suggests. England exported more than wool, including some manufactured goods, had flourishing home industries, and was fully integrated into a complex trade network which included all western Europe.

It is true enough that England was primarily an exporter of raw materials and foods, but there was variety even in this. Besides the fleece-wool and woolfells, hides, some dairy produce, meat and timber were exported, probably running into hundreds of pounds a year. Exports of cereals were significant in times of plenty, as in Hull in 1307–8 when aliens alone took corn worth nearly £800.[41] Fish exports, mainly herring, were important locally especially at Yarmouth where in 1310–11 exports were valued at £1,396.[42] Minerals exported included salt and coal but were mainly tin and lead. These were also locally important near production areas and in good years might well have been worth £1,000–£2,000.[43] England also exported manufactured goods, notably cloth. There has long been a debate about the early fortunes of the English cloth industry. English cloth had been known as far away as Italy in the twelfth century, and a number of well organized urban weavers' gilds developed then. However, by the end of the thirteenth century some of these gilds claimed impoverishment, and when alien trade was taxed from 1303, it is clear that imports of alien cloths were high, running at some 12,000 cloths a year while exports of English cloth were low.[44] The decline of the English industry, however, should not be overstated. Some cloth industries were relocated in country areas, others in suburbs away from municipal and gild control, yet other industries continued in town centres, as at Salisbury.[45] Edward II was moved more than once by cloth producers to discuss ways of encouraging home industries; the matter was on the agenda for discussion in council at the parliament of 1322, and the export of fullers' earth and teasels were prohibited in 1326.[46] These industries, together with much family production, continued to clothe the majority of the English home market and some continued to find overseas buyers. The export is sometimes overlooked because few standard cloths of assize were recorded. Most English cloth was valued and charged duty at 3d in the pound so that exports were incorporated in the total valuation of miscellaneous goods.[47]

Most exports were through eastern ports, particularly through Boston and Lynn, probably still drawing on the old cloth fairs, but exports can be found through almost all English ports in Edward II's reign, from Hull in the north to Bristol in the west. The range of cloth was wide, with a few of the cloths of assize specified as top quality scarlet, but many of those valued were lighter cloths, sometimes described as worsted, says, serges, and blanket. Some were of Lincoln or Beverley and in the west cloths were described as russets, *grisancos* and Mendips. The figures available are patchy, and the trade was clearly small and was probably still declining in the 1320s, but it was still there, and exports were quite probably worth £1,750 a year even then. Moreover, what we can see is only the trade carried by aliens. Apart from cloth, a few manufactured belts, gloves, purses, and tin pots were also exported from London. And exports of ale from Lynn could reach a value of nearly £1,000 a year.[48] None of these goods rivalled the value of wool exports which were probably worth £200,000 and £230,000 at their peak, but those exported by aliens alone were worth several thousand pounds a year, and indicate production of a reasonable quality, able to find an international market.

England's imports testify to active home industries and include those not normally thought of as the imports of colonial economies. Apart from the 12,000 cloths a year (many of which were undoubtedly made from English wool), some articles of cloth, leather and metal in consignments of mercery and batteryware, and wine, spices and other luxury foods, there were a number of raw materials. Most notable among the industrial materials were dyes and mordants for a cloth industry clearly well beyond the homespun level, producing good quality cloth worth dyeing. Woad was imported all round the country, and total amounts might well be beyond 1,000 tons a year worth over £4,000: Southampton alone received 512 tons worth £2,734 in 1310–11.[49] Some alum and much more potash were imported to fix the dyes.[50] Iron and steel were imported for the metal industries. This was a lesser trade than that for the cloth industry but could still be substantial: in Lynn in 1322–3 imports of steel (probably about 170 barrels) were worth £364 and iron was worth £103 10s, while in Sandwich and Dover in 1325–6 iron imports, mainly from Basque sources, amounted to £562.[51]

English ports had complex contacts with most of western Europe and were not dependent on one or two nationalities only. There were sharp regional contrasts in the direction of a port's trade, depending largely on its geographical position. The North Sea ports and the south east naturally saw large numbers of Dutch, German, and some Flemish ships and merchants; the Channel ports saw few of these but many more from northern France. Within that general pattern there were some striking local variations. Hull and Lynn received most of England's Norwegian trade. All the east coast ports down to London saw Hansard vessels, especially ships of Hamburg and Lübeck, but Hull saw most of those from Stralsund, Gotland and Stavoren. Some north French ships from Abbeville or Calais came to east coast ports with woad, and occasionally Bayonne ships brought wine to Yarmouth in return for fish. At Sandwich and Southampton there was a strong Iberian presence. Although nearer to Spain and Portugal, Exeter and Bristol were far less attractive to Iberians than the more populous markets of the south-east, which also lay close to the international centre of Bruges in Flanders. They saw less Iberian trade than might be expected and most of their alien visitors were from north France, Ireland and the Channel Islands.

The goods apart from wool handled by the ports also underline regional differences and the local attractions for aliens at this time. Newcastle exported coal.[52] Hull and Boston exported significant amounts of lead from Yorkshire and Derbyshire, and received much herring and codfish for re-distribution. Boston and Lynn dealt heavily in cloth, and Lynn exported much ale, drawing no doubt on the barley fields of her hinterland. At Yarmouth the herring fisheries provided a major export, and the trade dovetailed neatly with the wine trade.[53] London already showed its characteristics as a capital by handling the greatest amount and variety of goods and especially importing manufactured goods, and luxury spices and foodstuffs. It attracted all nationalities. At Sandwich and Dover small timber was a notable local export. Southampton's exports were mainly agricultural, but sometimes included tin coasted up from the west. Little of this went from the West Country ports which mainly exported cloth and agricultural goods.[54]

It is true that alien activity looks particularly strong in England's overseas trade at this time, but this is partly due to the nature of the tax records. The English share of trade was significant, and was growing fast under Edward II. The English merchants' share of the licenced wool trade in the early 1270s may have been under one-third, but under Edward II they became dominant, handling two-thirds of exports.[55] In the Bordeaux wine trade, although Gascon merchants were very active at the beginning of the fourteenth century, English shipping was particularly strong. English ports provided about half the shipping at Bordeaux in Edward II's reign, often over 300 ships a year, which carried just under half the tunnage exported. Since only perhaps one-quarter of the tunnage was destined for England, clearly English shipowners were enterprising enough to carry for other markets.[56] Alien wine imports steadily dropped in the 1320s and English merchants' imports rose, until a government inquiry set up in 1330 reported that now the English imported twice what the Gascons had done.[57] The alien trade in general merchandise also steadily decreased in the 1320s, but whether this was accompanied by an increase in English activity as in the wool and wine trades is unclear in the absence of taxation of English merchants.

The large numbers of aliens in England and the high profile of some, notably the Italians as Crown bankers, but also the Germans with their charters of privilege, and the Gascons who were able to negotiate their own trade terms in 1302, have also contributed to the description of the English economy as underdeveloped. The debate over the exact contribution of aliens to the development of the English economy continues. The overvaluation of the Italians' contribution was sharply challenged by Professor Postan in 1951 when he questioned 'the ability of the Italians to lead and the need of the English to follow'.[58] An excellent recent survey of Italian activities by Professor Prestwich has softened some of Professor Postan's arguments. Professor Prestwich accepts their relatively low significance in the production of goods and in teaching business techniques, but re-establishes the benefits and importance of their financial activity. Dr Lloyd's survey of alien trade has also indicated the useful role of Italian and German merchants in the more distant Baltic and Mediterranean trade, while the English energies were taken up with expansion in their nearer markets.[59]

The political historian can make use of the information in the customs records just as the economic and social historian can in making more precise the picture of England's commerce. England was a productive island with a considerable consumer market; attractive to aliens but with a strong mercantile and ship-owning community of its own; a country with strong home industries as well as being a supplier of a prime raw material; fully integrated into a complex international trading network and not dependent on the investment and technical leadership of another 'advanced' economy, although services which a particular group could offer would easily be utilized. England was in no way a drained or impoverished country; indeed its trade balance was decisively in its favour, bringing in enough silver to produce problems in itself, by helping to fuel the inflation which had a strong monetary element in 1305–10.[60] To speak of this situation as if it were similar to a colonial economy is misleading.

English kings enjoyed the political advantage of a strong home economy which they could tax. They could not but be aware of the importance of trade, and the need to encourage it. Government regulation had increased in the thirteenth century and continued under Edward II, who tried to encourage the cloth industry, and whose setting up of a staple system was both to protect English wool merchants and to use as a lever in foreign affairs.[61] Government interest in trade was both to promote the general prosperity of the realm, and to ensure its own regular revenue, one-third to one-half of which in peacetime was now drawn from customs duties.

Yet Edward squandered the stability that this promised and left himself open, among all the other accusations, to charges of greed and of stripping and ruining his realm. His financial position was not, of course, the main reason for his downfall but it was a contributory one partly stemming from, and partly independant of the others. The central reason for his deposition was wholly political: Edward's long-term ineptitude in antagonizing almost all the great political figures on whom a king normally relied for support. The early fourteenth-century baronage expected to be asked for advice, to have reasonable access to the king's ear, and to receive a reasonable amount of royal patronage. Whether through weakness of character as is often said, or through a strong but misguided perception of his royal right to choose whatever counsellors he wished, Edward allowed first Gaveston then Despenser to block the channels of access and patronage. Moreover the king's violence against the rebels in 1322 and the subsequent confiscation of estates, even if understandable as an emotional reaction against those he blamed for Gaveston's murder and the restrictions of his prerogative, must rank high in a list of political errors. It increased fears for life and for property rights, and few of high rank were left who were able or willing to stand against Edward and Despenser. As the author of the *Vita Edwardi Secundi* wrote, 'no one however great and wise dares to cross his will. Thus parliaments, colloquies, and councils decide nothing these days. For the nobles of the realm, terrified by threats and the penalties inflicted on others, let the king's will have free play. Thus today will conquers reason.'[62] When Isabella finally appeared in open opposition with the support of her son who was so nearly of an age to rule, Edward found his main political support had gone. But other reasons for his deposition were given in the accusations against Edward, including his loss of territory, his persecution of certain churchmen, and his greed in 'stripping his realm'. That his financial pressures were not just an afterthought but had raised much anger, is shown by the criticism of them in chronicles and parliamentary petitions. Perhaps the criticism was even more bitter, because for once it was not of a king struggling for solvency in the face of circumstances outside his control – inflation, increasing war expenses, bullion shortages – but of a king with adequate revenues pushing for yet more. The customs revenues played a large part in providing his solvency, but Edward failed once more to make the most of his potential strengths.

### Notes

1  M. Prestwich, *War, Politics and Finance under Edward I* (1972), pp.221–2; M. Prestwich, *Edward I* (1988), pp.535–6.
2  M. Mate, 'High prices in early fourteenth-century England: causes and consequences',

*EcHR*, 2nd ser., XXVIII (1975); *Foedera, Conventiones, Litterae* . . ., ed. T. Rymer (RC, 1818) II. i. 263, 286; *Rot. Parl.* I. 295.

3 *Flores Historiarum*, ed. H.R. Luard (RS, 1890) III. 217–8; *Vita Edwardi Secundi*, ed. N. Denholm-Young (1957), p.136; *The Brut*, ed. F.W.D. Brie, EETS, 131, (1906), p.225; Sir Thomas Gray, *Scalacronica*, trans. Sir Herbert Maxwell (Glasgow, 1907), p.70.

4 Prestwich, *War, Politics and Finance*, p.221.

5 N. Fryde, *The Tyranny and Fall of Edward II* (Cambridge, 1979), pp.94, 105; M. Buck, *Politics, Finance and the Church in the Reign of Edward II* (Cambridge, 1983), p.193.

6 Fryde, *Tyranny and Fall*, p.75.

7 G. Harriss, *King, Parliament, and Public Finance in Medieval England to 1369* (Oxford, 1979), p.524.

8 J.F. Willard, *Parliamentary Taxes on Personal Property 1290–1334* (Cambridge, Mass., 1934), p.344; W.E. Lunt, *Financial Relations of the Papacy with England to 1327* (Cambridge, Mass., 1939), pp.410–1.

9 Fryde, *Tyranny and Fall*, p.94.

10 M. Buck, 'The Reform of the Exchequer, 1316–1326', *EHR*, XCVIII (1983), 246–7, 254–5; Buck, *Politics, Finance and the Church*, pp.166–89; Fryde, *Tyranny and Fall*, pp.89–90, 100–1.

11 Prestwich, *Edward I*, p. 537.

12 Brotherton Library, Leeds, Ms. 29, (Anonimalle Chronicle), f.257.

13 Buck, *Politics, Finance and the Church*, p.176; Buck, 'Reform of the Exchequer,' p.254.

14 Ibid., p.258.

15 *Flores*, III. 218–9; *Vita Edwardi Secundi*, pp.136, 139; *Brut*, p.225; H. Johnstone, 'The Queen's Household', in T.F. Tout, *Chapters in the Administrative History of Medieval England*, V (Manchester, 1930), 274–5 (Isabella's dower lands were worth £4,500 a year, although £8,493 arrears were owed in 1324; her total grant from the Exchequer was 3920 marks a year, or £2,613 6s 8d); *Foedera*, II. i. 650.

16 Harriss, *Public Finance*, pp.148–9.

17 For the level of trade see E.M. Carus-Wilson and O. Coleman, *England's Export Trade, 1275–1547* (Oxford, 1963), pp. 36–43, 122.

18 Calculations based on T.H. Lloyd, *Alien Merchants in England in the High Middle Ages* (Brighton, 1982) Appendix 1; M.K. James, *Studies in the Medieval Wine Trade* (Oxford, 1971), p.10.

19 M. Prestwich, 'Italian Merchants in late thirteenth and early fourteenth century England', in *The Dawn of Modern Banking*, University of California Centre for Medieval and Renaissance Studies (New Haven, 1979), pp.79–80, 102–4.

20 Prestwich, *Edward I*, pp.533–4.

21 R.W. Kaeuper, *Bankers to the Crown. The Riccardi of Lucca and Edward I* (Princeton, 1973), pp.129–30, 149, 164–9.

22 R.W. Kaeuper, 'The Frescobaldi of Florence and the English Crown', in *Studies in Medieval and Renaissance History*, 10 (1973), 63, 67; Prestwich, 'Italian Merchants', p.79; Prestwich, *Edward I*, p.534.

23 Lloyd, *Alien Merchants*, pp. 179–80, 183.

24 *Rot. Parl* I. 444; *SR*, I. 156; *CFR 1307–19*, p.68.

25 *English Historical Documents*, III, ed. H. Rothwell (London, 1975), 527–39.

26 Kaeuper, *Bankers to the Crown*, pp.144–5; T.H. Lloyd, *The English Wool Trade in the Middle Ages* (Cambridge, 1977), p.60; N.S.B. Gras, *The Early English Customs System* (Cambridge, Mass., 1918), p.71.

27 Kaeuper, 'The Frescobaldi', pp.72–92.

28 N. Fryde, 'Antonio Pessagno of Genoa, King's Merchant of Edward II of England', in *Studi in Memoria di Federigo Melis*, II (Naples, 1978), 168; Lloyd, *Alien Merchants*, pp.178–81; *CFR 1307–19*, pp.132, 187, 191, 281–2.

29 Lloyd, *Alien Merchants*, Appendix 1; James, *Wine Trade*, Appendices 2, 3.

30  Buck, 'Reform of the Exchequer', p.246.
31  Prestwich, *War, Politics and Finance*, p.178; Harriss, *Public Finance*, pp.145–6.
32  Harriss, *Public Finance*, pp. 146–52, 523–4.
33  PRO E101/163/1, f. 135; James, *Wine Trade*, pp.9–14, see also M. Powicke, *The Thirteenth Century*, (2nd ed., Oxford, 1962), pp.304–7.
34  Willard, *Parliamentary Taxes*, p.344; Sir J.H. Ramsay, *A History of the Revenues of the Kings of England, 1066–1399* (Oxford, 1925), II. 148, Table B; Lunt, *Financial Relations*, pp.392–3, 396, 402, 407, 409–11 shows that over £195,000 came from papal grants. He includes income from two tenths granted to Edward I in 1306 and 1307, but collected by Edward II, and a crusading tenth of 1311, which might be counted a loan.
35  R.L. Baker, 'The English Customs Service, 1307–1343. A Study of Medieval Administration' *Trans. American Philosophical Soc.*, new ser., 51 (Philadelphia, 1961), pp.13–22.
36  Kaeuper, *Bankers to the Crown*, pp. 155–6.
37  Lloyd, *Wool Trade*, pp. 111–2.
38  PRO E101/78/4a; James, *Wine Trade*, pp.14, 80–3. Dr Lloyd has pointed out that the decline in the wool trade can be correlated clearly with factors directly affecting wool markets. 'Overseas Trade and the English Money Supply in the Fourteenth Century' in *Edwardian Monetary Affairs (1279–1344)*, ed. N. Mayhew, British Archaeological Reports, 36 (Oxford, 1977) p.105.
39  Various tables and analyses are provided in Carus-Wilson and Coleman, *England's Export Trade*; James, *Wine Trade*; Lloyd, *Alien Merchants*; Lloyd, *Wool Trade*.
40  F. Balducci Pegolotti, *La Pratica della Mercatura*, ed. A Evans (Cambridge, Mass., 1936), pp.258–69; T.H. Lloyd, 'The Movement of Wool Prices in Medieval England', *EcHR* Supplement, 6 (1973), p.70.
41  PRO E122/6/1.
42  PRO E122/148/13, 30, 31.
43  Figures are hard to come by for tin, but in 1340 Bardi exports alone were worth £724. Exports of lead from Hull alone had reached a value of £1,231. J. Hatcher, *English Tin Production and Trade before 1550* (Oxford, 1973), pp.91–5, 103, 110–11, 114–5; PRO E122/55/19, 20, 56/14, 26, 57/2, 6/1.
44  Lloyd, *Alien Merchants*, p. 111, and Appendix 1.
45  E. Miller, 'The Fortunes of the English Textile Industry in the Thirteenth Century', *EcHR*, 2nd series, XVIII (1965), 64–82; A.R. Bridbury, *Medieval English Clothmaking. An Economic Survey* (1982), pp.31–2.
46  J. Conway Davies, *The Baronial Opposition to Edward II. Its Character and Policy*, (Cambridge, 1918), p.583; *Calendar of the Plea and Memoranda Rolls preserved among the Archives of the Corporation of the City of London at the Guildhall, AD 1323–1364*, ed. A.H. Thomas (Cambridge, 1926), p.44; *Calendar of Letter Books of the City of London: Letter Book E*, ed. R.R. Sharpe (1903), p.211.
47  The following paragraphs are based on the surviving particular accounts, PRO E122.
48  PRO E122/93/18.
49  Lloyd, *Alien Merchants*, pp.75, 81–2; PRO E122/40/7a.
50  Imports of potash could be high, and reached 172 tons in Hull, 1305–6, PRO E122/55/19.
51  *The Making of King's Lynn*, ed. D.M. Owen, Records of Social and Economic History, new series IX (1984), no.408; PRO E122/124/29.
52  J.B. Blake 'The Medieval Coal Trade of North East England: some Fourteenth Century Evidence', *Northern History*, II (1967), 13–14.
53  PRO E101/163/4.
54  Hatcher, *Tin Trade*, p.162; note 43 above.
55  Lloyd, *Wool Trade*, pp.50–9; Carus-Wilson and Coleman, *England's Export Trade*, pp.41, 43; figures for 1322–6 are clearer in Lloyd, *Alien Merchants*, Appendix 1.

56  PRO E101/161/3, 162/1, 5, 6, 163/4; James, *Wine Trade*, p.81.
57  James, *Wine Trade*, pp.14, 80–3, and Appendices 12–14.
58  M.M. Postan, 'Italians and the economic development of England in the Middle Ages', reprinted in M.M. Postan, *Medieval Trade and Finance* (Cambridge, 1973), pp.335–41.
59  Prestwich, 'Italian Merchants', passim; Lloyd, *Alien Merchants*, pp.127–43, 154–6, 166–209; see the full discussion of the relationship of England and Italy at this time by R. Britnall in the forthcoming volume of the *TRHS*.
60  See note 2 above; Lloyd, 'Overseas Trade and the Money Supply', pp.96–108, 121–2; M. Prestwich, 'Currency and the Economy of Early Fourteenth Century England', also in *Edwardian Monetary Affairs*, pp.45–58.
61  Conway Davies, *Baronial Opposition*, p.583; *English Historical Documents*, III. 544–6; Lloyd, *Wool Trade*, pp.102–17.
62  *Vita Edwardi Secundi*, p.136.

# 3
# Conflict and Consensus in English Local Society*

Nigel Saul

*Royal Holloway and Bedford New College*
*University of London*

The cohesiveness of English local society in the late Middle Ages is a quality which has received considerable emphasis in recent work on the period. Particularly valuable has been Michael Bennett's discussion in his *Community, Class and Careerism: Cheshire and Lancashire Society in the Age of Sir Gawain and the Green Knight.* Not only is the closely-knit structure of society highlighted here more clearly than ever before, but the importance of that structure to the maintenance of stability is demonstrated more amply as well. Crucial to the argument is the role of the gentry – the group 'which above all imbued the concept of (county) community with real social meaning'. In the two counties under review it is shown that they formed overlapping networks of proprietors whose members acted within 'a framework of trust, consensus and cooperation'.[1] In matters concerning the settlement and disposition of property these men were drawn into dependence on one another by the absence of anything resembling an official system of land registration. They were involved in reciprocal obligations as feoffees, and they regularly acted as witnesses to one another's deeds. At a less formal level they were drawn together by intermarriage and by the widespread practice of farming out youngsters for upbringing in each others' households; while in the political arena they were brought into association in such capacities as justice of the peace, knight of the shire and commissioner of array by the interest which they all had in ensuring that local affairs were run to their mutual advantage. In all these areas of life they were sustained by solidarities which were flexible enough to accommodate disagreement and yet at the same time resilient enough to withstand factional pressure.[2]

---

\* Earlier versions of this paper, which replaces the one originally delivered at Leeds, were read at seminars in the Universities of Kent and London. I am grateful to the audiences on those occasions for their helpful and constructive comments. I am also grateful to Philip Morgan and Christopher Whittick for reading the paper in typescript.

A parallel, and perhaps older, tradition of scholarship takes an altogether less sympathetic view of the workings of local society. On the evidence of the Plea Rolls it sees that society as being characterized less by cooperation and consensus than by tension and conflict. Peasant communities are pictured as being divided by disputes over ownership of property and access to common land, and their gentry overlords as riven by apparently unending feuds and outbreaks of gang warfare. In the words of Professor Hilton, 'members of gentry families appear with such considerable frequency [in the Plea Rolls], in proportion to their total numbers, that disorder appears almost to be a by-occupation of their class' – and that in a group 'whom one might have expected to have been the protectors of the social order from which they gained their livelihood'.[3] Some of this violence took the form of nothing more 'reprehensible' than the poaching of the magnates' parks.[4] But much more of it was rooted in the natural conflicts of the age. The gentry, it is argued, were engaged in a struggle for control of scarce resources. Sheer necessity drove them into competition with one another. Compelled as they were to maintain a comfortable style of life on incomes frequently unequal to the demands placed upon them, the acquisition of more land represented the only way out of their predicament. To some extent the control exercised locally by the magnates or centrally by the Crown placed some limitation on their natural factiousness, but rarely was it sufficient; and when, as in the later Middle Ages, royal control went at least partially into retreat and the keepers of the peace were granted some of the powers once exercised by the Justices in Eyre, the gentry, from whose ranks the JPs were drawn, found themselves in possession of new weapons with which to pursue their rivalries. Packed juries and drummed-up indictments became the all but inevitable characteristics of a society which found its ultimate and most anarchic expression in the Norfolk of the mid-fifteenth century.[5]

To an extent the conflict between these two points of view is explicable in terms of the selective use of evidence. The impression of harmony is derived from sources such as charters, enfeoffments and marriage agreements which show the gentry working in cooperation with each other; while that of conflict is derived from a very different set of materials, namely the Plea Rolls, which by their very nature are revealing only of conflict. Nevertheless it is doubtful if the discrepancy can be explained solely in these terms: it is simply too great, and it leaves unresolved the problem of reconciling to each other the two sets of impressions. The strains involved in any attempt to do this have been felt by a number of writers on the subject. Ailsa Herbert, for example, comments that 'crime in Herefordshire was endemic and went largely unpunished' in the early fifteenth century (even in the reign of Henry V), but then goes on to say that at the same time the courts 'experienced an increasing volume of litigation, which must suggest that the law was still largely respected'.[6] Similar unease is felt by Philip Morgan in his analysis of the workings of the Cheshire military community. As points of contact between estates increased, he writes, 'so too did opportunities for conflict; throughout the fourteenth century relationships between families hovered uncertainly between demonstrations of group unity, aggressive litigation and outright violence'.[7] Gerald Harriss is, at first glance, a little less hesitant: he sees appeals to lordship, manipulation of the legal system and outright violence as all 'comprising an integral system of social control'. But even he leaves it to others to decide whether conflict or cohesion is to be regarded as the habitual conditon of this 'bastard feudal' society.[8]

The uncertainty felt by modern historians has its roots in the ambivalent behaviour of the gentry themselves. They had the ability to switch roles with apparently effortless ease. They appear first as poachers, then as gamekeepers; first as law-breakers, then as lawmakers. In parliament they appealed for better enforcement of the law; back home they were among the first to break it. In parliament they condemned the practice of maintenance; back home they were themselves the beneficiaries of it. In the long-running debate on the administration of justice they argued that peace could best be preserved by the granting of the determining power to themselves in their capacity as keepers of the peace. Yet, once they had gained that power, they used it ruthlessly and unhesitatingly as an instrument of factional warfare. And at no time did they show any more appreciation of the inconsistency in these positions than they did when calling on the king to vindicate his rights in warfare while yet withholding the grants of taxation that he needed in order to achieve that end.

To be sure, the Crown itself set a poor example in observance of the law. Time and again it gave its assent to statutes which it then ignored. The Sumptuary Ordinance of 1363, for example, was a dead letter from the moment of its passing.[9] So too was the statute providing for annual rotation of sheriffs: though first approved in 1340 and subsequently reaffirmed in 1343, 1351 and 1354, it was only in 1371 that it was finally put into practice.[10] The statute passed at Lincoln in 1316 prohibiting the appointment of stewards to the shrievalty probably fared no better; and the Ordinance of 1390 regulating the distribution of livery certainly did not.[11] Selectivity in the enforcement of statutes was as much a feature of the Crown's policy as was selectivity in their observance of that of its subjects.

Neither was respect for the law aided by the evident partiality with which it was administered. Jurors and justices alike allowed themselves to be bought by those who needed their favour. In an episode in the long-running struggle between the abbot and townsmen of St Albans, Sir John de Cambridge, a Justice of Common Pleas, allowed himself to become the willing agent of the former in drumming up indictments against his recalcitrant tenants. So notorious was his partisanship that a long petition was submitted to the king complaining of the friendship between him and the abbot, and adding for good measure that the local sheriff and coroner were also in the latter's pay. A few years later Sir John Inge, another justice of the Common Bench, played a similar role in the dispute between the Prior of Christ Church, Canterbury and his tenants at Monks Risborough (Bucks.). Under colour of an oyer and terminer commission, the justice and a local ruffian by the name of Sir John de Molyns, who was also one of the prior's councillors, received indictments drawn up by a jury composed almost entirely of Molyns' own adherents.[12] Since those named were already in prison and were in no position to appear, they were condemned to outlawry. In this case the manipulation employed was so crude and so blatant that the outlawry was shortly afterwards revoked. But the influence of the locally powerful over the judicial system was in general so pervasive that the central courts were rarely capable of either resolving by verdict the suits that came before them or of mounting an effective deterrent to criminal activity among the well-born and well-connected. Had those who were inconvenienced been confined to the ranks of the peasantry and the politically inarticulate, the injustice of it all would probably have caused little concern. But they were not. They included at least some of the gentry. For example, there was a Gloucestershire knight, Sir John de Berkeley of Dursley, who complained in about 1330 that he could not get justice in his native county because Sir Thomas de Berkeley of Berkeley, Roger Mortimer's son-in-law, held the king's ministers in the county at his fees and robes.[13] Sir John was a fairly rich knight and, though no relation (or friend) of the baronial house of the same name, was a man with influence in the shire. If someone of his local importance could find himself worsted, then it becomes easier to understand why the volume of complaint about the corruption of the justices, and of judicial administration more generally, reached such a pitch in the fourteenth century. It was the well-being of the gentry which was being threatened, not just that of their tenants.

In the light of these considerations it is possible to argue that gentry disenchantment with the law sprang from a strong suspicion that it no longer served their needs: that when the processes were so riddled with graft, and in any case were generally so slow, advantage seemed to lie with the use of extra-legal means.[14] There is much to be said for this view. But it is also open to serious objections. The growing volume of litigation, for example, which in one sense is evidence of the courts' failure to cope is another evidence of their success in attracting business. In the fourteenth century, at least, there is no sign of anything like the loss of confidence in the courts that is supposed to have occurred in the late fifteenth and early

sixteenth centuries.[15] On the contrary, there was an explosion of what
G.L. Harriss has called 'law-seeking and law-keeping'.[16] Over the century
as a whole the Rolls of the Court of Common Pleas grew steadily bigger,
despite a sharp fall in population over the same period. A typical roll of
Richard II's reign runs to some 400–500 membranes in length as against
some 200–300 membranes half a century earlier. Simultaneously there was
a shrinkage in the size of the Rolls of King's Bench (a forum for mainly
criminal business) roughly proportionate to the fall in population.[17] It
seems possible, even probable, therefore that, while resort to extra-legal
remedies remained constant or declined, there was an increasing resort to
legal ones. Such a pattern of behaviour hardly accords with a view of
society as being increasingly riven by violence. Much more it suggests a
commitment to the use of law which balanced, if it did not altogether
outweigh, the understandable temptation to employ self-help. The fact
that, like every human institution, the common law had its imperfections
is unlikely seriously to have undermined public confidence in it. What it
did, rather, was to stimulate an appetite for reform which the king and his
officers went at least some way to satisfy. Criticism of corruption was
answered in 1346 by an Ordinance prohibiting the taking of fees and robes
and thirty years later by the judges' complete renunciation of such fees.[18]
And demands for measures to limit the violent seizure of land were met by
the extension of conciliar jurisdiction and by the passing of the Statutes of
Forcible Entry.[19] Reality may not always have matched expectation; and
litigants may still on occasion have been driven to seek from the king and
council remedies which they could not find at common law.[20] But the
structure built up by Henry II and his successors proved a good deal more
durable than has sometimes been supposed. What has tended to obscure a
clearer appreciation of this point is the very different way in which the law
was viewed in the Middle Ages. Because of the relative weakness of the
agencies of enforcement, it was not accorded automatic respect: it was not
regarded as an external, as an end in itself which defined and regulated
every aspect of life. Rather it was seen as a bundle of remedies or strategies
which could be used or abused as necessary. In no area of life was this truer
than in that of proprietorship. The use that was made of the law here was
entirely self-interested. Legal process was seen less as a means of solving a
dispute than as a way of gaining a temporary advantage over an opponent.
It was appropriated by litigants for ends that were purely personal.

   Chief among these ends was, of course, the preservation and extension
of the family patrimony. It was with this rather than with any more
abstract notion that the idea of 'justice' was associated in landed society. A
manor that was lost had to be recovered because a lineage's reputation
depended on it. Richard II was suspected of disinheriting the Crown by
seeking peace with France through the devolution of the Duchy of

Aquitaine on his uncle John of Gaunt; and the same stigma was likely to attach to any landowner who was thought to have been less than whole-hearted in the safeguarding of his own property. Consequently justice, like law itself, was viewed in essentially subjective terms, and every litigant identified his own cause with it. Time and again petitioners rounded off bills of complaint to the king with words to the effect that the wrongs they had suffered were against reason or against law, and that right ought to be done to them. Whether they had any notion of justice as a more abstract, more objective idea is difficult to determine. Professor Crowder has recently argued persuasively that they did – or rather that there *was* a prevailing view of justice, powerfully influenced by the teaching of the Church, which provided a reference point for contemporary perceptions.[21] Assuming that he is right, it has to be allowed that in the course of a lengthy and difficult suit there would have been times when a litigant felt that the decisions of the courts bore little relation to 'justice' in this abstract sense. Miscarriages undoubtedly occurred, and the idealization of those who were its victims was one of the by-products.[22] But overall the risk of injustice was kept to a minimum. The 'tiered system' of litigation in civil cases at least – criminal ones were different – turning as it did on the use first of one writ and then of another, allowed a case to be reviewed from a number of different angles before a final decision was reached.[23] And the tendency of the great majority of cases to be settled by compromise, whether in or out of court, sharply reduced the sense of grievance likely to be felt by the 'losing' party had the case gone to a jury.

Because matters of reputation and honour were at stake quarrels between gentry families (quarrels commonly over land) were apt to be long and bitter. They would smoulder for generations, periodically flaring up and then dying down, only to erupt again later. Some of the most combustible of these disputes were ones that raged within rather than between families. One such – involving members of the Pashley family – became a cause célèbre in southern England in the late 1320s. Its origins lay in the dynastic ambitions of one Margaret de Basing, the woman with whom the Exchequer baron Sir Edmund Pashley consorted for the last years of his life. In a bid to secure an inheritance for the illegitimate offspring of her union with the judge this cold and calculating woman plotted the murders first of the judge himself and then of his sons by his wife Maud. Edmund the younger was murdered at Coulsdon (Surrey) on 13 March 1328; William, his elder brother, disappeared at about the same time. Only John, the second born, appears to have escaped her clutches. It was through his determination that a campaign of resistance was mounted, and for the best part of ten years Surrey and eastern Sussex were disrupted by a succession of raids and counter-raids until a compromise of sorts was patched up in 1345.[24] Other feuds, albeit ones less macabre than this, were no less vigorously fought. The struggle for the Langley inheritance in Gloucestershire, which was initiated by the abduction of Joan, the family heiress and wife of Sir John de Charlton and her subsequent remarriage to Sir John Trillowe, the man who carried her off, was also punctuated by the familiar sequence of raids, counter-raids and evictions. In this instance it was only terminated by the final break-up of the inheritance and its dispersal among those contenders who could wield the most muscle.[25] In the same county a struggle broke out only a few years later over the succession to Sir Simon Basset's manor of Lasborough. Lady Maud, Sir Simon's widow, and her sons Maurice and Edmund launched a raid on the manor in February 1377 in the course of which Margaret, Simon's granddaughter and the occupant, was assaulted and raped. The litigation between her and her husband on the one side and her uncles on the other dragged on until at least the second decade of the fifteenth century.[26] In all of these feuds the common factor was succession to an inheritance. What was at stake was access to wealth and thus to the chief source of status in society. But it was not only, nor even chiefly, the prospect of material gain that drove people to these lengths: frequently the costs of the dispute exceeded the value of the estate in question for years ahead.[27] Much more it was a sense of dynastic pride. Claimants to an estate saw themselves not only as aspirant proprietors but as heirs to a family tradition which it was their duty to maintain. Their consciousness of the past was sharpened by a preoccupation with heraldry and buttressed by the compilation of genealogies. One such genealogy – this, a particularly detailed one – was drawn up by the Morleys in the fifteenth century to support their claim to the manor of Glynde (Sussex), which the Waleys family had held before them.[28] Schemes of heraldic decoration conveyed the same message, but to a wider audience. An exceptionally grand display in the church at Trotton (Sussex) appears to have had its origins in the insecurity felt by a young lord newly entered into his inheritance. Sir Thomas de Camoys, the lord concerned, was not of the direct line of descent; he was a collateral, who succeeded on the death of his namesake and kinsman Sir Thomas in 1372. To demonstrate to his tenants the legitimacy of his descent he had the wall of the church decorated with a pictorial scheme commemorating the forebears with whom he wished to be associated.[29] In like manner, though in more modest fashion, John and Christina Cressy commissioned a pair of brasses to mark their successful acquisition of the manor of Dodford (Northants) at the end of a long and bitterly fought battle over the succession to the Keynes inheritance. One was to commemorate themselves, and the other Christina's parents, neither of whom had ever seen, let alone lived in, the manor. Commemoration in this instance served as a disguise for the 'newness' of the new lords.[30]

The tenacity with which the gentry defended their interests both exacerbated the feuding between them and added greatly to the difficulty of resolving it. But whether it also added to the general level of violence is much harder to establish. In the opinion of Peter Coss it did. Peoples' instinct, he has written, was to resort first to arms and only secondly to litigation.[31] The analysis he offers of the break-up of the Langley inheritance adds weight to his opinion. But it is more difficult to accept it as a general observation on the relationship between law and the use of force. More often the latter was invoked only secondarily, and in conjunction with proceedings in the courtroom.[32] Its purpose was to bring additional pressure on the other party to submit. Its scale, therefore, was limited, and its use directed against property rather than person: homicide, though not unknown, was uncommon.[33] The longer, more complex and more violent disputes were to that extent exceptional. But they are also the ones that are more rewarding to analyse. Because they placed the greatest strains on the fabric of society, they offer by far the best opportunity to see how resilient were the bonds that held that society together.

The origins of the dispute over the manor of Norton Veel (Somerset) are obscure.[34] By the time the case reached the courts, as it did in the 1330s if not earlier, the positions of the two parties were well established. Sir Peter le Veel, the plaintiff, claimed that the manor had been settled on his grandparents, Robert and Hawisia le Veel, by one Walter de la Hide. Thomas de Stapeldon, the defendant, countered by claiming that he had been granted a life interest in the manor by his kinsman Sir Richard de Stapeldon.[35] On the face of it Thomas's case appears the more convincing. Norton was one of the manors which his elder brother Walter, Bishop of Exeter, had bought for the purpose of endowing his numerous relatives: it had been acquired in 1315 from Sir William Paynel by the bishop and Sir Richard jointly, and the latter had then demised it for life to Thomas.[36] Peter's case on the other hand presents a number of problems. The settlement to which he refers cannot be traced among the surviving records; and the only evidence for an earlier connection between his family and the manor is a fine of 1302 in which Paynel used Hawisia le Veel as deforciant to settle the manor on himself and his wife jointly with remainder to his wife's right heirs.[37] Hawisia's employment in this capacity, however, is difficult to explain other than on the assumption that she had some previous connection with the manor or some blood relationship with Margaret Paynel. The most likely explanation is that she was one of the right heirs to whom the fine referred, and that her reversionary rights were nullified by the sale to the Stapeldons.

In any event, in the 1330s it was clearly the Stapeldons and not the Veels who were in possession, and Sir Peter was obliged to sue in Common Pleas for recovery. In 1334 his action was remitted by *nisi prius* to be heard by Sir William Shareshull and his colleagues at Bedminster, near Bristol, on 10 December. Thomas attended, but Peter did not. So the case was adjourned to the Quindene of Easter, when Peter arranged to be represented by his attorney, a Devonian called Richard de Wodewill. Thanks to an unfortunate misadventure, however, Richard was never given the chance to speak for his client. While travelling to Bedminster, so it was later alleged, he had stolen a horse from one Stephen Tracy, and on the raising of the hue and cry had been captured and placed under arrest. Peter reacted to this news by challenging Thomas's own attorney, on the grounds that he was not the attorney originally named. Further exchanges followed, but the court eventually found in Thomas's favour, and ordered judgement to be given on the matter of seisin. At this point another member of the Stapeldon clan, Sir Richard of 'Bywestcombe', entered the court to say that it was not Thomas but he who was the owner of the disputed manor: for, although Sir Richard de Stapeldon had granted a life interest in the manor to Thomas, he had subsequently alienated the reversion to Richard of 'Bywestcombe'; and so it was he to whom Peter should reply. Peter nevertheless insisted that Thomas should reply. Both sides placed themselves on a jury, and judgement was given on this matter and on the substantive issue in favour of Peter.[38]

There matters rested for half a century. In the absence of any evidence to the contrary Peter may be presumed to have recovered seisin and to have remained in undisturbed possession. But in the late 1380s or early 1390s, towards the end of the lifetime of his son, another Peter, the le Veels were once more expelled. This we know only by implication; but that implication is clear, for in 1391 Peter the younger is found making a bid to re-enter. According to a jury which met at Bridgwater on 9 June that year, he came to Norton at the head of an armed gang and temporarily at least re-occupied the place. He dismissed the agents and officials appointed by his adversaries, who were now said to be Sir Thomas FitzNicol and Sir Philip Dauntsey, and replaced them with his own; and a mob owing allegiance to him ransacked the house of Hugh, the vicar, with a view to seeking out and killing Philip Dauntsey.[39] The involvement in the dispute for the first time of FitzNicol and Dauntsey is a little puzzling, and is explicable only on the supposition that they were Stapeldon's feoffees – Stapeldon himself is at no point mentioned in the inquisition, yet Veel is known to have been at odds with him only nine years before;[40] and the two men themselves, moreover, had no previous connection with the manor. Shortly afterwards the fighting at Norton spilled over into the streets of neighbouring Taunton, where a band of Sir Peter's men set about John Murye, an official of the sheriff: weapons to the value of 40s were abandoned in the course of the struggle and later picked up by the town bailiff. The Sheriff of Somerset could no longer overlook what was going on, and with grim irony he despatched Murye to Norton to arrest the troublemakers. On his arrival there Murye immediately recognized Sir Peter in a room in the gatehouse, and exchanged words with him. But his attempts to effect an arrest were rebuffed, and his fistful of writs was snatched from him and cast to the winds. A few days later, however, he was back, this time in the company of William Manyell, the Constable of Taunton, and the two men, evidently dismissing an assault on the manor as impracticable, contented themselves with extracting an oath from Sir Peter to the effect that he would be present at the session of the justices of the peace at Taunton on 6 May. Needless to say, he did not attend – though it is possible that death prevented him, for he is known to have died at around this time.[41]

Whether the struggle was kept up by his sons we cannot say, but it seems unlikely.[42] For already in the unpromising conditions of the spring of 1391 the makings of a settlement were to be discerned. With the entry of FitzNicol and Dauntsey into the dispute the divisions between the two sides suddenly became less clear-cut. FitzNicol, as we have seen, was almost certainly Stapeldon's feoffee at Norton. But only a few years before, in another capacity, he had been witness to an enfeoffment made of the manor by Stapeldon's adversary, le Veel;[43] and in Gloucestershire, where he and le Veel held other estates, they sat alongside each other at sessions of the peace.[44] FitzNicol's several connections with Veel, therefore, undermined the strength of his commitment to Stapeldon, and created the conditions whereby a compromise between the two men might be reached. In this case, as in many similar ones in stateless societies which have been studied by anthropologists, it is the number and variety of ties linking individuals which provides the key to the cohesion of the group as a whole.[45]

The point emerges still more clearly from a study of the events that followed a crime committed in a different part of the country some forty years later. On New Year's Day 1434 Henry Longford, a Derbyshire esquire, was murdered in Chesterfield parish church, and his brother-in-law Sir Henry Pierrepont suffered severe maiming. The initiator of the attack was almost certainly one Thomas Foljambe, and the murderer, if not Thomas himself, was a member of his kin.[46] According to one of the juries that submitted indictments, it was Pierrepont who was responsible for provoking the affray, to the extent that just over a year before he and two allies had assaulted Thomas Foljambe the younger at Chesterfield. But the longer-term origins of the dispute lay in the escalating rivalry between the Pierrepont and Foljambe families. The Foljambes were fast becoming the most important landowning family in the Chesterfield area, but the interest of the Pierreponts represented an obstacle to their further advancement. At Michaelmas 1429 Pierrepont had obtained a grant of the farm of the manor for twenty years from the Countess of Kent; and four years later he obtained as well a lease of the fair which allowed him to levy a tax on the buyer of each animal sold. This last he was prevented from doing by Thomas Foljambe and his kinsmen. The two families had come into head-on collision.

In March 1434 a general oyer and terminer commission was issued to the Duke of Bedford, the Earl of Suffolk, Sir Humphrey Stafford and two judges, the chief purpose of which was to deal with the murder. Indictments were received from six hundredal juries and two grand juries. The first of the latter, headed by none other than the maimed man Henry Pierrepont himself, blamed the Foljambes for the affair, and furthermore alleged that one Richard Broun of Repton, gentleman, a common maintainer of quarrels, had tried to get Thomas Foljambe acquitted of felony. The second jury, on the other hand, placed responsibility on Pierrepont. They indicted him and two other gentlemen of assaulting and maiming a servant of Thomas Foljambe (and of assaulting Thomas Foljambe the younger) at Chesterfield, and in an effort to blacken his character still further accused him of aiding and abetting a murder committed as early as 1411. An idea of the political complexion of this jury is given by one of the other indictments which they brought forward. This said that on 24 June 1433 Henry, Lord Grey of Codnor brought 200 men to Derby with a view to influencing the outcome of the parliamentary election due to take place there. Grey was almost certainly an associate of Pierrepont; and a number of retainers of his were represented on the jury which had indicted Richard Broun and the Foljambes. But at this point the factional divisions begin to blur. The first jury, which was broadly sympathetic to Pierrepont and Grey, was also responsible for indicting men known to be currently or subsequently members of Grey's affinity: John Curzon of Kedleston and Henry Booth were both so indicted; Robert Francis, who had been omitted from the jury, was accused of taking livery from Grey; and then so too was Henry Bradbourne, who apparently did remain a juror. The second jury also showed themselves to be divided in their sympathies. When their more partisan members were absent, they indicted Foljambe's great ally Sir Richard Vernon of coming to Derby the day after Grey with his own, even larger, retinue and of distributing livery in the town at Christmas 1429. One of the men whose absence allowed this indictment to be made was one Henry Booth of Arleston, who is known to have been in receipt of Vernon's livery. But Vernon was by no means his only patron. At roughly the same time – the early 1430s – he was also receiving livery from Ralph, Lord Cromwell; and in addition he was a member of the council of Lord Grey. It was the existence of cross-currents like these that made possible a settlement of the dispute. All who were involved had far more to lose than to gain from its continuance; so they found it in their interests to promote reconciliation. They could not expect the oyer and terminer commission to do this for them; nor, indeed, did they, for in their eyes this was an intrusive instrument, as likely to disrupt as to bring harmony to the local community. Reconciliation could only be brought about by forces operating within local society itself – chiefly, that is, through the agency of the ties that bound men together. Even in so individualistic a society as Derbyshire these were sufficiently strong to undermine the forces that made for conflict. It might be a while before their effects were felt, but felt they eventually were; and in the case under review the point was reached in 1453 when a marriage could be arranged between Thomas Foljambe junior's son Thomas and a daughter of Sir Nicholas Longford.

Paradoxically, then, conflict in medieval society contained the seeds of its own destruction. Arising as it did out of the differences that separated people, it was also stifled by them – for the greater the number of claims on peoples' allegiance, the more difficult they would find it to commit themselves to any one, and the greater would be the pressure to effect a settlement. In a typical gentry community the number of such competing claims was legion. They arose naturally out of the workings of local society.[47] Men's dependence on one another for assistance and co-operation meant that they were bound to be pulled this way and that in their loyalties. As kinsmen and neighbours they owed obligations to each other in the attestation of deeds and the provision of kin. As members of the office-holding elite they had conflicting responsibilities to the king to execute his orders and to their peers to ensure that local affairs were run to their mutual advantage. And finally as clients or retainers they were linked to the nobility by the complementary processes of service and sponsorship. Not all of these relationships, of course, were of equal weight and quality: though determining their relative precedence is not an issue that need detain us here. What is of far greater importance is the fact that they could all be relied upon to offset each other. Divisive tendencies were thus neutralized, and the formation of permanently hostile groups rendered all but impossible.

The restraining effect exerted by such cross-ties went a considerable way to compensate for the relative weakness of state authority in the Middle Ages. It limited peoples' resort to self-help, and provided a substitute for the discipline imposed by coercion. But by itself it was not a sufficient answer to the problem of keeping order in society. It provided a limited though useful role in bringing about a cease-fire. But if the cease-fire were to be converted into peace, more positive steps towards reconciliation would need to be taken: the disputants would have to be brought together again, and the issues dividing them somehow resolved. Traditionally, in societies where state power has been weak, these objectives have been achieved through the mediation of third parties. In Anglo-Saxon England there is evidence from as early as the seventh century that blood-feuds were brought to an end in this way. According to Bede, it was the intervention of Archbishop Theodore which halted the feud between two English kings after the brother of Ecgfrith of Northumbria had been killed by the Mercians.[48] Three centuries later mediators were involved in bringing an end (albeit this time only a temporary one) to a feud between the respective kindreds of Thurbrand and Uhtred, Earl of Northumbria. Thurbrand, a member of a rich Yorkshire family, had engineered the murder of Uhtred in 1016, as he entered the hall at 'Wiheal' to make his submission to Cnut. Uhtred's son Aldred avenged his father by killing Thurbrand, and the feud then descended to the latter's son Carl. But by the intervention of friends a settlement was made, and mutual reparations were paid over. Indeed, so complete did the reconciliation appear that Aldred and Carl planned to go on a pilgrimage together. But shortly after they set out the wounds were reopened. For some reason – we are not told what – the enmity was renewed, and Aldred was slain by his companion.[49] Unsatisfactory though the outcome was on this occasion, the implication of these two cases is nevertheless clear – namely, that resort to mediation was of regular occurrence in the settlement of disputes in the early medieval period.[50] Arising as it did from the vested interest that kinsmen and neighbours had in limiting the damage done to the social fabric by feuding, it formed the centre-piece of a system of control which was locally based and owed little or nothing to external coercion. It predated the growth of state power and was in large measure a substitute for it.

In the centuries after the Norman conquest, however, this inward-looking and largely self-sufficient system of peace-keeping came under increasing challenge from without.[51] The provincial autonomy which was its foundation was slowly undermined by the centralizing policies of the Norman and Angevin kings; and the local exercise of justice which was its guarantee was eroded by the decision of Henry II to open the royal courts to all men of free condition.[52] Slowly but inevitably, then, local communities had to adapt to the growing influence of the Crown and its agencies in their lives. Initially at any rate their reaction was not unfavourable. Disputants dissatisfied with the quality of justice dispensed locally could now take their cases to the highest tribunal in the land; and the fact that many did so is attested by the growing volume of business recorded on its rolls. But with the passage of time reservations began to set in. As early as the later years of Henry II it was being murmured that the king was more concerned to sell justice than to do right to litigants, and more interested in lining his own pockets than easing the burden on his subjects; and a generation later, when the terms of Magna Carta were being framed, it was laid down (clause 40) that the king was not to sell, delay or deny right or justice. The selling of justice, however, was much easier to denounce in principle than to prevent in practice, and in the thirteenth century matters seemingly went from bad to worse. Henry III, unable to obtain grants of public taxation, turned instead to the exploitation of justice, and netted huge amounts from the profits of the general eyre. From the national visitation of 1246–9 he raised no less than £22,000, and that at a time when the ordinary revenue of the Crown was only some £24,000; and from visitations of individual counties he raised sums of up to £400–£500.[53] Small wonder, then, that by the thirteenth century the Crown, so far from appearing the lion of justice, was cast rather in the role of a bird of prey – swooping down on communities and making away with their wealth. Visitations – particularly ones dealing with criminal business – which were once welcomed were now feared and resented, and communities often took measures to head off their arrival. Thus, when in the aftermath of the Peasants' Revolt news reached Hertfordshire that the king proposed to visit St Albans in person to punish the insurgents, a local knight by the name of Sir Walter atte Lee intervened to stop him. In a speech to the townsmen put into his mouth by the chronicler Walsingham he said that, were the proposed visitation to take place, untold destruction and dislocation would follow; to avoid this, he had interceded with the king, and had secured a moderation of his intentions: the investigation would now be conducted not by unknown people – not by 'strangers' – but by 'friends and neighbours of yours' drawn from the ranks of the local gentry. The loud applause which followed indicated his audience's approval of his action. But their optimism proved premature. After initial success with his investigations atte Lee ran into opposition from the townsmen. Rumours began to spread that the king was going to come to St Albans after all, and on 13 July he finally arrived – surrounded, Walsingham tells us, by thousands of archers and armed men.[54] A day or two later the 'bloody assize' began.[55]

The scale of the assault on local autonomy in the thirteenth and early fourteenth centuries was such that the gentry were obliged to seek ways of shielding themselves from it. At first they thought largely in terms of limiting the degree of direct contact between their own communities and the judicial agencies of the Crown. Thus, for example, they petitioned for observance of an informal rule that no county be visited by the justices in eyre more than once in every seven years. But later they developed a more comprehensive strategy designed to assert control over the very institutions that threatened them. Central to it were two key demands – firstly, that the determining power be granted to the keepers of the peace, enabling them to pass judgement as well as to receive indictments, and secondly, that the men appointed to the office of sheriff should not be outsiders but local men of substance with roots in the shires in which they served.[56] To neither demand was the Crown easily persuaded to accede, because the issues at stake were simply too important. Conceding the determining power would give the keepers – the justices, as they would become – the jurisdictional control over a wide range of offences previously reserved to the professional judges, possibly – indeed, eventually – including breaches of the labour laws; and appointing sheriffs of local origin would risk royal interest being subordinated to local ones, and allow private favour and partiality to enter into the proper execution of the king's business. For the best part of a century the arguments raged – favouring first one side, then the other. But in the end it was the gentry, in the capacity of their parliamentary representatives, who emerged triumphant. By the 1360s the determining power was finally won for good (having already been granted and withdrawn several times), and the great majority of sheriffs being appointed were men of local background.[57] Together these concessions went a long way to satisfying gentry aspirations. By reducing the degree of control which the king exercised over the institutions of local government they allowed the gentry correspondingly to increase theirs. As a result the threat which was posed to their values and traditions was neutralized by a process of assimilation and takeover – neutralized, but not entirely eliminated, however, as the events of July 1381 were to show: the regular circuits of the assize justices remained, and the Court of King's Bench could still be instructed to make periodic visitations of particular counties. But heavy-handed intervention was a thing of the past: of that at least the gentry could be sure.[58]

Within the developing framework of royal justice, then, much older behavioural patterns were embedded and preserved. Not all of these were concerned with the peaceful resolution of conflict: some, for example, had their roots in the old-fashioned thirst for vengeance – such as the procedure, later formalized as the appeal of felony, which allowed the victim or his kin to initiate the process of bringing a criminal to justice.[59] But the great majority appear to have been concerned with minimizing the inconvenience caused by feuding. Drawing as they did on the processes of conciliation and arbitration they were able to effect a settlement in all but the most intractable of cases.[60] Little or no coercive machinery was required – indeed, the system can be seen as a substitute for it. Nor were any unreasonable demands made of human nature: provided only that there were enough ties binding people together self-interest could be allowed to do the rest.

When the need to preserve the peace is understood in these terms, it becomes unnecessary to posit an antithesis between the rival claims of conflict and consensus. Consensus on certain underlying issues was the essential pre-condition without which no social intercourse could ever take place; but conflict was the no less inevitable by-product of the tensions which that intercourse generated. In the words of the German sociologist Simmel, it would be impossible to conceive of a social unit in which either the one state or the other was absent; or, even supposing that it was, such a unit would be entirely lacking in what he called 'real-life process'.[61] Throughout history the two have been almost inseparably interwoven in the social fabric, the interplay between them giving rise to the oscillations of behaviour noted above.[62] While it is true that at times the consequences for stability have been unsettling, the threat to the social fabric as a whole has always been contained. Either some mechanism has been forged to limit the extent of the violence – as with the development of multiple allegiances; or else the violence has taken a form which has had the effect of strengthening the state and not weakening it. In tribal Africa, for example, violence has been shown to have manifested itself in succession disputes which channelled into contests for the kingship ambitions which might otherwise have issued in secession: just as in medieval England it manifested itself in baronial rebellions which implicitly reaffirmed allegiance to the Crown by focussing dissatisfaction on the person of the king who wore it.[63] Not in every circumstance should violence be viewed in starkly negative terms. At times there was a positive aspect to its character which made it a valuable regulator of social relations.

The same point emerges from a study of its operation at a local level. In a community or society dominated by an established elite it offered almost the only means by which an outsider or newcomer could break in. The quarrel already noted between Sir John de Berkeley of Dursley and the Lord of Berkeley may probably be seen in this light.[64] And so too may the activities of Ralph Greyndour and his gang in the Forest of Dean half a century later. The Greyndours, being up-and-coming members of a highly individualist society closer in spirit to the Welsh Marches than to the rest of Gloucestershire, took strong exception to the lordship of the Berkeleys. For a decade they waged war on members of the family and their allies, and on one occasion they even plotted the murder of Sir Thomas himself. But in the 1390s they abandoned their campaign, and in the early years of the following century Sir John Greyndour – probably Ralph's son – is found as a retainer of Sir Thomas and a year or two later as Sheriff of Gloucester. Violence in their case brought its reward: it gained them entry to the elite, and led to the re-establishment of social equilibrium on the basis of a new consensus.[65]

In the context of gentry and magnate relations violence can also be seen as prescribing limits beyond which one or other of the protagonists would have been unwise to go – a point nicely illustrated by the feud in Sussex in the 1380s between Sir Edward Dallingridge and John of Gaunt, Duke of

Lancaster. Dallingridge, as self-appointed leader of the local gentry community, resented the challenge to his pre-eminence posed by the westward expansion of Duke John's interests in the county, and sought to halt it by mounting a campaign of harrassment against his officials. He was brought to trial by the duke, found guilty and imprisoned. But within a fortnight he was at large again. The duke, having made his point, realized that it would be unwise to press his advantage too far.[66] He therefore decided to draw back, having accepted that the effect of the feud had been to impose limits on the bounds of his power.

But whatever may be said for the necessary and constructive quality of conflict, there is no denying that in other ways it could be destabilizing, and that it was commonly seen as such by contemporaries: hence the concern which they showed to develop mechanisms by which conflict could be channelled towards peaceful resolution.[67] Considering how deeply the warlike ethic was embedded in medieval society this was not going to be easy; and until there was either a moderation of that ethic or an increase in the coercive power of the state it was unlikely ever to be wholly successful. But within the limits set by these two constraints society's achievement may be considered a not discreditable one. In the rising tide of cases entered on the plea rolls and in extensive use made of the processes of arbitration and conciliation may be discerned a growing willingness to involve the apparatus of law (whether formally or informally administered) in the settlement of disputes. The use of the courts may not in every case, of course, have been a substitute for the use of force: as often as not it was only one element in a comprehensive strategy in which force also played a part. But even where force *was* involved, there is no need, in trespass cases at least, to take at face value all the picturesque detail served up in the count. This was included merely to satisfy the requirements of the law, because unless the use of force was demonstrated the case could not be accepted by the central courts.[68] In many cases what may lie behind such anecdotage may be nothing more serious than the unauthorized collection of hedge clippings which lay behind the 'treading down of grass and other enormities, committed with force and arms, that is with swords, bows and arrows' alleged by one Henry Hull in an action in Common Pleas in 1466.[69] Form here has to be distinguished from reality; and the reality in late-medieval England may have been a good deal more humdrum than the legal sources, highly coloured as they often are, make it appear. Whether it corresponded to what we today would call 'peace' is beside the point. It was peace of a sort; and it proved adequate as the foundation of a vigorous and competitive society. Max Gluckman would have seen in it 'the peace in the feud'. Aristotle would have regarded it, as he regarded virtue, as an activity rather than a state. Perhaps in these two characterizations we will come as close as we ever will come to capturing its inner quality.

## Notes

1  M.J. Bennett, *Community, Class and Careerism: Cheshire and Lancashire Society in the Age of Sir Gawain and the Green Knight* (Cambridge, 1983), pp.39–40.

2  Bennett's *Community, Class and Careerism* is merely the fullest and most articulate exposition of the theme. In seminal form it was set out by K.B. McFarlane, 'Parliament and "Bastard Feudalsim"', *TRHS*, 4th Series, XXVI (1944), 53–79, reprinted in his *England in the Fifteenth Century* (1981), pp.1–21. More recently it has featured in J.R. Maddicott, 'The County Community and the Making of Public Opinion in Fourteenth-Century England', *TRHS*, 5th Series, XXVIII (1978), 27–43; idem, 'Magna Carta and the Local Community, 1215–1259, *Past and Present*, 102 (1984), 25–65; and S.J. Payling, 'Political Society in Lancastrian Nottinghamshire', (Oxford D.Phil. thesis, 1987). To these works may be added N.E. Saul, *Scenes from Provincial Life: Knightly Families in Sussex, 1280–1400* (Oxford, 1986), which demonstrates the network of ties binding together the gentry of east Sussex.

3  R.H. Hilton, *A Medieval Society: the West Midlands at the End of the Thirteenth Century* (1966), pp.252–3.

4  Ibid., p.255.

5  The clearest statements of this point of view are in A. Harding, *The Law Courts of Medieval England* (1973), pp.92–8; and idem, 'The Revolt against the Justices', in *The English Rising of 1381*, ed. R.H. Hilton and T.H. Aston (Cambridge, 1984), pp.165–93.

6  A. Herbert, 'Herefordshire, 1413–61: some Aspects of Society and Public Order', in *Patronage, the Crown and the Provinces*, ed. R.A. Griffiths (Gloucester, 1981), p.116.

7  P. Morgan, *War and Society in Medieval Cheshire, 1277–1403*, Chetham Soc., XXXIV (1987), p.116.

8  G.L. Harriss's introduction to McFarlane, *England in the Fifteenth Century*, pp.xxii, xix.

9  There are no records of prosecutions under it, and there is plenty of evidence that it was ignored. See, for example, Saul, *Scenes From Provincial Life*, p.173. It was probably intended to do no more than state an ideal.

10  SR, I. 283; *Rot. Parl.* II. 142, 229, 261, 265, 308. For comment see N.E. Saul, *Knights and Esquires: The Gloucestershire Gentry in the Fourteenth Century* (Oxford, 1981), pp.107–11.

11  Saul, *Knights and Esquires*, p.109; R.L. Storey, 'Liveries and Commissions of the Peace, 1388–90', in *The Reign of Richard II*, ed. F.R.H. Du Boulay and C.M. Barron (1971), p.147.

12  Both cases are discussed by J.R. Maddicott, *Law and Lordship: Royal Justices as Retainers in Thirteenth- and Fourteenth-Century England* (Past and Present Supplement, 4), pp.35–40.

13  PRO SC8/157/7832, printed in Saul, *Knights and Esquires*, p.226.

14  The inadequacy of one of the central courts – in this instance King's Bench – in a slightly later period is stressed by M. Blatcher, *The Court of King's Bench, 1450–1550* (1978), in particular chap. 4.

15  Blatcher, *Court of King's Bench*, pp.10–33.

16  Harriss, in McFarlane, *England in the Fifteenth Century*, p.xxii.

17  This shrinkage occurred very suddenly in the aftermath of the Black Death.

18  Maddicott, op. cit. pp.46, 75–81.

19  D. W. Sutherland, *The Assize of Novel Disseisin* (Oxford, 1973), pp.173–4.

20  As argued by G.O. Sayles in Appendix VI to his introduction to *Select Cases in the Court of King's Bench under Richard II, Henry IV and Henry V*, Selden Soc., LXXXVIII (1971), pp.lxv–lxvi. He is criticized by J. Post for misinterpreting the document concerned ('Courts, Councils and Arbitrators in the Ladbroke Manor Dispute, 1382–1400', ed. J. Post, *Medieval Legal Records, edited in memory of C. A. F. Meekings* by R.F. Hunnisett and

J.B. Post (1978), p.302n). But there may still be grounds for believing his general argument to be true (Saul, *Scenes From Provincial Life*, p.92).

21  C.M.D. Crowder, 'Peace and Justice around 1400: A Sketch', *Aspects of Late Medieval Government and Society: Essays presented to J.R. Lander* (Toronto, 1986), pp.53–81.

22  In the Robin Hood ballads, for example, it is the outlaws who are cast as heroes, and the enforcers of the law, notably the sheriff and the king's justices, as the villains. The text of the main cycle, the 'Gest of Robyn Hode', is most conveniently accessible in R.B. Dobson and J. Taylor, *Rymes of Robyn Hood* (1976).

23  R.C. Palmer, *The Whilton Dispute, 1264–1380* (Princeton, 1984), p.212.

24  Nigel Saul, 'Murder and Justice, Medieval Style: the Pashley Case, 1327–8', *History Today*, XXXIV (August, 1984), 30–35.

25  P.R. Coss, *The Langley Family and its Cartulary. A Study in late medieval 'Gentry'*, Dugdale Soc. Occasional Papers, 22 (1974).

26  Saul, *Knights and Esquires*, pp.190–3.

27  This is certainly the impression given by the length of the Whilton dispute (for which see note 23, above,). It is difficult to relate the costs of litigation to the annual values of lands being fought over, but there are some suggestions in Saul, *Scenes from Provincial Life*, pp.93–4.

28  *The Glynde Place Archives: A Catalogue*, ed. R.F. Dell (Lewes, 1964), no.1.

29  On the north wall of the nave were four armoured figures wearing jupons decorated with the Camoys arms. Curiously, in the light of their dress, a hunting scene appears to have been intended, because the westernmost figure holds a dog on a lead. Katy Powell, who has made a study of the paintings, dates them to c. 1380. The patronage of Sir Thomas is therefore a near certainty, and his guiding principle the need to establish lineage at least a fair likelihood. (I am grateful to Miss Powell for her advice on this matter).

30  Nigel Saul, 'Two Fifteenth-Century Brasses at Dodford, Northants.', *Trans. Monumental Brass Soc.*, XII, iii (1977), 210–4.

31  Coss, *The Langley Family and its Cartulary*, p.14.

32  The one obvious exception is the abduction of an heiress – which, as in the Langley case, could usually be relied on to mark the beginning of a feud. But how often was abduction an act of violence? One suspects that it was often in reality an elopement. In a society in which partners were usually chosen by parents, there were bound to be rebellions by those who wished to choose their own. For a possible instance see J. Post, 'Sir Thomas West and the Statute of Rapes, 1328', *BIHR*, LIII (1980), 24–30.

33  For an example, see below p.47.

34  The manor, now known as Norton Fitzwarren, lies a couple of miles west of Taunton.

35  PRO C260/104/21; CP40/302 m. 290.

36  *Pedes Finium, commonly called Feet of Fines for the County of Somerset, 1 Edward II to 20 Edward III, A.D. 1307 to A.D. 1346*, ed. E. Green, Somerset Rec. Soc., XII, (1898), p.51. For comment see M. Buck, *Politics, Finance and the Church in the Reign of Edward II: Walter Stapeldon, Treasurer of England* (Cambridge, 1983), p.21.

37  *Pedes Finium . . . Richard I to Edward I, A.D. 1196 to A.D. 1307*, ed. E. Green, Somerset Rec. Soc., VI (1892), p.319.

38  PRO CP40/302 m. 290.

39  PRO KB9/168 m. 24. The attack on the vicar's house may also have been occasioned by a search for the manorial archive. I owe this suggestion to Philip Morgan.

40  Stapeldon had been outlawed in 1382 in an action of debt brought by Veel. The record and process were summoned into Chancery on 11 December 1384 (PRO C88/57 no. 58).

41  The Escheator of Gloucestershire was ordered to take custody of his lands on 12 September 1391 (*CFR 1391–6*, p.46).

42  At least there is no evidence of its continuance. Sir Peter had three sons who survived to manhood – Thomas, Henry and Robert (*CCR 1381–5*, p.442; *CPR 1391–6*, p.245; *CPR 1385–9*, p.69).

43   CCR 1385–9, p.155, being a grant by Sir Peter to Hugh Berde clerk and John Gust, their heirs and assigns, of the manor of Norton Veel, dated 26 May 1386. The witnesses were Sir Thomas Trivet, Sir Thomas Fichet, Sir Baldwin Malet, Sir Thomas FitzNicol and Sir John Poulet – all of them quite substantial men.

44   For appointments to the bench see *CPR 1381–5*, pp.138, 246. Sir Peter le Veel senior had held the manors of Charfield and Tortworth (Gloucs.), both a few miles south-east of Berkeley (*Cal. Inqs. Post Mortem*, VIII, no. 466). The FitzNicols held the manors of Hill and Nympsfield, the former lying a mile or two to the south-west of Berkeley (*Cal. Inqs. Post Mortem*, XIV, No. 129).

45   This is the argument advanced by E. Colson, *The Plateau Tonga of Northern Rhodesia: Social and Religious Studies* (Manchester, 1962), M. Gluckman, *Politics, Law and Ritual in Tribal Society* (Oxford, 1965) and idem, *Custom and Conflict in Africa* (Oxford, 1955), chap. 1, 'The Peace in the Feud'. The thesis is challenged by J. Black-Michaud, *Cohesive Force. Feud in the Mediterranean and the Middle East* (Oxford, 1975), where it is suggested that the feud is a relationship between the feuding parties: played according to a recognized set of rules, it provides the foundation of the internal political hierarchy and serves to engender external ties of temporary dominance. The theory is an attractive one in the context of Mediterranean societies. But whether it can be applied to gentry society in northern Europe is not so clear – not in the present state of knowledge, anyway. We simply do not know if feuds of the kind discussed above were 'played' according to any generally accepted set of rules. Futher research may shed light.

46   I am summarizing the discussion of the case in S.M. Wright, *The Derbyshire Gentry in the Fifteenth Century*, Derbyshire Rec. Soc., VIII (1983), pp.128–33. For further observations see S.J. Payling, 'Political Society in Lancastrian Nottinghamshire' (Oxford D.Phil. thesis, 1987), p.256.

47   As Michael Bennett has conclusively shown in *Community, Class and Careerism*, chap. 2.

48   Bede, *Historia Ecclesiastica*, book IV, chap. XXI.

49   D. Whitelock, *The Beginnings of English Society* (Harmondsworth, 2nd edn., 1954), pp.44–5.

50   For the background to this subject see *The Settlement of Disputes in Early Medieval Europe*, ed. W. Davies and P. Fouracre (Cambridge, 1986).

51   In writing this and the following paragraphs I have been influenced by the discussion of the problems faced by peasant societies today in adapting to the growth of external influences in J. Migdal, *Peasants, Politics and Revolution: Pressures towards Political and Social Change in the Third World* (Princeton, 1974).

52   The best discussion of these changes is now to be found in W.L. Warren, *The Governance of Norman and Angevin England, 1086–1272* (1987).

53   These figures are taken from J.R. Maddicott, 'Magna Carta and the Local Community, 1215–1259', *Past and Present*, 102 (1984), 47.

54   T. Walsingham, *Historia Anglicana*, ed. H.T. Riley, 2 vols. (RS, 1863–4), II. 23–9. Sir Walter atte Lee had good qualifications for taking on the role that he did. He was a substantial local landowner, holding manors at Datchworth, Clothall, Cockhamsted (in Braughing), Waterford (in Stapleford), Albury and Chamberlayns (in Brent Pelham) (respectively *VCH Hertfordshire*, III. 79, 223, 310, 477, 478; IV 5, 96). He had already served four times as knight of the shire for Hertfordshire, in the parliaments of January 1377, 1379, and January and November 1380; and he was to serve again in 1385, 1386, February and September 1388, January and November 1390 (*Return of Members of Parliament*, I (1878), pp.195, 202, 204, 206, 208, 226, 229, 232, 235, 238, 240). He was to serve as Sheriff of Essex and Hertfordshire in 1389–90 (*PRO List of Sheriffs*, p.44). The late-fourteenth century effigies of a knight and his lady in Albury church, illustrated in *VCH Herts*. IV, opposite p.10, are probably those of him and his wife.

55   Sir Charles Oman, *The Great Revolt of 1381* (London, new edn., 1969), p.96, says that

Richard arrived on 12 July, but the earliest date for letters issued there is the 13th (*CPR 1381-5*, p.25).

56 For the background to these arguments see Saul, *Knights and Esquires*, chap. IV. Also relevant is the account in Harding, *Law Courts of Medieval England*, pp.86–123.

57 J. Post, 'The Peace Commissions of 1382', *EHR*, XCI (1976), 98–101; Saul, *Knights and Esquires*, chap. IV.

58 Richard II's manipulation of local government in the last years of his reign is perhaps the exception that proves the rule, because it was one of the factors that led to disenchantment with his kingship. Among the charges levelled against him in the deposition articles are that he kept his favourite sheriffs in office beyond the statutory one year and that he interfered with parliamentary elections (*Rot. Parl.* III. 419–20.

59 For the survival of the appeal see C. Whittick, 'The Role of the Criminal Appeal in the Fifteenth Century', in *Law and Social Change in British History*, ed. J.A. Guy and H.G. Beale, Royal Historical Society Studies in History, 40 (1984), pp.55–72.

60 The one celebrated dispute that was most emphatically not resolved by these methods was of course that between the Pastons and their various enemies arising out of the death-bed bequest to them by John Fastolf of his inheritance. But the problem here was that the Pastons tried 'to climb too high too fast'; and so county society turned on them (C. Richmond, 'The Pastons', *History and Archaeology Review*, 2 (1987), 24).

61 G. Simmel, *Sociologie* (1908), quoted by S. Roberts, *Order and Dispute: An Introduction to Legal Anthropology* (Harmondsworth, 1979), p.45.

62 See above, p.40.

63 Gluckman, *Order and Rebellion*, pp.7–29; idem, *Politics, Law and Ritual*, chap. 4.

64 See above, p.41.

65 Saul, *Knights and Esquires*, pp.179–80, 291.

66 S. Walker, 'Lancaster v. Dallingridge: A Franchisal Dispute in Fourteenth Century Sussex', *Sussex Archaeological Collns.*, 121 (1983), 87–94.

67 One might also mention the dishonour which would fall upon a lord who permitted disorder in his retinue.

68 J.H. Baker, *An Introduction to English Legal History* (2nd edn., 1979), p.57.

69 Harding, *Law Courts of Medieval England*, p.111.

# 4

# *Piers Plowman* – A Poem of Crisis: an Analysis of Political Instability in Langland's England

Helen Jewell
*University of Liverpool*

Practically everything about *Piers Plowman* has been disputed: whether the versions are the work of one author, the length of the separate versions, their dates, and, of course, the interpretation of the poem. Scholarly opinion does now believe the three versions to be the work of one man, but the dating remains obscure. The A text, of approximately 2,560 lines, formerly dated to around 1362, is now placed later in the decade, around 1367–70, with revision in 1369–70. The B text, of approximately 7,300 lines, formerly dated to March to May of 1377, is now put at 1377–9, the C text, a substantial revision of similar length, at one time dated to 1392, has now been brought back to 1385–6, or 1387 at the latest.[1]

My own interest in this subject has sprung from using *Piers Plowman* with history students at the University of Liverpool, and sensing the need for a study which focuses on the patently changing political circumstances in which the different versions were composed. Because of the former dating of the A text to 1362, this survey will begin with the early 1360s; the critical point to begin indeed is surely with 1360 itself, the year of the Calais peace. The remainder of Edward III's reign will be reviewed and the first decade of Richard II's will be considered, viewed more as the aftermath of the events previously examined than for any developments they themselves fostered. The backcloth is, then, largely the twenty-five years following the Calais peace.

In 1360 the peace of Bretigny, ratified at Calais, had marked the turning point of Edward III's career. Contemporaries were not to know at the time that Edward had, as Professor Le Patourel put it, 'shot his bolt'.[2] Just over twenty years of warfare with France, including the victories of Sluys (1340), Crecy (1346) and Poitiers (1356), had left the English feared on the continent, prestigious and undefeated, though very significantly the 1359 expedition had not been a success. The peace, therefore, opened with the English seemingly in a good position. By contrast, when the war with France resumed in 1369, things went from bad to worse for the English, militarily and diplomatically. The lack of success abroad fuelled criticism and discontent at home. Edward III's reign closed with the upheaval of the Good Parliament of 1376 fresh in memory, and Richard II's began with domestic uncertainty, and soon saw court extravagance become an overt political issue. The greatest peasant uprising in English history was sparked off in 1381, and the older and larger English university was racked by heretical activities until Wyclif's condemnation at Blackfriars in 1382, which damped heresy down at Oxford. More than London could be described as 'turbulent'.[3] How had things gone amiss?

Let us begin by looking at the 1360 situation. In 1360 there was no reason to foresee great political upheaval on the horizon. During the year, the king, who was popular, reached the age of forty-seven. Though elderly by medieval standards, the victor of Crecy was still a force to be reckoned with on the international stage, and patently felt himself still vigorous – he was to set sail intending foreign campaign in person as late as 1372. His supportive wife Philippa, whose date of birth is uncertain, was about forty-seven in 1360; she had borne her last child only in 1355, and seems to have continued to exercise on harmonious influence on her family until her death of plague in 1369. The royal princes were a loyal set of sons, of varied ability. In 1360, aged thirty, Edward the Black Prince was still unmarried; he was a European chivalric hero, but not politically astute, as Professor Prestwich has remarked.[4] Lionel of Antwerp reached twenty-two in the course of the year, John of Gaunt became twenty, and Edmund Langley attained eighteen: they were all in early manhood and already being provided for. Lionel was married to the de Burgh heiress of the earldom of Ulster and the Clares; it was to their household that Geoffrey Chaucer was attached in 1357 as a page.[5] John was married to the Lancaster heiress; Edmund had been given the northern estates of the Warennes after the death of the last earl in 1347. These princes were soon to enjoy titular promotion: in 1362 Lionel was made Duke of Clarence, Gaunt Duke of Lancaster, and Edmund Earl of Cambridge. I agree with Professor Prestwich that Edward III's management of this brood had been 'remarkably successful'.[6]

Edward had also handled the magnates well, surrounding himself over the previous twenty years with high hereditary dignities while building up an aristocracy of civil and military service – the phrase comes from Powell and Wallis.[7] In securing the necessary funding over two decades of war, the king had had to share power and policy with the magnates, and indeed with the Commons in parliament. The upshot of this, as Dr Harriss has displayed, was that the Commons learned political argument and some techniques of parliamentary opposition in a protracted defensive dialogue with the Crown.[8] Parliament increased in importance as the occasion where war was explained and justified, and where tax was granted, in a delicate balance between the king's needs and community grievances. From the 1340s onwards, complaint was most immediate about prerogative levies and royal officials' exactions, and grew to take in the expenditure and management of taxes. The Commons had not achieved very much by 1350, but in the following decade they achieved much more. Dr Harriss comments that the Commons' predicament educated them keenly, evolving parliamentary techniques, political maturity and corporate political identity.[9]

During the 1360s, the decade of the A text, however, economic and political pressures began to shake the stability of England noticeably. The major economic determinant of the period was the demographic situation. The Black Death of 1348–9 had reduced the population of England drastically: the death rate nationally is now estimated at between 30 and 45 per cent.[10] Renewed plagues in 1361–2 and 1369 in particular checked any demographic recovery from the 1348 catastrophe, and set England on a population decline which was only to be reversed in the later fifteenth century. Contemporary chronicle reference to the 1361–2 plague as characteristically a *mortalité des enfants* may be very significant.[11] Medieval historians are only slowly waking up to the consideration of the age profile of a community, and the timing of the Peasants' Revolt may be more significant in relation to the plagues of 1361–2 and 1369 than to that of 1348.

Those sectors of English society present in parliaments, Lords and Commons together, as landlords and employers of men, had suffered economic dislocation in the period following the Black Death. Class resentment spits out from the wording of the Statute of Labourers of 1351. 'Against the malice of servants, which were idle and not willing to serve after the pestilence, without taking excessive wages', the king had, in 1349, ordained that servants should be bound to work for the salaries and wages customary in the places where they ought to work in the twentieth year of the king's reign, or the five or six previous years, on pain of imprisonment. In the first parliament after the plague it was given the king to understand, 'by the petition of the commonalty, that the said servants, having no regard to the said ordinance, but to their ease and singular covetise, do withdraw themselves to serve great men and other, unless they have livery and wages to the double or treble of what they were wont to take the said twentieth year'. The commonalty praying remedy, the Statute of Labourers was enacted, pegging wage rates to 1346 or four years before. The clauses tackled the problem comprehensively, covering first the liveries and wages of carters, ploughmen, drivers of the plough, shepherds, swineherds, dairyworkers and all other servants, and plugging the potential loophole of wheat allowances in agricultural workers' pay arrangements. Any enterprise on the part of the workers was checked by the requirement that they serve by the whole year, or by other usual terms, and not by the day, and day rates at times of peak agricultural demand were pegged for haymaking, mowing and reaping, though an increasing scale within August had to be allowed to reapers. The rates were specifically 'without meat or drink, or other courtesie' demanded, given or taken, and the hiring of workers was to be done openly, workmen bringing their tools in their hands to the merchant towns, there to be hired 'in a common place and not privy'.

The statute next tackled agricultural piecework, setting maximum rates for threshing wheat and rye, barley, beans, peas and oats. Servants were to be sworn twice a year to keep the Ordinances, and none were to leave the towns they lived in during the winter in summer if there was work for them there, exception being made for some areas where labour traditionally migrated seasonally in search of work. Refusal to take the oath or perform it was to be met with a term in the stocks or in gaol, and the statute ordered the construction of stocks for the purpose in every town by the following Whitsun.

The statute next turned to workers of a less exclusively rural kind. Carpenters, masons, tilers and other 'workmen of houses' were pinned down in their wages, for instance the master carpenter, tiler and thatcher all to 3d a day. Seasonal variations in the building trade were acknowledged here too, plasterers being paid more between Easter and Michaelmas, and 'without meat or drink'. Carriage rates were not to exceed the charges in 1346. Finally, 'cordwainers and shoemakers' were to sell as in 1346, and 'goldsmiths, saddlers, horsesmiths, spurriers, tanners, curriers, tawers of leather, tailors and other workmen, artificers and labourers and all other servants not here specified' were to be sworn before the justices to practise their crafts as in 1346, punishment for transgression being fine and ransom and imprisonment at the justices' discretion. Liability to imprisonment rose from forty days for the first offence to a quarter of a year for the second, and 'double pain' thereafter. Hostlers and victuallers were subject to investigation, and the statute awarded recovered excess payments to those who sued the statute breakers, or these were given to the collectors of fifteenths to be set against the whole tax levy on the town where the excess was taken.[12]

This first prices and incomes policy of any English parliament had been imposed against the free play of economic forces, and in the 1360s the propertied classes still hoped to see effective prosecution of breaches of the labour laws, execution being in this decade removed from the experimental justices of labourers and made over to the normal justices of the peace.[13] The JPs were given enforcement of the labour legislation permanently from 1368, patently with Commons' approval. A parliamentary petition for remedy against 'the malice and grievous dearness affecting servants, labourers and artificers' in 1368 sought, in furtherance of what it termed 'the ancient statute', that JPs in each county be commissioned to hear and determine offences at the suit of parties, and that double restitution be made to those who sued; the king's response was that the statute and ordinance of labourers and artificers should be kept and duly executed, through the justices of the peace as requested, but that recovery of single damages should suffice.[14]

From published peace rolls of the early 1360s one can see the labour offences being vigorously pursued. Putnam's edition of the Yorkshire East Riding Roll from 1363–4 draws attention to some 93 cases of excess wages, 46 of departure from the locality, 11 of departure from a master, and 42 cases of refusal to work at legal wages, or at all.[15] Adam son of Robert took 5d for threshing a quarter of wheat; Matilda daughter of Agnes de Stakeston was not willing to work except at day rates, and went outside the vill; Clement Scherman, reaper, took 4d a day in autumn, with food; Nicholas de Clyveland, 'mawer', took 7d a day and went outside the vill; William de Grauncemore withdrew from the service of the Prior of Bridlington contrary to statute.[16] Many of the entries, like the above, are tersely recorded, but some add a touch of colour conveying a trace of the aggressiveness of the situation. Matthew de Penreth of Hunmanby and John son of Robert withdrew from Hunmanby for the sake of getting more, namely 4d a day; Simon Faber of Huggate and Joan his wife would not swear before the constable to keep the statute of the labourers.[17] As the labour legislation settled into the commission of the JPs, whose regular Quarter Sessions date from 1362, the machinery was to hand for the routine enforcement of what had begun in 1349 and 1351 as essentially emergency legislation. This development was to the advantage of the governing classes, and to the resentment of the workers, whose enterprise remained thereby strait-jacketed at law.

After the new plagues of the 1360s the nature of the confrontation between lords and peasants seems to have taken a turn for the worse. The surviving peasants increasingly resented the personal disqualifications of villeinage, and the restrictions of the labour legislation, while the lords increased their efforts to hold on to traditional rights and obligations against economic pressures.[18] All three versions of *Piers Plowman* comment on the current ability of scarce labour to command its price. As A says:

. . . no beggar eat bread that beans in come,
But coket, or clermatyn, or of clean wheat,          [fine white-flour breads]
Nor no halfpenny ale in no wise drink,
But of the best and brownest that brewsters sell.

Labourers that have no land [to] live on [but] their hands
Deign nought to dine a day [on] night-old worts.        [day old vegetables]
May no penny ale them pay, nor piece of bacon,
But if it be fresh flesh, or fish fried,
And *chaud* and *plus chaud* for chilling of their maw[19]
                [hot and piping hot lest they chill their stomachs]

That the provision of food was a point of friction between employer and labourer is borne out by the Peace Rolls' presentments of workers who secured food as well as pay. The East Riding roll previously cited uses such phrases as *cum mensa, et cibum, et victum, cum esca* and *cum prandio*, variously translatable as with board, with food, lunch, dinner; the variations, since they tend to appear in entries in blocks, may be stylistic preference rather than technical distinctions between types of food or times of meal. J. Day has recently drawn attention to the relative inelasticity of wages compared to prices in times of customary or statutory wage controls, with the comment 'it was fringe benefits like a meal ration, payments in kind or a shorter working day that varied according to the condition of the labour market.'[20] The government's reaction to this free for all was roundly unpopular with the workforce. The A text continues:

But he be highly hired else will he chide
That he was workman made warie the time,                    [curse]
And then curse the king and all the council after
Such laws to look, labourers to chaste.

In the B text of the lines considered above, the cuisine is extended from frying to include baking, and in C the grievance is turned, I think significantly, from the original councillors to the current law enforcers:

And then he curses the king and all the king's justices
Such laws to learne labourers to grieve[21]                    [teach]

Entering *Piers Plowman* as early as the A text, be it early or late 1360s, this passage illustrates the day to day friction between labourers and their employers, and the passage's retention in B and C shows us that this was no passing 1360s phenomenon.

The twenty-five years under review were in fact ones of acute economic change. As estimated on the Phelps–Brown Hopkins scales, legislation notwithstanding, building labourers' wage rates in general rose sharply in southern England between 1350 and 1370, from a 2d a day plateau to a 3d a day one, while building craftsmen's wages rose from 3d a day in the years before 1350 to 5d a day between 1350 and the early 1360s, money in England remaining relatively stable.[22]

While employer and employee groused and blustered, the manorial economy, feeding a reduced population, apparently coped in normal times. But agriculture before technological skills was very much at the mercy of climate, and famine could never be forgotten: its threat stalks all three versions of *Piers Plowman* and its attributes are familiar:

> Hunger in haste then seized Waster by the stomach
> Wringing him so by the guts that water ran from his eyes

and so on.[23] Wheat prices, tabled as decennial means, in shillings per quarter, rose from 5 (25p) in the decade 1341–50 to 7.1 (35½p) in 1351–60, 8.3 (41½p) in 1361–70, 6.8 (34p) in 1371–80, falling back to 5.5 (27½p) in 1381–90.[24] The particular dearth in the dry April of John Chichester's London mayoralty of 1369–70 is singled out in the B text as something not to be forgotten.[25]

Studies of individual industrial activities, notably cloth making and tin mining, which offer the only sets of records complete enough for a quantitative analysis of industrial and commercial activity, have suggested that output did not fall to match the population decline, indeed, barely falling at all. In modern parlance, productivity held up well against demographic fall. This is not to say, however, that all commercial activity throve. The raw wool export trade, on which the buoyancy of the customs duties depended, was in decline. Total exports, of some 35,000 sacks of wool per annum in 1350, declined, with fluctuations, over the next decades, being at 20,000 in 1380. Though total cloth exports rose in the same period, approaching 5,000 cloths per annum in 1350, and reaching around 30,000 per annum by 1390, this economically beneficial export of labour was not exploited to benefit the government's revenue.[26]

Peacetime, of course, brought a reduction in military expenditure, but there was a deficit in government expenses. Dr Harriss has shown how Edward III spent lavishly on building and display in the 1360s – over £15,000 was spent on reconstruction at Windsor, 1362–5, and £24,000 in building Sheppey Castle 1361–9, and odd thousands were spent on improving royal hunting lodges and resting places including King's Langley 1360–77, and Sheen 1363–8.[27] No direct taxation, that is tenths and fifteenths, was sought from parliament in the ten years of peace from 1360, but the renewal of the wool subsidy in parliaments in 1362, 1365, 1368 and 1369 gave this indirect taxation a kind of renewable permanence.

Parliaments met in the 1360s every year except for 1364 and 1367.[28] During this decade sessions were relatively tame. Nonetheless, at the end of the 1368 session the former steward of the household, John de la Lee, was committed to the Tower in a White Chamber session of prelates, dukes, earls, barons and some of the commons, being unable to clear himself on several articles and points brought against him, an early occurrence of the lords trying a royal official against whom petitions had been brought in parliament, and the forerunner of more extensive proceedings of this kind.[29]

To sum up for the 1360s, when the A text was composed, it is plain that the effects of the plagues and consequent economic legislation were beginning to bite. Contemporaries were able to notice this, comment on it, and expect the comment to be understood. Petitions to parliament in 1362 and 1363, concerning respectively the high price of chaplains and diverse mischiefs referred to 'la grand pestilence' and 'les pestilences et grantz ventz'.[30] The plague's position as the chronological starting point of phenomena was clearly understood by Langland: A says 'since the pestilence time' parishes have been poor; a marriage boom has been noted – 'many pair since the pestilence have plight them together'; and 'since the pestilence time' the friars have been particularly active stirring up questions.[31] The A text already encapsulates some stirrings of social conscience: in the fair field full of folk:

> Some put them to plough and played full seldom,
> In planting and sowing, working full hard
> Won that these wasters with gluttony destroy.

While Piers the Ploughman makes a bargain with the knight:

> I shall swink and sweat and sow for us both
> And also labour for your love all my lifetime
> In covenant that you keep Holy Church and myself
> From wasters [and wicked men] that would me destroy.

Piers also binds the knight:

> Look you tean no tenant                                    [injure]
> and
> Misbede you not thy bondmen.[32]                           [abuse]

A primitive biblical communism runs through all three versions: from A the lady Holy Church tells the dreamer that God 'commanded of his courtesy in common three things', namely:

> clothing – from chill you to save
> . . . meat at meal, for meseise of thyself          [want of ease]
> And drink when you thirst, but do it not out of reason.

This is repeated almost exactly in B, and more tersely in C.[33]

But England's economic and political stability was actually more shaken than contemporaries could be expected to realize or interpret correctly. Economic understanding was naive. The propertied classes expected to be able to put the clock back to the good old days through labour legislation imposing maximum wages and stipulating contractual terms. Sumptuary laws were passed in 1363 to repress those upstarts who managed nonetheless to afford upmarket consumables: the governing classes were obviously sensitive to the show of wealth by the lower orders. Righteous indignation colours the language of this sumptuary legislation as it had the Statute of Labourers: the 1363 law was to check 'the outrageous and excessive apparel of divers people against their estate and degree'. A hierarchy was set out. Grooms were to have one flesh or fish meal a day, 'the remnant of other victual as of milk, butter and cheese, and other such victuals according to their estate', and were limited to clothing made of fabric not exceeding 2 marks cost for the whole cloth. They were to have nothing gold or silver, embroidered, enamelled or silk, and their wives and children were similarly blocked in their sartorial ambitions. Up a rung on the social ladder, people of handicrafts and yeomen were limited to cloth costing 40s, and were not to be decked with 'stone, cloth of silk or silver, girdle, knife, button, ring, garter, brooch, ribbon, chains' or any manner of things of gold or silver, or any manner of apparel embroidered or enamelled, their wives and children similarly.' At the bottom of the pyramid, 'carters, ploughmen, drivers of the plough, oxherds, cowherds, shepherds, dairyworkers, and all other keepers of beasts, threshers of corn, and all manner of people of the estate of a groom attending husbandry, and all people that have not 40s of goods and chattels, shall not take or wear any manner of cloth but blanket and russet wool of 12d, and shall wear girdles of linen according to their estate, and come to eat and drink as in the manner that pertain to them and not excessively.'[34] This particular legislation was repealed after two years, but the wording should be borne in mind when reading Langland's descriptions of clothing and feasting.

In the 1370s, towards the end of which the B text was composed, the situation grew markedly worse: McKisack called this a disastrous decade.[35] The king grew older and less vigorous, and eventually became positively senile before his death. Queen Philippa had died in 1369, and Clarence predeceased her. A malign influence on the king was rising to favour some three years before the queen's death, when a *domicella* of hers, by name Alice Perrers, was in receipt of a king's gift of two tuns of wine yearly, and favours began falling more richly from 1367.[36] Alice, whose husband William of Windsor was promoted to the lieutenancy of Ireland from 1369 to 1371, and 1374 to 1376, and summoned to parliaments from 1381 to

1384, is generally seen as the prototype of the poem's maid Meed, ensconced at Westminster, the centre of royal government, where she and her retinue threaten social harmony and justice.[37] In the A text Meed is:

> . . . wonderfully clothed,
> Purfiled with pelure, the purest on earth        [bordered with fur]
> Crowned with a crown, the king has no better,
> All her five fingers were fretted with rings
> Of the purest perries that prince ever wore        [precious stones]
> In red scarlet robed and ribboned with gold.

B goes into greater detail of the jewelry and robe, C cuts back the description a little.[38] Meed's actions, however, are even more telling than her appearance:

> She may nigh as much do in a month ones        [at one time]
> As your secret seal in seven score days

says Conscience to the king in A; B and C reduce the time to six score days.[39]

Alice's notoriety was certainly at its height about the time of the B version: the Good Parliament of 1376 passed an Ordinance against women pursuing business in the king's courts by way of maintenance, singling her out by name, though she was restored to favour in the next parliament. The first parliament of Richard II renewed the attack on her; she was called 'principal promoteress' of specific mischiefs and found guilty, the lords of parliament considering the 'damages and villainies committed by her to the king and the realm.'[40] Whether Perrers by intention, or only by subsequent identification, Meed was escorted to London by sheriffs and law officers whose portrayal pillories also the corruption of local administration.[41]

In the normal course of events, the decline of an elderly king might have been compensated for, at least in part, by the prospect of the succession of as famous a son as the Black Prince, but contemporaries were deprived of this comfort as the prince, after several years of ill-health, predeceased his father by a year, leaving only a ten year old boy to succeed his grandfather in 1377. As the old king declined, divergent policies on peace and war, and within the war party, on the appropriate methods and areas for campaign, created uncertainties and differences of opinion. The personal ambitions of John of Gaunt became an important factor here, and the ground was laid for that violent unpopularity of the duke's which was so manifest at the time of the Peasants' Revolt. Lancaster had been sent to Calais in 1369 on the resumption of war, to small result, and led an army through France in the winter of 1373–4, to little effect. Between these events, he had married, in 1371, Constance, elder daughter and co-heiress of Pedro the Cruel, on whose behalf the Black Prince and Gaunt had intervened in Castile in 1366. His ambitions with regard to the Castilian throne were patent – he assumed the style King of Castile and Leon certainly in 1372, and is referred to as 'Uncle Spain' after Richard II's accession. These Iberian ambitions were undoubtedly suspected of colouring Gaunt's attitude to the Anglo-French war. He was not a military commander of the calibre of his first father-in-law the Lancastrian earl Henry of Grosmont, and his widespread unpopularity in 1377–8 has been convincingly connected to the disturbed situation in the ill-defended south-east, where his conduct as Keeper of Pevensey was questionable.[42] His clumsy and unconstitutional protection of John Wyclif in 1376–7, when his Savoy palace was threatened by Londoners, shows him no respecter of legal form. 'Time honoured Lancaster' has been too kind a judgement.

England in the 1370s seems to be lacking in both military and political leaders. In this decade, parliaments met in each year from 1371 to 1373, and from 1376 onwards.[43] In a wave of anti-clericalism the 1371 Commons ousted clerical ministers of state, including the chancellor, Bishop Wykeham of Winchester, who had opened the proceedings. Bishop Brantingham of Exeter, the treasurer, and Peter Lacy, a canon of Lichfield and Durham, the keeper of the privy seal, were removed at the same time, specifically because 'men of holy church are not justiciable in all cases'.[44] Wykeham, incidentally, came to the chancellorship again in 1389, and Brantingham to the treasurership in 1377 and 1389. One of the biggest public blunders in parliamentary history occurred in 1371, when Lords and Commons made a parish-based grant of £50,000 to the king, on the assumption that there were over 40,000 parishes in the country; there proved to be under 9,000.[45] With mis-information on that scale in the corridors of Westminster, one can hardly argue that the government was in competent hands. The political background to the critical 1376 parliament is superbly analysed in George Holmes's *The Good Parliament*, which brings out a disorganized and corrupt court, having signally little success in its expeditions to France or Ireland, a court attacked by the Good Parliament for, in Holmes's phrase, 'squandering the king's money and surrendering his conquests'.[46] By this time, most of the territories ceded at Bretigny had been won back by the French. The king's chamberlain, Lord Latimer, and his mistress, Alice Perrers, and a leading financier Richard Lyons all came under attack in the parliament. Dr Holmes takes the view that in 1376 a peculiarly offensive court policy unified for a short time all the politically important classes in disaffection. The case is extremely well argued, but leaves open for us the question how much disaffection existed, at slightly less explosive level, widely, in the period under review?

General discontent continued. In 1372 parliament tried to discipline sheriffs and escheators, and in 1373 petitions came up about purveyance, labour legislation and villeins. Of the five edited Lincolnshire Peace Rolls from 1360–75, the Lindsey 1373–5 roll contains in its editor's view an 'exceptionally large' proportion of offences against the labour laws, 151 in a total of 485. The Lindsey roll testifies to frictions between employers' interests and workers' enterprise similar to those revealed in the East Riding over a decade before, though the cases are often given more detail, with, for example, the dates of the breach of the contract: William formerly servant of Robert de Belesby was hired to serve the Abbot of Humberstone as a ploughman from St Martin's day until the same feast a year later, but the Sunday after St Martin's day 1373 he withdrew from the abbot's service, against the statute; William Runfare of Saltfleet Haven was hired at St Hilary's day 1371 to serve William Skott of Saltfleet Haven as a fisherman for a whole year, and stayed in his service only until the feast of the Purification next following, then withdrew against the statute.[47] There are straightforward cases of overcharging: Hugh Sauupe and Thomas de Pumfrayt of Halton, common mowers of Halton, took for scything each acre of meadow there, from William Marchall of East Keal and others 5d *et prandium* contrary to statute; a band of mowers jacked up their wages from 5d to 8d an acre in the employment of the Abbot of Louth Park, and Priors of Ormsby and Alvingham, each receiving 20s in excess wages.[48] Food was still a sore point, *et prandium* and *et cibum* regularly appearing in the charges, and on occasion *et mensam*, and some bulk payments of food are recorded – Thomas, shepherd of John the Vicar of Laughton by Wragby, took as his stipend for half a year in 1372 8s and for each three weeks two bushels of pure wheat, and refused to work otherwise, to the contempt of the king, taking over the period 8s excess; Roger de Gedenay and Thomas his brother, thatchers, refused to work at their trade at day rates, but at a lump sum to get excess wages (*in grosso pro excessivo salario habendo*), and took from Stephen Bell of Langworth in 1373 11s and two bushels of wheat and two of barley worth 2s, for roofing one house, though the roll records indignantly that they finished the work in nine days; Robert servant of John de Asgardby, ploughman, received wheat and one mark for his salary in 1374 and 1375, where the allowance for servants used to be half wheat and half peas, and 8s wages, a useful piece of information for us.[49] The greater details in this roll bring out more clearly than the East Riding roll the aggressiveness in the situation. Robert Raulyn of Middle Rasen, mower, withdrew to get more money; two other inhabitants of the same vill went to get a greater wage, and William Masoun of Limber, assigned by the constables there to serve one Robert

Saper as mower refused to submit to the constables' justice *(noluit se justiciari per constabularios)* and withdrew from the vill rebelliously *(per rebellitatem suam)*; Adam Theker of Stainfield, similarly, ordered to take the oath to keep the statute, wholly refused to do so, in contempt of the king; Emma wife of Richard Stepyng of Tealby, ordered by the constable there to take the oath refused to swear and would not submit to justice 'except at her own will'.[50] An unusual entry, showing the willingness of the gentry class to use the law to the full, tells how William de Skipwyth, knight, having hired John Wrighte of Alvingham to work as a carpenter at South Ormsby, to build a hall, prosecuted Wrighte with a writ of attachment when he withdrew before he had finished the work. The writ was directed to John Coke bailiff, but Wrighte resisted him and refused to submit.[51]

Rosamond Sillem, the editor of the five rolls, commented 'an examination of the Lincolnshire peace rolls proves that the picture of lawlessness suggested by the petitions of the Commons and the words of Langland is by no means exaggerated'. She was referring particularly to petitions in the Good Parliament, including two pressing for the enforcement of the labour laws and two relating to purveyance, and she linked the Good Parliament petitions expressly with Peace's bill against Wrong in the B text, while Richard Kaeuper sees Wrong as 'clearly a royal purveyor, whose sins in this fictional petition are only amplifications of the charges encountered in many an historical petition against purveyors'. Sillem also commented that outside the economic sphere the Lincolnshire indictments for homicide and lesser crimes of violence confirmed 'the vivid impression of the lawlessness of rural England given by contemporary writers such as the author of *Piers Plowman*'.[52] A similar picture of lawlessness emerges from Furber's Essex peace sessions of 1351 and 1377–9, though neither Essex roll is a record of all the activity of JPs in the county.[53]

It was in the late 1370s that Dr Bolton thinks labour enforcement became more vigorous, 'when the shortage of labour really began to bite,' and some 200 of the 280 extant indictments before Essex JPs 1377–9 involved labour offences, 170 being offences about wages and contracts: for example 'Richard Blake reaper takes 3d per day and food and 6d for an acre'.[54] The rolls reveal a rebelliousness and breakdown of order in Essex, significantly a county which was about to play a major part in the Peasants' Revolt. Gilbert Rougge of Sturmer, labourer, for example, was indicted as 'a rebel against the constables, unwilling to swear or justify himself', and it was presented that 'no constable of Dunmow hundred has done his duty of making labourers swear to serve and take wages according to the statute'.[55]

The accession of Richard II in 1377 merely added the disadvantages of a royal minority to an already grim situation. It has been shown that in the first parliament of the reign fifteen of the Ordinances of 1311 surfaced as the basis for fourteen common petitions, though how widely this was then appreciated is unclear.[56] The first parliament revived the prosecution of Perrers, in the second, in October 1378, the Commons sought to get the names of the great officers and councillors and governors of the king reported to them, and there was tied to the wool subsidy grant a request it be spent purely on defence, backed with the appointment of treasurers. In the third parliament, in April 1379, the graduated poll tax was only granted after the appointment of a committee of magnates to investigate 'l'estat du roi' – whose brief ranged widely over the financial state of the kingdom.[57] There were ample grounds for criticism of the government's expensive and ineffective war policy, and ground too for rooting out as public examples those who had used office or financial influence to profit personally. The king's minority made his own protection the more poignant a necessity. It is the B text of *Piers Plowman* which introduces the fable of the rats and mice wishing to bell the cat, including the comment:

> Ther the cat is a kitten the court is full elynge                    [wretched]
> Witness holy writ, who so will it read
> *Ve terre ubi puer rex est.*[58]                    [Woe to the land where a boy is king]

This passage was more or less retained in the C text – Richard II only ended his minority at the age of twenty-two in 1389.

To sum up, in the 1370s, towards the end of which the B text was composed, there had been a marked deterioration in stability. The replacement of a king who had become incompetent by a minor brought no short term relief. No one either politically able or morally scrupulous emerged to take the situation in hand. The war was going badly abroad, and even basic home defence was so ill-provided that private persons of public spirit were driven to shoulder the burdens of public defence. John Philipot, the London grocer and mayor 1378–9, in 1378, the year he was one of the parliamentary grant treasurers, equipped a fleet which captured the pirate John the Mercer, and the following year Philipot defrayed the cost of one of the two stone towers erected below London bridge for securing the city and shipping by barring the river passage by a chain across.[59] That the king's advisers, demonstrably rewarding themselves generously, sensed political opposition is suggested from the locations of parliaments. From 1338 onwards, all the meetings designated in the *Handbook of British Chronology* as parliaments and related assemblies met at Westminster or London until June 1371 when the great council met at Winchester. Provincial sessions, always disadvantageous to the Londoners, followed in 1378 at Gloucester, and in the next decade, within our period, in 1380 at Northampton and in 1384 at Salisbury. This provincial location may well reflect the influence of Gaunt, whose unpopularity in the capital, and not only there, was intense. Stubbs attributed parliament's meeting at Gloucester in 1378 to Gaunt's 'fear' of the Londoners. There may be more to the movement of parliaments from London than personal animosity between London citizens and the royal government: Stubbs remarked, after considering the various medieval parliaments held outside the capital, 'the inference from this long list is that the liberties of England were safest at Westminster'.[60]

In fairness, it should be pointed out that the 1370s saw some developments which affected England for the worse but were not entirely direct consequences of English action or failure. These factors affected war, diplomacy, and the state of the church. One was the change in French war tactics, adopting scorched earth policies and refusal to engage, tactics to which the invading English could find no satisfactory answer. Another was the involvement in the war on the French side of the Castilian fleet, which menaced England's naval war front. A third was the outbreak of the papal schism in 1378, from which time there was a lack of church leadership which was to hamper international diplomacy and the disciplining of heretics such as Wyclif. Gaunt's Castilian ambitions had bearing on the second of these developments, and English diplomatic involvement on the third, but the first was not contributed to deliberately by English choice of action, though it developed as reaction to earlier English war tactics.

The sensitivity to social injustice was not abated in the 1370s. The B text adds to Piers' lessons for the knight the comment (it follows the 'misbede not thy bondmen' line):

> Though he be thy underling here, well may it happen in heaven
> That he be worthier set and with more bliss, *Amice ascende superius*
> [Friend, rise higher]
> In charnel at church churls be evil to know     [hard]
> Or a knight from a knave there[61]

– the sort of after-death equality which was the logical rounding off of the Genesis lordlessness 'when Adam delved and Eve span'.

The 1370s left unfortunate legacies for the next half decade, the years preceding the C text. The new government kept up the old government's practices, for example the poll tax, and the opposition kept up the same stance against household influence and affinity. There were parliaments each year 1380–86: the January 1380 parliament launched an attack on the administration, setting up another commission to supervise details of royal administration and finance. At the November 1380 parliament at Northampton the Commons boldly rejected the chancellor's demand for

£160,000 as 'very outrageous and utterly intolerable', though they went on to grant the third poll tax, thus bringing to a head a dangerous coincidence of 'grinding war taxation' and 'utter exhaustion and frustration'.[62] The timing of the Peasants' Revolt of 1381 suggests that this poll tax triggered the rebellion, but the situation was already explosive. Rural wage labour was already aggrieved by the constraints of the labour laws and 'significantly, the fury of the revolt seems to have been most intense in the area for which we have evidence of the greatest efforts to enforce the labour laws';[63] rural tenantry was already discontented by the landlords' efforts to enforce controls: Dr Dyer suggests manorial supervision of the customary land market may have tightened – 'on some manors one gains the impression of some administrative slackness in the two decades after the plague, followed by more stringent controls in the 1370s'.[64] The towns were not immune from the consequences of the demographic changes and the fiscal demands of unsuccessful war; their workers were also subject to the labour legislation, and their inhabitants were often resentful of oppressive elite government structures. There was widespread hatred of lawyers, and 'the administration of justice now emerged as a political issue between different levels of society'.[65] Abler politicians of the day assessed the matter quite accurately: in the 1382 parliament the revolt was blamed on court extravagance, a weak executive, tax burdens and inadequate defence, and the point was made 'if the governance of the kingdom be not rapidly amended, the realm itself will be utterly lost and destroyed for all time'.[66] The Lords and Commons vehemently refused to enfranchise serfs. Richard II, increasingly concerning himself with the work of government from around 1383, as Mr Taylor some time ago pointed out, had some success in developing a household-centred government in the mid-1380s, only drawing more intense aristocratic opposition to himself, backed by 1386 by Commons criticism of misgovernment, as Dr Tuck makes clear.[67] The parliamentary attack on royal extravagance in the autumn of 1385, opened up by Dr Palmer, deserves as much attention as the more famous follow-up attack on de la Pole in 1386.[68] In 1386 ministerial responsibility to parliament for personal and official conduct was at stake, and this can be linked back to the 1371 replacement of ecclesiastics, one purpose of which at least was expressly to replace churchmen with lay ministers answerable for offences in royal courts.[69] If the C text may be safely brought back to 1385 or 1386 we need go no further.

Langland's England was hardly free from political crises and disturbances. Langland was obviously concerned about politics, which are alluded to in Piers Plowman much more than in the works of Chaucer, and he was concerned about them in the context of morality, which must in his day have been far less separable from what we might call abstract politics. Expedient *realpolitik* had made little acknowledged inroad into the Christian idealism which still, in the late fourteenth centry, flavoured the civil laws of states, international diplomacy, and, even, the public policy of the business world. I am not sure that we have to try to locate in Langland a consistent view of desirable political principles, either across the three versions, or even within any one of them. Only a blinkered political theorist never voices an inconsistency, or raises an opposite interpretation often to treat it ambiguously seriously or satirically. The Bible itself, often referred to by Langland, is full of contrary recommendations.

Dr Anna Baldwin has recently worked out an elaborate account of Langland's attitude to government in the abstract, and his own experience of it in practice.[70] Using the C text, which she dates to before 1387, she argues that absolutism triumphs in the Visio section (that is the Vision of Piers Plowman section) in that version, and that the commons, commune, community, who appear as co-legislators in B, are relegated in C to mere suppliers of necessities. I cannot personally accept that the textual changes between B and C will always bear the implication Dr Baldwin puts upon them, and certainly I cannot accept that they exclusively carry those implications. However, the argument that Langland had come to believe that law, and legislators in parliament, had been corrupted, and that hope lay in the imposition by the king of natural law principles, is worth looking at in the light of the 1380s, the period of composition. This imposing of law by the king would be a function of the king's prerogative equity, and the only restraints would be reason and conscience. If Baldwin is right about the Visio king of the C version, we should have to fit this view into events as follows. If the text is from 1385, it would be from the year when the October Parliament attempted to curb royal extravagance, and would be supporting what Mr Taylor termed 'the drift of Richard II's policy towards personal government'.[71] If C dates from 1386, Langland would be being tolerant of the royal disregard of the parliamentary strictures of 1385, and, if the text is from late in the year, he would be reacting against the October 1386 Wonderful Parliament. The Lords Appellants' activities in 1387–8, culminating in the Merciless Parliament, might indeed be sufficient, if the C text were so late, to switch off idealists from expecting remedies to be imposed on the king through altruistic human agencies. But if Langland did move in this direction, patently he was not reflecting a widespread trend, or if he was reflecting a widely held view, Richard's subsequent acts must have greatly disappointed any supporters of the idea, rendering the ideal of a despotic king proving more reasonable and just than an advised monarch so unlikely as to become rapidly untenable.

One of the major problems in this field is what, if at all consistently and precisely, Langland meant by commons. As Mr Taylor and Mr Pronay remarked in the context of the *Modus Tenendi Parliamentum* 'in the use of the terms community and commonalty we are dealing with one of the most vexing of medieval expressions'.[72]

In some contexts in *Piers Plowman* communes or commune appears to be purely the common people, and this usage seems clear in the C prologue line:

that the commons should their commons [food] find

and in the C lines:

As a king to claim the common at his will
To follow and to find him and fetch at him his consayl.[73]

In a more sophisticated political usage it may represent the community as possibly in the B prologue:

Might of the communes made him to reign

and

For to counsel the king and the commune save

but these mixed references are disputable and occur within lines of each other yet do not have to have the same implication: commune in the latter line could be 'common profit'.[74] To equate the House of Commons with the Commons in a poem of the late fourteenth century would be to attribute to author and readers a very acute recognition of a technicality.

Both the B and C texts set Reason to preach before the king that he should love the Commons:

. . . he counselled the king his commune to love

is followed up in B by:

It is thy treasure, if treason ne were, and treacle [remedy] at thy need

C follows it with:

The comune is the king's treasure, Conscience knows well.[75]

Both passages are a considerable change from the A text wherein Conscience preached to the people urging wasters to work and priests and prelates to practise what they preached. Perhaps Langland originally never entertained the thought of needing to tell Edward III that the Commons were his treasure.

It is only in B and C that we are shown the king who proclaims himself head of the law and is reproved by Conscience that he may only take what he needs with reason on condition he rules well.[76] There were absolutist theories abroad in England in the 1370s – see Wyclif's *De Officio Regis* of 1378. But there seems to have been much more sign of alarm about absolutism. Certainly there was some awareness of the king's growing use of civil law procedures as distinct from common law ones, and parliament complained in 1385 that 'divers pleas concerning the common law, which ought to be examined and decided by the common law are of late drawn before the Constable and Marshal of England, to the great damage and disquiet of the people'.[77] Parliament's members, Lords and Commons alike, would of course be the last people in the realm to lose faith in their own role as restrainers of arbitrary kingship, and we should not expect them to share any view demoting their own role.

The governed, however, whether granted a share in law-making or condemned to fetch and carry, can expect something in return: law, love and loyalty (lewte) from the king

> . . . holding with no party
> But standing as a stake that sticks in a mere                    [boundary]
> Between two lords for a true mark[78]

and it can be argued that Richard II fell conspicuously short of this level of impartiality.

Dr Baldwin's opinion that Langland put his trust in the absolute monarch is not the inference drawn (from one of the same passages) by Dr Pearsall, and the year of the publication of Baldwin's book saw Janet Coleman declare that the poet of *Mum and the Sothsegger* (ascribed variously to the last quarter of the fourteenth century and to 1406) and the poet of Digby 102 (a collection of complaint poetry including part of a C text of *Piers Plowman*, written about 1400) and the C text itself, all defend the role of the middle class in the possession of political power.[79] Earlier, R.H. Jones took the view that both *Piers Plowman* and *Richard the Redeless* emphasized royal responsibility for order, justice and the common good, and that Gower, sharing this opinion, came to despair of Richard II as a suitable ruler.[80] Moreover, Langland did not remove some of his less absolute passages outside the Visio section: the last two passus of C, surviving scarcely changed from B, draw from Dr Baldwin the comment that Langland 'began by demonstrating the value of absolutism; he ends by demonstrating the responsibility of the commune'.[81]

It seems to me that the ideas which were gaining hold in the 1380s were the reverse of absolutist, and that the moves to effect ministerial responsibility, through from 1371 to 1386, cannot be totally separated from the responsibility borne by the king. Calling to account is in the air, this principle is the same whether it is tax treasurers, castle keepers, the chancellor or the king. The accounting has to satisfy a group of people, be it the lords, the members of the Commons or a wider concept of populace. The common theme is dissatisfaction, which has reached a level at which passivity expires. There is as much dilemma facing the man wishing to find Do Well, Do Better and Do Best in the political world as there is in the spiritual. There had been a quarter century of instability in politics, religion and economic conditions all at once. Langland's work is a product of this instability, and a reflection of it.

## Notes

1   The texts cited are G. Kane, *Piers Plowman: the A Version* (1960); A.V.C. Schmidt, *William Langland: The Vision of Piers Plowman: a critical edition of the B text* (1978); and D. Pearsall, *Piers Plowman by William Langland: an edition of the C text* (1981). The extracts taken from these texts have been modernized where I thought this would be helpful to readers unfamiliar with Middle English. Schmidt, p. xi, regards B as 'on the whole the most enjoyable version', and E. Salter, *Piers Plowman an Introduction* (2nd ed., Oxford, 1969), p.106 recommended B as 'satisfactory as an introduction to Langland's characteristic thought and methods of work'. Anna P. Baldwin, *The Theme of Government in Piers Plowman* (Cambridge, 1981), p.3, however, thinks C, the final version, clearer in what Langland says about government. Pearsall, p.13, calls the poem 'a poem of crisis'. M. Drabble, *The Oxford Companion to English Literature* (Oxford, 1985), pp. 764–5 draws attention to recent interpretative works.
2   J. Le Patourel, 'Edward III and the Kingdom of France', *History*, XLIII (1958), 189.
3   Ruth Bird, *The Turbulent London of Richard II* (1949), passim.
4   M. Prestwich, *The Three Edwards: War and State in England 1272–1377* (1980), p.277.
5   F.N. Robinson, *The Works of Geoffrey Chaucer* (2nd ed., Oxford, 1966) p.xx.
6   *Rot. Parl.* II. 273; Prestwich, *Three Edwards*, p.276; see too M. McKisack, 'Edward III and the Historians', *History*, XLV (1960), 1–15.
7   J.E. Powell and K. Wallis, *The House of Lords in the Middle Ages* (1968), p.351.
8   G.L. Harriss, 'War and the Emergence of the English Parliament 1297–1360', *Journal of Medieval History*, II (1976), 35.
9   Ibid., 52–3.
10  J. Hatcher, *Plague, Population and the English Economy 1348–1530* (1977), p.25.
11  Ibid., p.63; *The Anonimalle Chronicle*, ed., V.H. Galbraith (Manchester, 1970), p.50 (entry for 1361).
12  SR, I. 311. Excesses were given over to the triennial tenths and fifteenths granted in 1348 and 1352, in the latter instance, with other labour penalties, affording taxpayers about 6 per cent relief, B.H. Putnam, *The Enforcement of the Statutes of Labourers during the first decade after the Black Death 1349–59* (New York, 1908), pp.99, 106, 128.
13  Ibid., passim; Putnam, *Proceedings before the Justices of the Peace in the fourteenth and fifteenth centuries, Edward III – Richard III* (1938), p.xliii–xlvi.
14  *Rot. Parl.* II. 296.
15  B.H. Putnam, *Yorkshire Sessions of the Peace, 1361–1364*, Yorkshire Archaeological Society Record Series, C (1939), p.xxxii.
16  Ibid., pp.50–51.
17  Ibid., pp.51, 62.

18  C. Dyer, 'The Social and Economic Background to the Rural Revolt of 1381', in *The English Rising of 1381*, ed. R.H. Hilton and T.H. Aston (Cambridge, 1984), pp.21–30.
19  P[iers] P[lowman] A, VII, lines 287–95.
20  J. Day, *The Medieval Market Economy* (Oxford, 1987), p.198.
21  *PP* A, VII, lines 296–9; B, VI, 303–17; C, VIII, 326–40.
22  E.H. Phelps-Brown and S. Hopkins, 'Seven Centuries of Building Wages', *Economica*, new series, XXII (1955), 195–205; Day, *Market Economy*, p.198.
23  *PP* A, VII, lines 159–60 et seq.; B, VI, 174–5 et seq.; C, VIII, 171–2 et seq.
24  Hatcher, *Plague*, p.51.
25  *PP* B, XIII, lines 268–70.
26  A.R. Bridbury, *Economic Growth: England in the later Middle Ages* (Hassocks, 1975), pp.24–6, 32; E.M. Carus-Wilson and O. Coleman, *England's Export Trade 1275–1547* (Oxford, 1963), pp.122, 138; J.L. Bolton, *The Medieval English Economy 1150–1500* (1980), p.291.
27  G.L. Harriss, *King, Parliament and Public Finance in Medieval England to 1369* (Oxford, 1975), p.484.
28  *HBC*, p.563.
29  Powell and Wallis, *Lords*, p.367.
30  *Rot. Parl.* II. 271, 279.
31  *PP* A, Prologue, line 81; X, 191; XI, 59.
32  Ibid., A, Prologue, lines 20–3; VII, 27–30; 39, 44.
33  Ibid., A, I, lines 20, 23–5; B, I, 20, 23–5; C, I, 20, 23–4.
34  *SR*, I. 380–2.
35  M. McKisack, *The Fourteenth Century* (Oxford, 1959), p.384.
36  M. Galway, 'Alice Perrers' son John', *EHR*, LXVI (1951), 242.
37  Baldwin, *Theme*, p.1.
38  *PP* A, II, lines 8–13; B, II, 8–16; C, II, 9–16. *Rot. Parl.* III. 66 petitioned to check the use of all manner of 'perree, pelleure, draps d'or, ribane d'ore, drap de soye' by those unable to spend £40 per year, 1379.
39  *PP* A, III, lines 134–5; B, III, 145–6; C, III, 181–2.
40  *Rot. Parl.* II. 329, 374; III. 14.
41  *PP*, A, II, lines 121–49; B, II, 158–88; C, II, 171–99.
42  J. Sherborne, 'John of Gaunt, Edward III's Retinue and the French Campaign of 1369', in *Kings and Nobles in the Later Middle Ages*, ed. R.A. Griffiths and J. Sherborne (Gloucester, 1986), pp.41–61, points out that the royal princes in military commands at this time suffered as 'members and agents of governments which muddled through each year's warfare, torn between aggressive and defensive thinking'; *CPR 1370–4*, p.197; *Rot. Parl.* III. 6; E. Searle and R. Burghart, 'The defense of England and the Peasants' Revolt', *Viator*, III (1972), 365–88.
43  *HBC*, pp.563–4.
44  *Rot. Parl.* II. 304.
45  Ibid., II. 303–4.
46  G. Holmes, *The Good Parliament* (Oxford, 1975), p.63.
47  R. Sillem, *Records of Some Sessions of the Peace in Lincolnshire*, Lincoln Record Society, XXX (1936), pp.xlvi, 15–16, 20.
48  Ibid., pp.19, 99.
49  Ibid., pp.46, 54, 100.
50  Ibid., pp.21, 22 (2 entries), 31, 81.
51  Ibid., p.61.
52  Ibid., p.xiv; R.W. Kaeuper, *War, Justice and Public Order, England and France in the later Middle Ages* (Oxford, 1988), p.334; Sillem, pp.xlvi–vii.
53  E.C. Furber, *Essex Sessions of the Peace, 1351, 1377–9*, Essex Archaeological Society Occasional Publications, no. III (Colchester, 1953) passim.

54 Bolton, *English Economy*, p.213; Furber, *Essex Sessions*, pp.69, 47, 167.
55 Ibid., pp.158, 169.
56 J.G. Edwards, 'Some common petitions in Richard II's first parliament', *BIHR*, XXVI (1953), 200–13.
57 J.S. Roskell, *The Impeachment of Michael de la Pole Earl of Suffolk in 1386 in the Context of the Reign of Richard II* (Manchester, 1984), pp.22–4, discusses *Rot. Parl.* III. 12–14, 35–6, 37–8, 57.
58 *PP*, B, Prologue, lines 194–6; C, Prologue, 204–6.
59 *DNB*, XLV, 160.
60 *HBC*, pp.564–5; W. Stubbs, *The Constitutional History of England*, III (5th ed., Oxford, 1903), 401.
61 *PP*, B, VI, lines 46–9.
62 *Rot. Parl.* III. 89; Kaeuper, *War, Justice and Public Order*, p.351. Sir Goronwy Edwards, *The Second Century of the English Parliament* (Oxford, 1979), pp.34–5, 38–40, describes in detail the parliamentary procedure granting this socially explosive tax.
63 Kaeuper, *War, Justice and Public Order*, p.370.
64 Dyer, 'Social and economic background', p.27.
65 A. Harding, 'The Revolt against the Justices' in Hilton and Aston, *English Rising*, p.170.
66 *Rot. Parl.* III, 100.
67 J. Taylor, 'Richard II's Views on Kingship', *Proceedings of the Leeds Philosophical and Literary Society*, XIV, v (1971), 197; J.A. Tuck, *Richard II and the English Nobility* (1973), pp.87–106.
68 J.J.N. Palmer, 'The Parliament of 1385 and the Constitutional Crisis of 1386', *Speculum*, XLVI (1971), 477–90; and 'The Impeachment of Michael de la Pole in 1386', *BIHR*, XLII (1969), 96–101; Roskell, *Impeachment of de la Pole*, passim.
69 Powell and Wallis, *Lords*, p.370.
70 Baldwin, *Theme*, passim.
71 Taylor, 'Richard II's Views', p.198.
72 N. Pronay and J. Taylor, *Parliamentary Texts of the later Middle Ages* (Oxford, 1980), p.39.
73 *PP*, C, Prologue, line 143; III, 374–5.
74 Ibid., B, Prologue, lines 113–5. A. Middleton, 'The idea of public poetry in the reign of Richard II', *Speculum*, LIII (1978), 94–114, focuses on the notion of common or commune.
75 *PP*, B, V, lines 48–9; C, V, 180–1.
76 Ibid., B, XIX, lines 468–83; C, XXI, 465–79, discussed by Baldwin, *Theme*, pp.7–11.
77 Powell and Wallis, *Lords*, p.383.
78 *PP*, C, III, lines 378–81.
79 Pearsall, *Piers Plowman*, p.37 (note 140); J. Coleman, *English Literature in History 1350–1400: Medieval Readers and Writers* (1981), p.113.
80 R.H. Jones, *The Royal Policy of Richard II: Absolutism in the later Middle Ages* (Oxford, 1968), pp.147–8. Jones also thinks the might of the Commons rather than the will of God makes the king reign, in Langland's view.
81 Baldwin, *Theme*, p.56. Why does she change tense in this sentence?

# 5

# The Good Parliament and its Sources

John Taylor
*University of Leeds*

I

The Good Parliament has on the whole received favourable treatment at the hands of chroniclers and later historians. Fourteenth-century chroniclers were unanimously well disposed to this assembly. The *Anonimalle* account called it 'the great parliament',[1] while the *Brut* which perhaps more than any chronicle embodies popular judgements and opinions, said of the Good Parliament that it was, 'the grettest that was sen meny yere afore'.[2] John Malvern's continuation of the *Polychronicon* describes the Good Parliament as 'maximum parliamentum'.[3] Whether these descriptions refer to the size, the duration, the achievements of the Good Parliament, or indeed to a combination of all these features is perhaps uncertain. The name itself derives from Walsingham's contemporary history. What appears to be the earliest draft of Walsingham's contemporary chronicle contains a heading relating to this parliament, 'quod multum bonum a quibusdam dicebatur'. A later version of the text was amended to read 'quod bonum a pluribus vocabatur'.[4] The whole of this portion of the chronicle was seemingly removed from Walsingham's later account. In Walsingham's revised text the assembly is described simply as 'parliamentum maximum'.[5] At the close of the fifteenth century Robert Fabyan in his *New Chronicles of England and France* gave a brief description of its proceedings, but did not identify the parliament by name.[6] Nonetheless Walsingham's description of 'the good parliament' was destined to survive. In the sixteenth century Stow knew certain early drafts of Walsingham's contemporary history as found in B.L. Ms Harley 3634, a part of which he translated.[7] In his *Annals or General Chronicle of England* he refers to the assembly of 1376 as 'a parliament commonly called the Good Parliament'.[8] Stow almost certainly took the title from Walsingham. Since the seventeenth century the parliament of 1376 has invariably been know as the 'Good Parliament'.

Historians and antiquarians have generally considered that its name is well deserved, although with some reservations concerning the extent of its lasting achievements. Stubbs, who did not have access to the account in the *Anonimalle* chronicle, said that the Good Parliament 'asserted some sound principles without being the starting point of a new history.'[9] Tout was more positive. He wrote that although the Good Parliament 'was certainly no starting point of a new history . . . its importance can hardly be over-rated when looked at from the stand point of political, social, or administrative history'.[10] In a valuable work devoted to the assembly Dr Holmes has recently emphasized the importance of the Good Parliament stating that 'such an exceptionally dramatic and well documented episode . . . provides an unusual insight into the politics of medieval England'.[11]

What makes the Good Parliament stand out among the parliamentary assemblies of the Middle Ages? It is no exaggeration to say that it is the best recorded parliament of the entire medieval period. Apart from the account on the parliament roll the Good Parliament gave rise to the most interesting description of the medieval Commons known to survive, namely that found in the *Anonimalle Chronicle* as well as to Walsingham's contemporary narrative. Shorter descriptions are found in the *Brut* and *Malvern*. We possess a sermon by Thomas Brinton which was preached in the course of the Good Parliament. It seems likely that Langland's fable of the rat parliament in the B text of *Piers Plowman* also refers to this assembly.[12]

Such descriptions reflect rather than explain the interest aroused by this parliament. Concerning that interest there can be no doubt. John Malvern's continuation of the *Polychronicon* says that songs were composed about the Speaker, Sir Peter de la Mare, 'de quo et factis suis habitus per tempus illud multa metrice valde subtiliter erant composita', an indication perhaps of the extent to which Peter de la Mare and the deliberations in the Commons captured the imagination of contemporaries.[13] At first glance it is not immediately obvious what aroused that interest. Compared with the later parliaments of the fourteenth century the political achievements of the Good Parliament were limited. The Good Parliament certainly succeeded in impeaching certain of the king's councillors as well as in punishing lesser offenders. The charges against Latimer and Lyons included such matters as advancing loans at excessively high rates of interest, the brokerage of royal debts, and selling licences to export wool to ports other than the Calais wool staple. Latimer was charged with extortion in Brittany and responsibility for the fall of the fortresses of Saint Sauveur in Normandy and Bécherel in Brittany. Charges were also brought against John Neville, Adam Bury, Willian Elys and John Pecche. Alice Perrers, the mistress of Edward III, was banished under an *ad hoc* ordinance.[14] Nonetheless these charges scarcely amounted to a major attempt at political change, while many of the acts of the Good Parliament itself were to be reversed in the parliament of January 1377.

As contemporary sources testify, however, the actions of the Good Parliament were perceived as being of some significance at the time. In part this may have been due to procedural developments in 1376. Prior to 1376 we know relatively little about parliamentary procedure. Although used as a handbook to parliament in the later Middle Ages the *Modus Tenendi Parliamentum* is clearly unreliable as a guide to the actual procedures followed by parliament in the fourteenth century. It is likely, however, that in the fifty years or so after the permanent incorporation of the Commons into parliament some form of procedure had developed. This may have owed something to the presence of common lawyers who imported into the working of parliament procedures first developed in the courts of law. Certainly by 1376 some elements of procedure had developed among the Commons as can be seen from the *Anonimalle* description of the knights of the shire who go to the lectern with their muttered grace before and after speaking.[15] In all probability the Good Parliament itself marks an important stage in this process. It witnessed, for example, the first use of impeachment, and provides the first significant indication we have of the evolution of the office of Speaker. If Peter de la Mare's protestation in this parliament appears to have been carefully rehearsed, at the same time it was almost certainly a product of the events of 1376.[16] Yet parliamentary procedure itself would scarcely have had a profound effect upon those members of fourteenth-century society who wrote the chronicles, and who, in any event, knew relatively little about the technicalities of parliament. It is altogether more probably that what interested writers on this occasion was the concerted action of the Commons, given expression, for example, in the memorable speeches of Peter de la Mare, and in the events of 9 May when Peter de la Mare insisted that all the Commons be assembled before he spoke to the Lords, 'and they were searched for in various places for more than two hours before they could be found'.[17] For the first time the Commons appeared to be acting as a single united body, and to be holding the political initiative. Although half a century of political development lay behind the Commons' actions at this time, their role in 1376 must surely have contained an element of novelty.

The extent to which the Commons were in fact an independent political force in 1376 is still perhaps a matter of legitimate debate. Suffice it to say that the commons at this time contained among them men of substance and influence. In the Good Parliament the knights appear constantly to have taken the initiative. Nonetheless they almost certainly acted in conjuction with the Lords. Malvern's continuation of the *Polychronicon* says that the Commons were secretly inspired by the Black Prince.[18] Whatever the truth of that suggestion, the knights of the shire whose speeches only are recorded in the *Anonimalle* account, were linked to the magnates by social, economic, and territorial ties. The influence of the magnates when they chose to assert it, was considerable. The fact is that the interest of magnates and Commons almost certainly coincided in 1376.

If the interest taken in the Good Parliament is primarily explained by the actions of the Commons, other features were almost certainly present. From the descriptions of the assembly as 'the great parliament', 'the greatest that was seen', 'parliamentum maximum', it seems likely that the Good Parliament impressed contemporaries by its duration and its size. It lasted longer than any parliament that had previously met in England.[19] As regards its composition the *Anonimalle* account tells us that in addition to the magnates, bishops, barons and bannerets of standing there were '280 knights and esquires and citizens and burgesses for the community of diverse cities and boroughs and counties.'[20] How the author arrived at these figures we have no means of knowing.[21] We cannot be certain either how the attendance at this parliament compares with that on previous occasions. Nonetheless the Good Parliament appears to have been 'remarkably well attended'.[22] The length of its sitting and its numbers would appear to have constituted a part at least of its significance.

The language in which the debates in the Commons were conducted may also have some bearing on the interest which they aroused. The *Anonimalle* account reports the proceedings in the language of that chronicle which is French. Walsingham, who wrote a Latin chronicle, employed Latin for his description of the Good Parliament, including what professes to be an abstract from a speech of Peter de la Mare. The period of the 1370s witnessed, however, important changes in the use of the two vernaculars, and it is difficult to believe that an assembly of knights and burgesses meeting in 1376 would have conducted their debates entirely in French. The gradual withdrawal of clerical proctors from parliament may also have aided the use of the English vernacular among the Commons.[23] The Good Parliament could therefore have been the first important parliamentary occasion on which the proceedings among the Commons were conducted at least partially in English.

As regards the interest aroused by this assembly, Tout wrote that 'the Commons held set debates in the chapter house, and these debates were thought worthy of record in the chronicles of distant monasteries'.[24] Yet despite an undoubted wider interest the debates were of most immediate concern to London based writers, and to chroniclers such as Walsingham in centres not too far distant from the capital. Although copied into the chronicle of St Mary's, York, the *Anonimalle* account almost certainly derives from a London and parliamentary source. The *Brut* is likely to have been of London origin. Langland and Brinton were present in London at the time of the Good Parliament. It was in London that songs and ballads were composed about Sir Peter de la Mare.[25] In the light of these considerations we should consider the reporting of the events of 1376 in three main areas; at St Albans with the work of Walsingham, in the accounts, official and unofficial, which appear to emanate from within parliament, and in the writings of Brinton and Langland.

## II

Walsingham's account of the Good Parliament which was written shortly after the events of 1376–7, appears to have formed the opening section of his *Chronica Maiora*. In the Rolls Series edition of the St Albans chronicles the account occupies pp.68–101 of the *Chronicon Angliae*. As printed in that edition it is taken not from the main St Albans manuscript (B.L. Ms Royal 13. E. ix) but from what appear to be earlier versions of the text.[26] These versions were in all probability the work of Walsingham himself and represent his earliest impressions of the Good Parliament.[27] If that is the case it is worth noting that it was the Good Parliament which prompted Walsingham to begin the work of chronicle writing. No other chronicler began his narrative at this point. Prior to Walsingham's account there are in fact few, if any, good descriptions of parliament in the chronicle sources. With one or two exceptions earlier parliamentary assemblies appear to have raised relatively little interest among monastic chroniclers and as we see from Walsingham's own narrative the reporting of parliamentary history was a subject which presented particular difficulties to a monastic writer.[28] Nonetheless in other respects a monk at St Albans was well placed to comment upon events in London. The abbey was a prestigious community as well as being a calling place for travellers. One of those travellers in 1376 was almost certainly Sir Thomas Hoo, knight of the shire of Bedfordshire in the Good Parliament, and a member of a family which had long associations with the abbey. The evidence of the St Albans chronicle suggests that Sir Thomas was one of Walsingham's principal informants on these events. Sir Thomas himself features in Walsingham's narrative which contains the well known description of the knight's dream.[29] According to Walsingham's account Sir Thomas at the time of the Good Parliament dreamed that he was listening to the Commons' debates. In his dream he noticed seven gold coins lying on the floor. Believing these to be lost he sought their owner. In the choir he found a number of choir monks whose leader told him that the coins were not lost but were in fact the gifts of the Holy Spirit given to Sir Thomas and the Commons to reform the abuses in government. Sir Thomas related the dream to his colleagues who not unnaturally took it to be a sign of divine assistance.[30]

If, as seems certain, the source of this episode was Sir Thomas himself, the story of his vision is almost certainly authentic. The knights undoubtedly played a central role in the work of the Good Parliament and, from Walsingham's account, Sir Thomas clearly believed that he and others in the Commons had a mission to reform the central government.[31] Other details in Walsingham's narrative also suggest an informant with inside knowledge of this assembly. Thus Walsingham knows something of the charges against Latimer and Lyons, recording accurately the loan of 20,000 marks by Latimer and Lyons to the king for which the king paid 10,000 marks.[32] The general content of the military charges is given including the accusation that Latimer impeded the despatch of help to Bécherel.[33] Walsingham refers to the intercommuning committee as well as to the election of a continual council to assist the king.[34] He gives prominence to the actions of Sir Peter de la Mare, and records what professes to be an extract from his speech.[35] All this suggests access to a well informed source.

Walsingham also preserves details not found elsewhere and which fit into the general pattern of events. Information concerning the charges against Latimer found only in Walsingham's account includes, for example, mention of Latimer's financial transactions with regard to the city of Bristol and Sir Robert Knolles, the imprisonment of a messenger from La Rochelle, and the betrayal of information to France.[36] The intervention of Neville in the parliamentary debate as reported by Walsingham seems likely.[37] Certain details in Walsingham's account which read oddly may be explained by the fact that Sir Thomas supplied him with details concerning the proceedings of the Good Parliament which did not feature in its final decisions. Thus Walsingham's account of the procedure adopted in appointing the intercommuning committee appears at first sight unlikely. He suggests that the committee was appointed in stages, beginning with the bishops, then the barons, and finally the earls. Nonetheless this procedure may well have been suggested during some preliminary stage in the negotiations and before the Commons asked for the whole delegation on 9 May as reported in the Anonimalle account.[38] Walsingham differs from other sources also in the names of this committee, including the Bishop of Rochester in place of the Bishop of St Davids as mentioned on the roll, and the Bishop of Bath as mentioned in the Anonimalle account. This again may be due to different individuals having been approached at separate stages in the course of the parliament.[39]

Yet if Walsingham is better informed on the Good Parliament than has often been supposed, he makes a number of errors which arise in part from his lack of a specialist knowledge of parliamentary assemblies. His most obvious slip is to locate the setting of the meeting of the Commons at

St Pauls and not Westminster.[40] His account of the afforcement of the continual council which was proposed on 26 May when a delegation of lords went to the king, places it incorrectly at the end of the proceedings of the Good Parliament, 'cum iam finis parliamenti instaret'.[41] Walsingham did not know the names of the councillors, and after writing 'electi sunt ergo' left a blank in the manuscript. In addition to errors and omissions Walsingham's narrative is also distorted by his animus against Gaunt.[42] Of the thirty-four pages which the printed text of the *Chronicon Angliae* devotes to the Good Parliament less than half can be said to be focused on the parliament proper. The remainder is a type of 'Chronique Scandaleuse'.

Nonetheless even this part of the narrative has its value. From Walsingham's account we learn something of the outlook of the community at St Albans. Walsingham's prejudices were undoubtedly shared in a large part by the monastic community, and one powerful influence may well have been the abbot, Thomas de la Mare, who was probably favourably disposed to the acts of the Good Parliament. At St Albans Gaunt was clearly viewed as a sinister influence seeking to undermine the work of this assembly. Thus Walsingham speaks of Gaunt's bribes to the accusers of Latimer, and of his intrigues to secure the succession to the throne.[43] These charges are not confirmed in other sources. If in recounting these events Walsingham's outlook does not quite amount to an 'apologia pro baronibus', it was without doubt indicative of a good deal of contemporary feeling about Gaunt. The cause of this outlook may well have been dislike of Gaunt's role in the Good Parliament, reinforced by a critical attitude towards his support for Wyclif, which Walsingham reports in detail.[44]

It is perhaps scarcely surprising that this account of the Good Parliament failed to find a place in the later versions of the St Albans text. Its removal almost certainly took place *c*. 1399 in a period of political revolution. This removal may have been on account of a general dissatisfaction with the text and its overall view of the Good Parliament, but more likely it was specifically due to the inadvisability of allowing the references to Gaunt to remain. The description of the Good Parliament is found now in its fullest form only in a fragment of Walsingham's contemporary history contained in B.L. Ms Otho. C. ii. A slightly abbreviated version which was once used as a *Polychronicon* continuation in Ms Bodley 316, but which was removed from that manuscript, is discovered in B.L. Ms Harley 3634.[45] Ms Bodley 316 originally belonged to Norwich Cathedral Priory. Wymondham, a dependency of St Albans where Walsingham was prior from 1394–6, was only a few miles from Norwich. It is likely that the continuation was copied at Wymondham, and the substitution made at Norwich, before the manuscript came into the hands of Thomas of Gloucester, who gave it to his new foundation at Pleshey. This must have occurred before 1397.

The process of revision was to be carried further. In the main St Albans manuscript which contains the text of Walsingham's contemporary history (B.L. Ms Royal 13. E. ix), and which was written in the 1390s, certain quires were removed, and the whole narrative from 1327 to 1377 replaced by a briefer version. It is probable that this was done at the time of Richard's deposition, and it seems likely that the original text of the Royal manuscript once contained a narrative similar to that found in the fragments which have been described. The narrative which was substituted in the Royal Ms devotes barely two pages in its printed version in the Rolls Series to the affairs of the Good Parliament.[46] It says only that the king asked for subsidies which were resisted, that officers of the king were removed and that complaints were made against Alice Perrers. The charges against Richard Lyons and Adam Bury are mentioned, as is Peter de la Mare's role in the parliament. The St Alban's account of the Good Parliament represents therefore one remarkable example of the rewriting of history in late medieval England.

### III

In addition to Walsingham's account the Good Parliament is recorded on the parliament roll.[47] Although the roll is an invaluable source for these proceedings it does not represent the order in which business came before the Commons. The chancery clerks, whose business it was to produce the record, arranged their material in a different fashion, often inverting chronological order, and putting down first matters only arranged at the end of the session. Nonetheless despite its chronological limitations the parliament roll of 1376 preserves many of the known facts concerning the Good Parliament.

Deriving in all probability from a parliamentary source also is the unique description, written in French, which is transcribed in the *Anonimalle Chronicle* of St Mary's, York. This account is perhaps best regarded as an unofficial record of the proceedings in the Commons' chapter house compiled by a chancery clerk.[48] How 'unofficial' this description was we have no means of telling. When contrasted with the parliament roll, however, and with the roll's silence regarding the Commons' procedures the account seems unlikely to have been governmentally inspired. It may owe its existence to the personal interest of the author, or again it may have been commissioned by some member of the Commons. In contrast to Walsingham's narrative the description reveals a degree of skill and expertise not commonly associated with monastic writings. It is perhaps one illustration of the important role played by chancery clerks in the development of a contemporary literature. Whatever its origin it constitutes a type of parliamentary reporting hitherto unknown in medieval England, and which was not to be resumed for some two centuries. A comparison between this account and that found on the parliament roll serves to indicate those features which impressed themselves upon its author.

The parliament roll of 1376 enabled Stubbs to produce a reasonably adequate account of the events of the Good Parliament.[49] The roll mentions for example the financial, military and administrative charges which were brought against Lyons, Latimer, Neville, Elys and Pecche. It alludes to the intercommuning committee to aid the Commons, and the continual council to help the king. Where the author of the *Anonimalle* chronicle shows his unique knowledge is in providing an exact chronology of the parliament up to Monday May 26, in relating the speeches and proceedings of the Commons in the chapter house, and in describing in detail the role of Peter de la Mare, nowhere alluded to on the roll.[50] These are features which render his account independent of the official version. Also included in the *Anonimalle* account is a statement of the number of those present in parliament.[51] The *Anonimalle* account is also fuller than the roll on the activities of Richard le Scrope and William Walworth, and mentions, which the roll does not, both Adam Francis and John Pyel.[52]

If the *Anonimalle* account contains information not found on the parliament roll, the roll in its turn contains information not discovered in this description. Thus the roll mentions the customs granted by the Commons at this time.[53] It gives (except in the case of the Calais staple) a fuller account of the financial charges against Latimer and Lyons than that found in the *Anonimalle* account. It mentions such details as Lyons' 4d tax in the pound upon letters of exchange.[54] The roll also preserves the replies of Latimer, Lyons and others, to the charges brought against them, and unlike the *Anonimalle* account, mentions the accusations against Neville together with his replies. This information occupies almost an entire side of the seven printed sides which the roll devotes to these charges.[55] The intervention of Michael de la Pole and William Wingfield in the examination of Reginald Love, a London merchant, found in the roll, is again not mentioned in the *Anonimalle* account.[56] Finally, unlike the *Anonimalle* account the roll relates the charges against William Elys, farmer of petty custom at Yarmouth, and deputy of Richard Lyons, and John Pecche, a senior London alderman and seller of sweet wines inside the city of London.[57] These omissions in the *Anonimalle* account serve to indicate the limitations of its otherwise excellent description.

Apart from omissions and additons there are also differences between the *Anonimalle* account and the parliament roll which are seen in their

descriptions of the intercommuning committee, and the continual
council. The roll mentions the intercommuning committee at the
beginning of its account but does so only in the briefest fashion.[58] There is
no suggestion in the roll that the Commons asked for, let alone nominated
the committee.[59] This version differs from the *Anonimalle* account where
Peter de la Mare requested on Friday 9 May that twelve councillors, whom
he mentioned by name, be appointed to assist the Commons in their
deliberations. The councillors joined them on Monday 12 May.[60] The list
of names of those on the committee also differs slightly in the two
accounts. Whereas the *Anonimalle* description has the Bishop of Bath, the
parliament roll has the Bishop of St Davids. Where the *Anonimalle*
account and Walsingham give Roger Beauchamp as a member of the
committee, the roll has Henry le Scrope. This may be due to last minute
changes in the composition of the committee. A second point of
difference concerns the continual council where the roll speaks of ten or
twelve councillors, while the *Anonimalle* account mentions nine.[61] The
names of these councillors are found only in the *Anonimalle* account,
although the roll does give the limiting factors on the work of the council.

Comparison with the parliament roll therefore shows overall the high
standard of reporting of this 'anonymous account'. There are few positive
errors. Among possible inaccuracies are a statement referring to the 'ditz
evesqes' which seems to confuse the committee of twelve with the later
continual council.[62] The account of Richard Stafford's removal from the
council is again unlikely, and is confirmed by no other source.[63] It is
perhaps improbable that the king swore before the lords to banish Alice
Perrers from his presence.[64] Nonetheless the absence of error is negative
evidence for the claim that this source constitutes an eye-witness account.
The strongest argument for such a claim is the remarkable knowledge of
parliamentary procedure which its author reveals. Thus we have the
speeches, questions and answers among the Commons in the critical
debates. There is the recording of a parliamentary language, and of a
parliamentary procedure. The words of Sir Peter de la Mare's protestation
are exactly noted. There can be no doubt therefore that this account
emanates from within the Commons and was the work of an author who
took a particular interest in the speeches of Peter de la Mare. Parliamentary speeches of such a quality had almost certainly never before been
heard in the lifetime of that audience.[65] A first impression might also
suggest that this author's quality of observation was unusual. Yet exactness
in detail is to be found elsewhere in the chronicles. The unusual feature in
this description is the writer's intimate knowledge of parliamentary
procedure, and his command of a specialized vocabulary. His expertise is
revealed throughout. Only the author of this account attempted, for
example, to give precise numbers of those attending parliament. It is

possible in this case that the author 'took his figures from the sheriff's returns to which he may have had access'.[66] This again suggests that he was a privileged observer.

Finally it should be noted that the account does not describe the whole proceedings of the Good Parliament. It gives an exact chronology only for the first half of the assembly, that is to say, up to Monday 26 May. The parliament itself did not end until 10 July. After 26 May the account in the *Anonimalle* chronicle ceases to give accurate dates, and describes the remainder of the parliament only in the briefest fashion.[67] Perhaps the very length of the assembly defeated its unknown author. Given the care with which the monks at St Mary's copied their sources it is unlikely that the description which reached St Mary's was fuller than the account which they transcribed. We can only speculate as to why this tradition of parliamentary reporting was not continued in the fifteenth century.[68]

### IV

It is perhaps not surprising that the Good Parliament is recorded in certain of the chronicles as well as in descriptions which emanate from within parliament. More remarkable perhaps is the fact that its actions are reflected in other types of writing. Thomas Brinton, a Benedictine monk who became Bishop of Rochester, devoted one of his best known sermons to the work of the Good Parliament. It is possible that Brinton played some part in the proceedings for he is named in the *Chronicon Angliae* as one of the members of the intercommuning committee to meet the Commons.[69] Brinton was perhaps the best known preacher of his time concerning himself with the social and political issues of the day.[70] In the only copy of his sermons which survives (B.L. Ms Harley 3760), the sermon which refers to the Good Parliament is listed as No. 69.[71] Internal evidence suggests that it was delivered on 18 May 1376, after the king's grant of an intercommuning committee to advise the Commons (13 May), and before the first meeting of the Commons with the committee. The sermon which was delivered therefore at a critical juncture in the affairs of the Good Parliament is likely to have been preached to a convocation of clergy held in London.

In his sermon Brinton reflected on the state of England. Whereas the king of France had many councillors the keys of the kingdom of England hung at the girdle of a woman (Alice Perrers). The lords temporal, confessors, preachers, whose duty it was to speak out against this state of affairs held their peace. Parliament which should have taken action was in danger of being compared to the parliament of the rats and the mice in the fable, which decreed that every cat should have a bell attached to its neck

but which took no steps to implement its decision. The sermon appears to
have been a plea for action, and the use of the fable an illustration of the
consequences of inaction on the part of parliament and others.[73]

More intriguing is Langland's use of the rat fable which is found in the
prologue to the B text of *Piers Plowman*.[74] Although Langland's poem is
poised 'between allegory and description of real life', it seems likely that in
so far as any one historical parliament prompted his reflections it was the
parliament of 1376.[75] In determining the manner in which Langland used
the fable the date of composition of his poem is clearly of some
significance. As far as the B text is concerned a date after 1376 seems
almost certain. In the first place it is likely that Brinton's sermon was itself
the source of Langland's knowledge of the rat fable, for this fable is the
only one discovered in the three versions of Langland's poem. Although it
is possible that Langland's knowledge of the fable may derive from the
homily books of Bozon and Bromyard the probability is that this unique
example of Langland's use of fable literature was the result of a strong
contemporary stimulus. This stimulus is likely to have been provided by
Brinton's sermon, which made the story familiar as a weapon of political
controversy, and which was 'better suited to act as a stimulus than a
general and otherwise quiescent knowledge of fable literature'.[76] There are
also in the prologue to the poem allusions (B.xix 426–7, 439–42) which
appear to refer to the rivalry between the popes which followed the
outbreak of the Schism. This would give a date of composition after 1379.
It seems likely therefore that the B text was written during the period
1377–9, and possibly even later.[77] At that time Langland would have
been aware of the outcome of the proceedings of the Good Parliament.

In Langland's poem the fable takes the form of an assembly of rats and
mice who hold a council. They are alarmed by the actions of a cat. A rat
suggests that the cat should be belled so that everyone will know the cat's
whereabouts. The rats applauded the suggestion, but no one dared fix the
bell. At last a wise mouse came forward and advised his companions to
leave the cat alone. The cat had his uses for the mice and the rats could
not govern themselves. Even at first glance the moral of this fable scarcely
accords with that of the story as used by Brinton. In his account Langland
appears to underline the advantages of the court, and the problems
inherent in any attempt by parliament to control its actions. Although it
is always hazardous to give a purely political interpretation of Langland's
themes, and his subject in this instance was almost certainly 'the perennial
issue of power in society' there seems no reason to believe that Langland
with his conservative instincts would have welcomed moves by the
Commons to limit the actions of the Crown and the court.[78] The ultimate
outcome of the Good Parliament might well have confirmed that
impression, and helped to shape his image of the assembly. The fact that

the Good Parliament almost certainly gave rise to the use of the fable in both Brinton and Langland illustrates again the interest which the assembly aroused among contemporaries.

What light Langland's account of the Good Parliament throws upon his basic political outlook and that of his contemporaries is a question which we cannot here consider in detail. If it appears unlikely that Langland came later to entertain theories of royal absolutism expressed in the C text of his poem, at the same time he may during the later 1370s have felt reservations concernng the objectives of the Good Parliament. Monarchy, however arbitrary, was better than attempts to muzzle it.[79] Like other of his contemporaries Langland's views on kingship were no doubt to change during the course of the reign, and the dialogue which he urged between king and Commons belongs in all probability to a later period.[80] To the question how far Langland's outlook reflected that of his contemporaries there can be no easy answer. Nonetheless the comparative ease with which the acts of the Good Parliament were reversed in the months which followed its conclusion suggests that, despite the chronicle accounts, contemporary opinion was not all of one persuasion. Although Langland was in all probability writing sometime after the Good Parliament it may be that his outlook reflected a body of opinion, already in existence in 1376, critical of the actions of this assembly, but which found little or no expression in the chronicle sources.

In conclusion it can be said that the accounts of the Good Parliament occupy a special place among fourteenth-century descriptions of parliament. Although no one account is perhaps more detailed than the descriptions of the Merciless Parliament found later in the chronicle of the Monk of Westminster, collectively they provide a fuller picture of a medieval parliamentary assembly than any other parliamentary portrayal that we possess. In addition these sources raise particular problems of provenance and bias. Walsingham, together with the author of the *Anonimalle* description, Langland, and others, record and comment on the proceedings of the Good Parliament from different centres. They illustrate therefore the widespread impression which the assembly made upon contemporary opinion. With the exception of Langland there can be no doubt that, as recorded in these sources, that impression was a favourable one. Thus in addition to the texts already mentioned, the author of the *Brut* wrote approvingly of the Good Parliament and of Sir Peter de la Mare as 'a trewe and an eloquent man'.[81] Malvern's continuation of the *Polychronicon* contains a similar picture, which also mentions the wisdom of the Speaker, and emphasizes his unusual eloquence.[82] The existence of these descriptions is all the more remarkable in view of the gap in the chronicle sources between 1340 and 1377.[83] The extent to which these views were representative of the political community as a whole must, however, remain a matter of conjecture. Again, whatever their bias in favour of the actions of the Good Parliament we should not ascribe to these writers the Whig notions of a later age. What they believed themselves to be observing in 1376 was almost certainly a brief, if dramatic, moment of political reform. Nonetheless they clearly saw in the Good Parliament features of unusual interest, and it is their reporting of these features which gave rise to some of the best descriptions of a medieval parliament known to survive.

## Notes

1 *Anonimalle Chronicle*, ed. V.H. Galbraith (Manchester, 1927 repr. 1970), p.79, n.4.
2 *Brut or the Chronicles of England*, ed. F.W.D. Brie (EETS 1906–8) II, 329. The *Brut* refers to the parliament of 1397 as 'the grete parlement', II. 352.
3 *Polychronicon Ranulphi Higden*, ed. C. Babington and J.R. Lumby (RS, 1865–86). VIII 384.
4 *Chronicon Angliae*, ed. E.M. Thompson (RS, 1874), p.68, and n4.
5 *Historia Anglicana*, ed. H.T. Riley (RS, 1863–4), I. 320. See pp.88.
6 Robert Fabyan, *New Chronicles of England and France*, ed. Henry Ellis (1811), p.486. Fabyan or his source suggests that because of the government 'the lande mayght not be plentuously of chafre, merchandyse, or rychesse.' Taxation had impoverished the people. See Eleanor Carus-Wilson, *Medieval Merchant Venturers* (1954), p.255. n2.
7 B.L. Ms. Harley 6217. The text is printed in *Archaeologia*, XXII, (1829).
8 *Annals* (1615), p.271.
9 Stubbs' account of the Good Parliament is found in *Constitutional History of Medieval England* (Oxford, 1875), II. 448–55.
10 *Chapters in the Administrative History of Medieval England*, (Manchester, 1923–35), III, 305.
11 G.A. Holmes, *The Good Parliament* (Oxford, 1975), p.3. This remains an essential study of the Good Parliament and its background.
12 See pp.92–3. Holmes' comment is worth noting that 'it is rather surprising that these magnificent sources which offer an unusual insight into medieval political life have not received more serious attention from modern historians,' *Good Parliament*, p.1.
13 *Polychronicon*, VIII. 385.
14 T.F. Plucknett, 'The Impeachments of 1376', *TRHS*, 5th series, I (1951), 153–64. See pp.90, 91.
15 A translation of the *Anonimalle* account of the Good Parliament is given in J. Taylor, *English Historical Literature in the Fourteenth Century* (Oxford), 1987), pp.301–13.
16 See J.S. Roskell, *The Commons and their Speakers in English Parliaments, 1376–1523* (Manchester, 1965).
17 *English Historical Literature*, p.305.
18 *Polychronicon*, VIII. 385.
19 See Tout's comments in *Chapters*, III. 305.
20 *English Historical Literature*, p.301.
21 See p.90–1 and the comments of M. McKisack, *The Parliamentary Representation of the English Boroughs during the Middle Ages* (Oxford, 1962), pp.75–6.
22 A. Steel, *Richard II* (Cambridge, 1941), p.24.
23 See the recent account of clerical proctors by J.H. Denton and J.P. Dooley, *Representatives of the Lower Clergy in Parliament 1295–1340* (1987).

24 Chapters, III. 305.
25 See n13, also *Polychronicon*. VIII. 385. Malvern's continuation was the one account to be composed outside London, see p.93.
26 See pp.87–8.
27 Ibid.
28 See pp.86–7.
29 See the valuable article by A. Goodman, 'Sir Thomas Hoo and the Parliament of 1376', *BIHR*, XLI (1968), 139–49. Walsingham says of Sir Thomas Hoo 'qui etiam iureiurando mihi retulit hoc quod narro'. This is not found in Ms. B.L. Otho C. ii which is the earliest version, but is added in the margin of Ms. Bodley 316. See *Chronicon Angliae*, p.70. It is likely that the dream occurred before 12 May, Goodman, op. cit. p.142.
30 *Chronicon Angliae*, pp.70–2.
31 On the knights in the Good Parliament see Holmes, op. cit. pp.134–9.
32 *Chronicon Angliae*, p.78.
33 Ibid., pp.76–8. See Holmes, pp.126–34.
34 Ibid., pp.68–70, 100–1.
35 Ibid., pp.73–4.
36 *Chronicon Angliae*, pp.77, 78, 79, 81, 82–3; Holmes, op. cit. p.133. Thomas Catterton, captain of St Sauveur, is also mentioned in Walsingham's account, *Chronicon Angliae*, pp.77, 261–4.
37 Ibid., p.80.
38 See Goodman, op. cit. p.142.
39 Ibid. See also Tout's comments to the effect that the art of parliamentary reporting was not yet far advanced, Chapters, III. 295 n.
40 *Chronicon Angliae*, p.70. This is an obvious slip on Walsingham's part.
41 *Chronicon Angliae*, pp.100–1 and n2.
42 *Chronicon Angliae*, pp.74–6, 92–3.
43 *Chronicon Angliae*, pp.85–6, 92–3.
44 Ibid., pp.115–21.
45 This version omits an account of Gaunt and his plots against the Commons. The duke was warned by one of his followers that the actions of the Good Parliament were strongly supported. The account is followed by further criticism of Gaunt, *Chronicon Angliae*, pp.74–5.
46 *Historia Anglicana*, I, 320–1.
47 *Rot. Parl.* II. 321–60. For the accounts found in the *Brut* and Malvern, see p.97.
48 See *English Historical Literature*, pp.203–5.
49 For his use of this source see *Constitutional History*, II. 448–55.
50 Some of De la Mare's speeches may find an echo in the parliament roll. See Plucknett, op. cit. pp.156, 158. *Rot. Parl.* II. 323. De la Mare is mentioned in the main chronicle accounts which describe the Good Parliament.
51 See p.84, 90–1 *Anonimalle Chronicle*, pp.79–80.
52 Ibid., pp.87, 89.
53 *Rot. Parl.* II. 322.
54 *Rot. Parl.* II. 323–4.
55 *Rot. Parl.* II. 328–9.
56 Ibid., 329.
57 Ibid., 327, 328. See Holmes' comments, op. cit. pp.109, 114–8.
58 *Rot. Parl.* II. 322.
59 On the intercommuning committee see J.G. Edwards, *The Commons in Medieval English Parliaments* (1958), pp.14–15.
60 *Anonimalle Chronicle*, pp.84–5.
61 *Rot. Parl.* II. 322; *Anonimalle Chronicle*, p.91.
62 *Anonimalle Chronicle*, p.88.

63 Ibid., p.92.

64 Ibid.

65 In this account particular attention is paid to Peter de la Mare's speeches. As evidence of a Commons' origin, the narrative speaks of the Bishop of Exeter and Sir Richard Scrope being assigned 'to us', *Anonimalle Chronicle*, p.88. See the comments of J.G. Edwards, *The Commons in Medieval English Parliaments*, p.17.

66 McKisack, *The Parliamentary Representation of the English Boroughs*, pp.75–6.

67 See *Anonimalle Chronicle*, pp.93–4.

68 This particular description may owe its existence to the element of novelty in the proceedings of the Good Parliament. The next notable description emanating from the Commons is the diary by a member of the Commons for Colchester in 1485. See N. Pronay and J. Taylor, *Parliamentary Texts of the Later Middle Ages* (Oxford, 1980), pp.177–93.

69 His name does not appear in the parliament roll or the *Anonimalle* account. On Brinton see *The Sermons of Thomas Brinton, Bishop of Rochester (1373–1389)*, ed. M.A. Devlin, 2 vols. Camden Society 3rd ser. LXXXVI (1954). There are some useful comments in Holmes, *The Good Parliament*, pp.103–4. Brinton is referred to by F.A. Gasquet, *The Old English Bible and other Essays* (1897), and G.R. Owst, *Literature and Pulpit in Medieval England*, (Cambridge, 1923). The *Chronicon Angliae* mentions Brinton as a member of the intercommuning committee, p.69.

70 A comparison with Richard FitzRalph, whose sermon book survives, is interesting. On FitzRalph see Katharine Walsh, *A Fourteenth-Century Scholar and Primate, Richard FitzRalph in Oxford, Avignon and Armagh* (Oxford, 1981), pp.182–238.

71 See the valuable article by Eleanor Kellogg, 'Bishop Brinton and the Rat Parliament', *Proceedings of the Modern Language Association* (1935), 57–68, which sets out the evidence for dating.

72 Devlin, op. cit. II. 315–21. There is a partial translation in Gasquet, op. cit. See the comments in Devlin, op. cit. I. xxv, and Owst p.579 seq.

73 On Brinton's sermon see the comments by Anna Baldwin, *The Theme of Government in Piers Plowman* (Brewer, 1981), p.17. Holmes suggests that it was the work of an author 'who had no sympathy for the policy of collusion with the papacy which the court had adopted in 1375'; *The Good Parliament*, pp.103–4.

74 *Piers Plowman*, B text, Prologue, 146 ff. On the general relationship between Langland's poem and the history of this period see *ante* pp.59–80.

75 This has been the general view since the time of Skeat. See M. Jusserand, *Piers Plowman, A Contribution to the History of English Mysticism*, (1894). For a recent comment see A.V.C. Schmidt, *The Vision of Piers Plowman* (Dent, 1978), p.xvi. Whether the person of Alice Perrers contributed to the portrait of Lady Meed, who represents the principle of avarice, remains an open question, but see pp.67–8.

76 Kellogg, p.67. See Owst, op. cit. p.583.

77 J.A.W. Bennett, 'The Date of the B Text of Piers Plowman', *Medium Aevum*, XII (1943), 55–64.

78 See Baldwin, pp.17–8 and Schmidt, p.xxv. In establishing Langland's meaning we cannot be certain whom precisely he means to signify by the cat, the rats, and the mice. In so far as there was an historical original the cat may represent the court of Edward III, the rats may be the lords, and the mice the commoners. The message, however, seems clear. The rats and mice should not attempt to bell the cat lest greater dangers befall them.

79 *English Historical Literature*, p.210.

80 See Dr Helen Jewell's comments on Langland's views, pp.75–8.

81 *Brut*, II. 330.

82 *Polychronicon*, VIII. 384–6.

83 J. Taylor, *The Universal Chronicle of Ranulf Higden* (Oxford, 1966), pp.25–9.

# 6

# The Defence of the Realm and the Impeachment of Michael de la Pole in 1386

James Sherborne
*University of Bristol*

The danger posed by the menace of French invasion in 1386 has long been recognized. Tout, for example, saw in it 'the last great panic of Richard II's reign', while others have seen 'the most serious threat that England faced in the whole course of the war' or, more emphatically, 'the most deadly threat to England throughout the entire Middle Ages'. Moreover the highly charged atmosphere of the parliament of October 1386 and the mood of national fear have been recognized. Professor Roskell has written of 'political crisis precipitated by the military panic', while Dr Palmer has observed 'the mere existence of the (enemy) camp at Sluys was an essential ingredient of the English parliamentary crisis' which led to the impeachment of the chancellor, Michael de la Pole, Earl of Suffolk, and the appointment for a year on 19 November of a reforming commission, an event which influenced politics in several ways for the rest of Richard II's reign. This paper in no way seeks to differ from these striking judgments.[1] Rather its purpose is to fill in some of the detail and to consider England's defence policy in 1386 and Article 3 of the impeachment which alleged neglect of keeping the sea.

Inadequacy of naval defence had in fact been a repeated complaint of the Commons in parliament since the renewal in 1369 of the war with France, soon joined by her powerful naval ally, Castile. These complaints were justified for France had learned that through raids upon the English coastline and attacks upon her merchant shipping enemy men and money might be diverted, defensively, to naval operations which, if conducted on any scale were expensive. England, however, was reluctant to accept the primary need for naval expenditure – it conflicted with her territorial objectives – but when no fleet was sent to sea, as in the summers of 1377 and 1380, the savaging of her shore was demoralizing and called forth protests about misguided strategy. By 1385, following earlier precedents, the most recent of which had been in 1369, France changed her naval tune, deciding to use her shipping to transport an army of invasion to England, hoping thereby to bring an end to hostilities.

In the meantime Castile had assumed a wider significance in English strategic thinking, as a military target rather than just a naval adversary. Following his marriage in 1371 to Constance, the daughter and heiress of the murdered King Pedro of Castile, John, Duke of Lancaster had cherished the hope that through his wife's claim he might acquire the throne of Castile for himself. After 1372, when he styled himself King of Castile, this thought was never far from his mind. It was, however, hard to gain the support he needed from English governments which until Buckingham's disastrous attempt to campaign in Brittany in 1380–1 were more interested in fighting in France. From 1381, however, with Cambridge's expedition to Portugal in that year and the crusade to Flanders in 1383 led by Henry Despenser, Bishop of Norwich, England adopted an oblique strategy by striking at France through her allies. In these terms an invasion of Castile had more than one attraction. France might be deprived of a powerful ally at sea, and after the Portuguese defeat of Castile at Aljubarotta in August 1385, the likelihood of English success in Spain became more tempting than before. Hence the endorsement of Lancaster's request for support for an expedition in 1386.

If the defence of the realm and the attack on Castile are two themes of this paper, the financing of warfare is another. Since 1371 the burden of taxation in the forms of a parish tax, lay and ecclesiastical subsidies and, for three years, poll taxes had borne heavily upon Englishmen, whose sense of fiscal obligation had in no way been encouraged by military or naval success. England indeed had not had a victory in the field since 1356, and by 1386 all the territorial gains won in 1360 by Edward III except Calais had been lost to the sustained counter-attack of an enemy which had prospered from England's inability to conceive or conduct an effective defensive strategy. Moreover English taxpayers were by no means convinced that war taxation was not being mis-spent. In similar fashion they believed that other revenues of the Crown, not subject to their grant, were being abused. Suspicion of the young Richard II and his friends and a growing distrust of de la Pole, chancellor since 1383, complicated the unhappy circumstances in which England found herself in the mid-1380s.

The keynote of the fractious parliament which sat from 20 October to 6 December 1385 was general disquiet about the king's finances and the need for their reform. This was combined with a fresh manifestation of a recurrent fear that taxes granted for the war might be misused. The grant of 1385 was of $1\frac{1}{2}$ for lay subsidies, the subsidy payable on 2 February 1386 and the moiety on 24 June. At the request of the Commons proceeds were appropriated to Lancaster's expedition to Castile, the defence of the Marches of Scotland, the relief of Ghent and the keeping of the sea. The

Commons, not for the first time, requested war treasurers, but their wishes were not fully granted. What they wanted was two lords, charged in parliament, who would by their special warrants authorize all spending by deputies acting under their instructions. The government was unprepared to go as far as this. Instead, two supervisors of taxation, Thomas Brantingham, Bishop of Exeter (and already twice treasurer of England) and John, Lord Cobham were appointed. They were to authorize all payments as advised by privy seal warrants from the council; thus the latter retained control and the Commons' purpose was overruled. Under the supervisors two London MPs and aldermen, John Hadley and Nicholas Exton, were appointed to 'take, receive and keep' the subsidy and, with the agreement and consent of Exeter and Cobham, restrict payments to the wars and the safeguarding of the sea. Hadley and Exton were required to certify to the Lower Exchequer all receipts and at the end of each week all payments they had made. As we shall see, 'this exceptional machinery for the collection and disbursement of the war grant' was not fully observed by the council. Hadley and Exton were not appointed until 30 January 1386, and within eight days receipts from the lay subsidy, payable from 2 February, were recorded in their name. Before this, however, in December 1385, John Hermesthorpe, an Exchequer official, had briefly acted as receiver of the subsidy and assignments to the value of £8,606 18s 9d were made on its anticipated yield to repay loans mainly to finance the relief of Ghent, with a much smaller provision for defence against the Scots.[2]

The appropriation of the 1385 grant was the result of distrust in the way the king and his council were believed to be indiscriminately spending extraordinary receipts. As for the keeping of the sea this was the product of accumulated experience and, most recently, of the events of 1385, when during July England was gravely threatened by an invasion force at Sluys, which was luckily diverted to the recovery of Damme after a surprise attack by the men of Ghent. The English council had anticipated a danger of this kind and from the expiry of a truce on 1 May, until the enemy soldiers dispersed from the fleet, the admirals, Sir Thomas Percy and Sir Baldwin Raddington served with 32 knights, 565 esquires, 569 armed men and 800 archers; they had mustered at Harwich and Orwell on 29 and 30 April. For at least part of their service the admirals patrolled the Flemish coast, as the enemy fleet gathered, with 21 ships, 6 barges and 6 balingers crewed by over 3,500 sailors. All this was at a cost of £12,285 4s 7d.[3] Such was the policy of the three great officers of state – de la Pole (Chancellor), Sir Hugh Segrave (Treasurer) and Walter Skirlaw (Keeper of the Privy Seal) who continued in office until October 1386. They needed no tuition in the importance of naval defence.

Before examining naval policy in 1386 some attention to Lancaster's expedition to Castile is necessary for three reasons, the demands its transport made on impressed shipping, the relatively heavy cost of the venture, and signs of financial embarrassment before it sailed. The first protection letters for Lancaster's army were issued in January 1386, and, judging by orders for the arrest of shipping of 12 and 15 March for assembly at Plymouth by 15 April and also by the duke's arrival there soon after that date, a sailing earlier than eventually proved practicable was planned.[4] One factor relevant to the council's sea-keeping policy might be that so many ships were taken up for Castile that this diminished resources needed for naval defence. In fact this was not so, for no ship which sailed to Castile was, after its return to England, engaged again in that year. What is true, however, is that the government could not collect transport vessels at the time it wanted them. This was one factor behind the delay. In April the duke found some 30 ships at Plymouth. By 10 June there were 49. Soon afterwards the fleet began to assume its final form, but the presence of 11 foreign ships on the paymaster's roll on 13 June suggests inadequate, or unavailable, domestic resources. Then, suspiciously, on 17 June, 25 West Country ships, including 9 from Plymouth itself, appear. One suspects they had been in port for some time, but that John Hatfield, the paymaster, had been unable to pay their crews. Finally on 30 June, the last essential component of the fleet, supplementary Portuguese transports and an escort of Portuguese galleys, arrived. Their assistance had been negotiated earlier in the year. Lancaster at last sailed on 7 July.[5]

Although before Easter, Hadley and Exton, the receivers of the war grant, had been paid over £29,000,[6] there are surprising pointers to financial distress before Lancaster's departure. In mid-April, for example, efforts were made to advance the payment of the moiety due on 24 June to 29 April, and in May some £6,000 was borrowed, including 1,000 marks from the king's chamber, 'to accelerate . . . the Duke of Lancaster's passage to Spain and other war business'. The loans were secured against a clerical half-tenth due on 17 June and the lay moiety payable some days later.[7] An urgent need is also suggested by a journey from Plympton to Bristol by a sergeant carrying letters from the treasurer, from Lancaster, and under the privy seal to collect taxation there of £100.[8] For the army the financial charges on the war grant were £26,666 13s 4d, half granted and half lent, almost exactly 50 per cent of the yield of £53,206 4s 8d received from the lay subsidies.[9] These payments are entered on the Issue Roll on 26 July, more than a fortnight after Lancaster sailed. Clearly these were delayed entries as the army would not have left England before receipt of cash. Transport costs amounted to £3,707 11s 4d spent on the non-Portuguese crews by John Hatfield.[10]

The financing of Lancaster's expedition appears to have been negotiated in the 1385 parliament. The *Westminster Chronicle* reported that the duke asked for £40,000 for his venture and that this was granted by the Lords and Commons. Here the sum stated is incorrect but, as in January and October 1382, Lancaster, it seems, made a submission of his needs which became the basis of an agreement. The words of Article 3 of de la Pole's impeachment in October 1386 suggest that the details of naval defence for the coming year and its finances were also settled, the Commons stipulating as a condition of a grant that a proportion should be devoted to the war at sea and spent in particular ways. The king and the Lords agreed to their demands.

The despatch of an army to Castile made obvious calls on English shipping, and for some months the council were concerned about the enemy's intentions. On 1 June Lancaster was told that as his fleet required a 'great part of the English navy', the realm would be harmed if anything went wrong. For this reason three men were ordered to provide for the ships' safe passages.[11] Naval defence received its first attention in 1386 in January, commendably early.[12] But at the same time English anxiety was to some extent lightened by negotiations with France which took place at Leulinghen and lasted for more than a fortnight after 1 March. All that resulted was a local truce until 1 May and, on 15 March, an agreement that if there was a wish to proceed to a general truce King Leo of Armenia should be told by 20 April. No expedition should sail before the following day. The French condition was that the Castilian plan be abandoned, but this the English refused.[13]

At Leulinghen neither side trusted the other. On 15 March, for example, the array of men at arms, armed men and archers was ordered throughout England to resist the enemy who 'gathering all their power on every side are purposing to invade the realm'.[14] From late March a flow of Chancery orders relating to coastal defence began. On 24 March Rye was the concern, following by Trematon (South Devon) and Porchester on 14 and 26 April. On 31 (sic) April proclamations in Sandwich, Dover (and for six miles around), Rye, Thanet and Oxney were ordered that all inhabitants should go with their families to Dover castle, Rye and Sandwich there to remain in safety; contrariants would be imprisoned. These were withdrawn on 14 May, but reimposed on 18 June, when inhabitants were ordered to take victuals with them.[15] English fears were justified, as in March Philip of Burgundy had received a grant from his duchy 'pour le passaige d'Engleterre' and soon Charles VI ordered the levying of an aide for an invasion force.[16] In February Calais had been briefly in danger and from March to May much was done to strengthen the town.[17]

For some time coastal defence orders continued to receive priority over the navy. The catalogue of these measures was extended in May with new commissions of array for Kent and Essex and attention to the king's castles in South Wales, Rye and Sandwich (again), Leeds Castle, Great Yar-

mouth and Lynn. Similar instructions, though at a reduced rate, continued in June with a further warning to Trematon, concern for Corfe and
Southampton, where 18 armed men guarded the new tower at the king's
expense, and new commissions for Suffolk and Nottinghamshire. On
2 June London aldermen were ordered to put their wards in array, and on
the next day the Abbot of St Augustine's Canterbury was told to array his
household.[18] The most striking order at this time was contained in privy
seal letters sent on 16 April to dukes, earls, barons, knights, esquires and
other members of the king's retinue 'ad proficiscendum in comitiva regis ad
certas partes in resistenciam inimicorum suorum.' These words leave it
unclear as to whether Richard II was contemplating a military or a naval
expedition. The thought, however, was only briefly sustained for apart
from signet letters sent on 12 May we hear no more of a royal intention to
campaign until late July.[19]

As for sea-keeping the first evidence appears on 26 January when four
sergeants at arms were ordered to take security from shipsmasters and crews
over a wide area for service to defend the realm in April. Their efforts are,
however, undocumented, and simultaneously they were diverted to collect
ships for Lancaster.[20] A month later, however, the naval policy agreed in
the recent parliament was fully set in motion. First, new admirals were
appointed on 22 February, Philip, Lord Darcy (north) and Sir Thomas
Trivet (west). Four days later these men contracted for naval service in
two phases. They were to start on 26 April with 'une petite armee' of 248
men at arms and 250 archers serving in ten vessels 'du guerre' for 40 days.
Then from 1 July they were to keep the sea for 91 days (July, August and
September) with 998 men at arms and 1,500 archers in 'une grande armee'
of 30 large ships, 12 barges, 12 balingers and 8 victuallers. Here was
appropriate and impressive forward planning.[21] The costing of these
operations had, we can assume, been worked out in the 1385 parliament.

The orders for the arrest of shipping which followed are inconsistent
with the schedule of the admirals. On 15 March, when negotiations were
still in progress at Leulinghen, the arrest of 30 ships, barges and balingers
'magis sufficientes pro guerra' was ordered in the northern admiralty for
assembly in the Thames on 15 April to serve with Darcy. Here the date of
assembly for a voyage to start on 26 April is fitting, but the number of
vessels required is three times that stipulated on 26 February for Darcy and
Trivet. Arrests in the west, also for assembly in the Thames, to confront
an invasion and to safeguard English possessions overseas, were required
on 28 March.[22] Neither could be executed as ordered and not until late
May were some 35 ships assembled in the Thames. They were manned by
over 1,100 sailors. Most of the vessels were surplus to requirements, at
least until 1 July when the 'grande armee' was scheduled to serve, and it is
not surprising that on 6 June crews were slashed to about 300 men. A

saving in wages of over £150 a week was made thereby. At the same time ships were temporarily put out of commission. The *Cog Thomas* of Hull of 200 tons, (master, John Cookson), with its crew reduced from 45 to 13 men, clearly was unprepared for a campaign. A fortnight later the council took more drastic steps. The crews of some ships disappear from the paymaster's account, others were left with skeletons of five or so sailors. With the imminent prospect of the admirals beginning the second phase of their campaign, the 20 June evidence casts a shadow over the strategy planned in February.[23] One complication is that in perhaps twenty cases crews which were paid off on 20 June reappear, though not of similar sizes, on 18 or 19 August. There is a two-fold suspicion. The sailors went unpaid, and this was a manifestation of the tightness in the council's money supply. On the other hand the ships involved remained under arrest, their owners receiving tontyght during the period when their vessels were crewless.

For all the alarms between March and June about coastal defence, the admirals did not come to the sea until several weeks after the appointed day of 26 April. Darcy was ready at Hull on 22 May and Trivet at Sandwich on 1 June. Each man had a retinue of 124 men at arms and 125 archers; the naval complement was 9 ships, 1 barge and 2 balingers, manned by 723 sailors.[24]

During their first voyage Darcy and Trivet captured a number of ships, several of which became, as was so often the case, the subjects of dispute. These included Castilian vessels, three of which were sold before 24 October 1386 for £1,255 17s 4d, and a fourth, much more modestly, for £100. In addition two ships of Sluys were taken. Other captures were controversial and became, prior to their release, the subject of council judgments. Two hulks, believed to be Flemish, in fact came from Piacenza and were eventually freed, as were a number of Genoese tarits which Walsingham, an unreliable witness in this matter, believed to be hostile. He accused de la Pole, sneeringly referring to him as a merchant's son, of impropriety in their release, but in fact this business was not concluded until 1387 when a Genoese ambassador negotiated a settlement with the council.[25] Knighton also criticized de la Pole for the release of two tarits of unspecified origin taken by Sir Baldwin Raddington operating out of Sandwich. The Commons, Knighton says, accused the chancellor on this matter in the October parliament. Two chroniclers are not lightly to be dismissed, but one suspects that the accusations were the consequence of ingrained prejudice by writers who reflected the unpopularity in 1386 of a man whose personal influence upon Richard II had long been suspect.[26] One futher capture by the admirals needs mention. A tarit of Aragon was taken 'in canali fflandrie'. The place of capture, along with that of a Castilian ship laden with Aragonese goods, was the result of intelligent manoeuvring near the enemy assembly point at Sluys.[27] An English naval presence there in September and later, as the momentum of enemy assembly was quickening, would also have been good strategy but, as we shall see, there was no English fleet at sea then.

The judgment on English naval strategy thus far is that the admirals' force sailed later than planned and that while it was unimpressive in scale, it at least provided a basic covering force by, as the indenture had stated, 'une petite armee'. All might have been very much better for English morale and security had the second phase of the February plan been executed with the 'grande armee'. But most unfortunately the council was obliged to abandon its original design and on 1 July Darcy and Trivet sealed fresh indentures to continue service for a further 40 days with their force unchanged except for the addition of some 50 sailors. Here was a huge contrast with the 2,500 soldiers and 54 fighting ships serving for 91 days planned in February. This was tempting fortune and, as we shall see, within weeks evidence of the enemy build-up starts for the first time to take on significant proportions. When the admirals completed their second voyage on 31 August, effective English naval defence action in 1386 ended. Their force might in a year when the sea was strongly kept have been suitable for the custody of the Narrow Seas. As it was, this was the smallest venture of its kind in any year between 1369 and 1388 when a naval policy worthy of the name was attempted. The cost of the soldiers and sailors was less than £3,700 very much less than had been determined in the recent parliament. The reason for this dramatic shift in policy is not hard to seek. The council, late in the day, had realized that whatever had been promised and whatever was desirable, it was running out of money. The 'grande armee' could not be afforded.[28]

Meanwhile in France and Flanders preparations increased. After the enemy's financial preparations in March, evidence of active forwarding of the invasion plan largely disappears until July. A serious fever, first mentioned on 17 May, struck Philip of Burgundy and this was almost certainly a delaying factor;[29] nevertheless, compared with 1385 when France sent an army to Scotland in June and an invasion force against England was substantially ready by mid-July, there is a suspicion of dilatoriness by the French council, punishing in its ultimate consequence. In later July, however, the picture rapidly changed. By 23 July Jean de Vienne, Admiral of France, was ordered to collect all shipping appropriate 'for the crossing'. The despatch of 100 large vessels from Brittany to Sluys was ordered at this time, and an agent was sent to La Rochelle to collect vessels. The first signs of troop mobilization also appear.[30]

The English council responded, and on 26 July we learn that Richard II planned to go to sea. On the 28th letters were sent to captains of his retinue ordering them to prepare because of rumours of an enemy invasion. A writ of 12 August ('quia certos rumores audivimus *iam de novo*') shows that fresh news from overseas had been received.[31] At this point there was only inadequate shipping, substantially undermanned, in the Thames and the need for greater resources was urgent. On 2 August the arrest at Southampton and in Norfolk and Suffolk of ships 'pro quodam viagio . . . ad obviandum inimicis Francie' was ordered. On 3 August a sergeant hastened to Hull, Lincoln, Grimsby and Boston to take and victual ships for the Thames. In London it was proclaimed that all willing to serve with the king's ships of war might freely do so, enjoying any profit they might gain. All landing places were to be safeguarded and, on 11 August, arrayers of men at arms and archers from the far north to Devon and Cornwall were ordered to prepare men to resist the enemy. On the next day commanders of coastal defences were appointed, and Newcastle, Boston, Hull and the Earl of Northumberland were told to prepare to resist.[32]

There was, however, an alternative strategy. The king, so de la Pole told parliament on 1 October, was anxious to invade France; thus the realm might suffer less harm than by defending itself at home. This was discussed at a great council at Oxford in the king's presence on 2 August, where parliamentary endorsement was thought necessary. But so too was another grant, for such was the state of royal finances that no undertaking at home, at sea or abroad could be afforded without the promise of new taxation. A preference for a military campaign is shown by the collection of foreign transport ships mainly from Holland and Zeeland. At this time Richard II was buying campaign horses.[33]

September 1386 proved a hectic month and as it advanced, fears of the French increased. Arrests 'pro quodam viagio (abinde) arripiendo versus Lescluys' were ordered. On 10 September there was a council meeting 'ad consolendum de resistencia contra inimicos'; a week later burgesses were called to Westminster, possibly with a view to borrowing money. In early September the mayor of the staple at Middelburg, William Brompton, was asked to send news to the council about the enemy and an armed balinger was sent to Sluys to reconnoitre.[34] Other scouting vessels were sent later. Money was short, and signet and privy seal letters were widely distributed requesting loans by 30 September. Two were sent to the executors of John Harewell, late Bishop of Bath and Wells, and of the late Guy, Lord Bryan. The council had small success in raising cash in this way, and during September only £733 6s 8d was forthcoming, and this thanks to the Archbishop of Canterbury and the Bishops of Coventry, Ely and Winchester. An instruction to four men from Boston to assess and levy a sum of 200 marks looks suspiciously like an unorthodox method of collecting a loan.[35]

The defensive orders of the council ranged round the English coastline, for inevitably it had no idea where the enemy would choose to attack. Kent,

Sussex and Hampshire continued to receive attention, as did Canterbury, the Isle of Sheppey and Queenborough, Rochester, Odiham and Portsmouth.[36] At Southampton Sir John Sandes commanded a garrison of 200 men, while Sir Simon Burley was responsible for 239 men at arms and 240 archers at Dover, Sandwich and Rye.[37] There were great fears for the east coast, where the worry was that despite a truce in June 1386 the Scots might cooperate with the enemy as they had done in 1385. Orwell, Norwich, Colchester and Lynn were warned 'contra adventum'; the sailing of ships was restricted; there was concern (a special interest at work here) for Howden, the treasurer's manor twenty miles inland from Hull; the Countess of Norfolk and the Earl of Pembroke were ordered to defend Framlingham as the king had particular information that the enemy planned to land at Orwell or in that area.[38]

Meantime the atmosphere in London grew more and more tense. The citizens, reported Walsingham, behaved like frightened hares, pulling down houses near the walls the better to resist. It is not surprising that they were frightened for, following a proclamation that all who had left the city should return by 20 September, came a precept to the aldermen on the 13th that householders should lay in food supplies for three months. This was enough to enduce a siege mentality.[39]

Something more tangible than rumour heightened alarm when evidence of the ambitious military engineering planned by the French for use after their landing became known. After disembarkation a large enclave surrounded by a wooden wall, punctuated by towers, would be created. Into this the army might enter for safety, rest and recovery, from it it could debouch on to the English countryside. Trees for this had been felled in Normandy, where its construction had begun in the previous year. In late September or early October sections were lost at sea en route to Sluys. Knighton had three transport ships captured, one by William Beauchamp, Captain of Calais. They were erected around Winchelsea. Walsingham's information was that two ships were taken and their contents set up to defend Sandwich. Froissart, who mistakenly believed the ville de bois, as the Religieux de Seint Denys described it, was made in Brittany, says the transport vessels were caught in a violent storm – a portent of the dreadful weather to come – off the mouth of the Thames. Some were blown up river, including one carrying sections and construction workmen. Whatever the detail, here was formidable proof that Englishmen were about to meet a disagreeably unusual experience.[40]

On 29 September over 4,250 men of the king's retinue arrived in London, under captains who included the Dukes of Gloucester and York, and the Earls of Arundel, Devon, Nottingham, Northumberland, Salisbury, Warwick, Oxford (soon, provocatively, to be made Duke of Ireland) and Derby (not yet called to parliament). Ralf Basset, Thomas Beaumont,

Hugh Burnell and Robert Willoughby were peers who brought retinues, as did Sir Henry and Sir Thomas Percy, Sir Hugh Calveley, Sir Hugh Segrave and Sir Thomas Trivet (recently returned from the sea).[41] They had been summoned on 6 September.

When they reached the capital, these men were uncertain what service would be required of them. It might be in France. On the other hand the king's first thought had been a naval expedition, and as recently as 24 September a royal writ had referred to the fleet about to sail to defend the realm. Parliament was intended to settle uncertainty about the king's purpose, but first there was the prior, and fundamental, consideration of a grant, the pre-condition of any enterprise. Yet even if a grant was made, a gap of some eight weeks would pass between the end of parliament and the first payment at the Exchequer, which might be expected to be, as it had been in 1378 and 1386, the following Candlemas. Thus any service undertaken would have to be funded by loans raised against the forth-coming subsidy, a dubious proposition when so much money was required. The end of September was therefore a demoralizing time, confused and uncertain. In the meantime, while peers of the realm remained in London for parliament, their men, and others gathered by commissions of array, were posted on exterior lines to defend the city.[42]

The leaders of the king's retinue served for 28 days, one month or for unspecified periods within the month after Michaelmas. By 31 October all had gone home, and dangerously so for on 15 October the council announced that the enemy would land by 1 November. Of this it had 'certain news'. Presumably an empty Exchequer explains the departure of the retinues. They returned home seriously underpaid, or not paid at all. Thus the Earl of Oxford, for example, who had a retinue of 16 knights, 120 esquires and 80 archers received on 26 October only £31 2s, enough for less than four days' wages. Salisbury received an assignment on 15 December for a mere £60 for his 2 bannerets, 7 knights, 84 esquires and 214 archers.[43] Once these men had withdrawn, the south-east was left almost undefended except for coastal levies.[44]

We shall never know how many arrayed men at arms, armed men and hobelars (summoned 11 September) or arrayed archers (12 September) came to London.[45] The government itself did not know, and the archers from Derbyshire, Devonshire and Staffordshire, who had been sent home unmustered and unpaid on 11 October, were unlikely to have been the only ones.[46] Once again money was the determinant, and only in three cases have payments by the Crown to archers been found. These were £2 19s (little more than two days' wages) to 70 archers from Herefordshire; £146 8s (roughly wages for about 14 days), to 360 archers from Mer-ionethshire, Caernarvonshire, the Marches and 'Wales'.[47]

Altogether 5,370 arrayed archers were summoned to London for

29 September from all shires except those of the Scottish border, Cornwall and counties along the coast from Norfolk to Hampshire; Lancashire archers were summoned for 5 October.[48] How long they served is uncertain, but for some it was only a short time. On 9 October the sheriffs and arrayers of Surrey, Middlesex and Sussex were told that all archers who had come from within 50 miles radius of London were to return home, remaining under array until further instructed. These men received no pay. Two days later archers from three other shires also returned for 'their ease and peace', but equally for the relief of those in whose neighbourhoods they had been posted. These men were also to remain in readiness for a further summons.[49] Walsingham wrote that some of them conducted everything but arson, and Knighton, using local knowledge, reported damage in Leicestershire by men from Cheshire. He says that soldiers from Wales, Lancashire and other distant parts, all unpaid, plagued the areas through which they passed on their jouney back from London.[50] It is probable that these men had left the capital long before 31 October.

Longer service may have been provided, unless cash equivalent to their wages for a month had been lent to the Crown, by men at arms and archers sent by Winchester, Bristol, Exeter, Nottingham, Oxford and Chichester. The costs were to be repaid from the yield of the next subsidy, levied and assessed by mayors and bailiffs. Wiltshire was to contribute to the costs of Salisbury. Here is another illustration of the hand-to-mouth finances of the government at this time.[51]

By November only the fleet in the Thames remained. By Michaelmas it had grown rapidly to ninety English vessels (tonnage approaching 10,000 tons), manned by over 3,000 sailors, and 45 foreign transport vessels. Crews' wages were generally in arrears and of the £4,779 4s 9d (wages) and £1,718 1s 6d (tontyghts) paid to John Bentley, the naval paymaster, more than half was not received by him before December 1386. On the 17th of that month he received £2,057 11s 11d. His last significant receipt was £1,065 18s on 19 February 1387, nearly three months after the fleet had been dismissed. Except for the fact that the enemy fleet remained at Sluys until mid-November, it is uncertain why these ships were held, for with the departure of the soldiers from London, there could be no army to transport to France, or soldiers to serve with a fighting fleet.[52]

It is to France and Sluys that we must return. Many enemy soldiers, like those mustered at Bruges in August, were caught up in prolonged and discomforting delay, waiting for Charles VI and his uncles to come to Sluys.[53] The French king had left Paris on 7 September and might have been expected in the north by Michaelmas. In fact he did not reach Bruges until 21 October.[54] Burgundy and Bourbon were with him at Lille on 18 October. Berry too may have been with the king at Lille.[55] The six-week interval between the French king's departure from Paris and his arrival at Bruges is as disconcerting as it is hard to explain.

On 29 October Charles VI came to Sluys and the signs were that shortly he would embark.[56] Rarely, if ever, had France assembled a greater force; there were thousands of soldiers and hundreds of ships. Ban and arrière-ban had been called out. The lowest army estimate has 8,000 knights, a great number of crossbowmen and other soldiers; the highest estimate, 103,600 men, was penned by a frightened Thomas Walsingham. Other estimates include Froissart's 60,000 men and the the well-informed Tournai chronicler with 25,000 men at arms and 600 crossbowmen plus 3,000 men at arms, archers and crossbowmen supplied by the towns. For Froissart the names of the great men of France and neighbouring lands who were present were a delight, reading like an aristocratic and chivalric roll of honour.[57]

On 18 September, when the French fleet was still collecting, it was commented that 'le roi a fait faire tant de navires que c'est le plus belle chose qu'on ait jamais vue'. This was also Froissart's opinion. Vessels had come, he said, from ports from Seville to Prussia. The Tournai writer has 1,200 to 1,300 ships, large and small, from Genoa, Castile, Scotland, Germany, Holland, Flanders, France and many other places. There was indeed a forest of masts. But by early November all was not well. Despite additional taxation and more borrowing, it is doubtful whether the French treasury, when it was ordered to pay wages, had adequate funds available. Many, particularly the rank and file, were owed cash with the result that they lived off the land in an undisciplined manner which added to Flemish discomfiture. One writer thought that the French expedition was aborted 'pour ce que le roi n'avoit point d'argent',[58] but there were other factors, the most important of which was deterioration in the weather; rain teemed from the skies and ill winds whipped up the sea. Hence there was divided opinion about the wisdom of the enterprise, and within a matter of days the venture was postponed until the spring of 1387. On or soon after 16 November, less than three weeks after his arrival at the sea, Charles VI left Sluys for Bruges.[59] Thus was England spared, and France suffered huge waste and anticlimax. Over months a fortune had been spent in laboriously amassing men, victuals and transport. At this time France like England was finding the cost of warfare almost more than she could afford.

On 28 November, not many days after Charles VI left Sluys, the most momentous parliament yet to meet in Richard II's reign ended its business. Anger against the government and particularly against the chancellor de la Pole, ran through its sittings. At its start on 1 October an undigested mass of soldiers, more than 10,000 men, had been summoned to defend London, perhaps the largest English force of its kind in the Middle Ages. They brought small comfort. In his opening speech, Michael de la Pole, the chancellor, concentrated on the king's proposal to lead an army overseas and the need for taxation. With the enemy almost at the gate the idea of an expedition to France may have seemed surprising and risky. But it had the attraction that Charles VI might be diverted from his purpose, preferring to remain to defend France. If, de la Pole said, the French project was agreed, provision for government during the king's absence must be made. Parliament would have none of the idea, which was brushed aside. Taxation, according to the parliament roll, was needed for defence, but Knighton differed. There were, he says, questions of the king's debts, the cost of his household and other expenses. An unprecedently large demand for four lay subsidies and four clerical tenths received short shrift.[60] There was a stalemate in defence policy.

Richard II was horrified by what ensued. Lords and Commons refused to proceed with the king's business, demanded the dismissal of the chancellor and treasurer, and announced that they had business to do with de la Pole which could not be conducted as long as he remained in office. One source, perhaps not strictly contemporary, but interesting in its words, adds colour by reporting that Gloucester, Arundel and Warwick declared that the 'enemy within' took precedence over the 'enemy without'. Although the chronology is unclear, it was perhaps at this point that the king, acting with the chancellor's advice, made an impotent attempt to dissolve parliament.[61] Lords and Commons refused to depart: the king withdrew to Eltham.

There his famous confrontation with Gloucester and Thomas Arundel, Bishop of Ely, took place. Angrily the king accused his subjects of plotting and spoke of calling on Charles VI 'to ask his counsel and aid and to submit to him rather than our own subjects'. These were strange words from a king whose chancellor had recently affirmed his zeal to invade France. On the other hand Richard undoubtedly lacked an innate belligerence towards France, as his recent sympathy for another attempt to negotiate a truce shows.[62] There was, however, a vast gap between approving negotiations in principle and calling on the French king to come to his rescue. It sounds as if Richard II was nearing the end of his tether. Now Gloucester and Ely alluded to the fate of Edward II and warned Richard that he too might be deposed. This was enough to bring the king back to Westminster where, on 23 October, de la Pole was dismissed, as were the treasurer and the keeper of the privy seal on the following day. The new chancellor was none other than Thomas Arundel. There followed the chancellor's impeachment including Article 3 which asserted that: Whereas the taxation granted in the last parliament was to be spent in a certain manner stipulated by the Commons and agreed to by king and lords, nevertheless its proceeds had been spent in another manner ('en autre manere') with the result that the sea had not been guarded as had been ordained. As a consequence many misfortunes had befallen the realm and would very probably do so in the future. This was the result of the recent chancellor's default.[63]

From this several points of interest emerge, the most important of which is that in 1385 a promise to fulfil the Commons' demand as to the amount of cash to be spent on sea-keeping had been made by king and lords. This had been disregarded, the money designated had been spent 'en autre manere', and as a result defence had been neglected with the most unfortunate consequences. The words of the Commons best make sense if we postulate, as suggested earlier, that the government had in 1385 undertaken a defined naval strategy, in line, it is suggested, with the terms of the indenture of Darcy and Trivet of 26 February 1386. The breach of this undertaking was the bone of contention in October 1386. But why had the money promised not been available? A study of the relevant Receipt and Issue Rolls of the Lower Exchequer provides some clues.

Receipts from the lay subsidy during the Michaelmas term of 1385–6 appear twice in the Receipt Roll of that term. First, there is the receipt of £8,606 18s 9d by John Hermesthorpe during December 1385. This has been referred to earlier and need not detain us. Secondly there is £29,208 10s received by the war treasurers, Hadley and Exton, between 7 February and 10 March 1386. To this must be added the receipt recorded in the Easter term of a further £15,444 15s 11¼d between 5 May and 23 July. This sum was not paid, as it should have been, to the war treasurers, but to the treasurer and chamberlains of the Exchequer, although £2,125 17s 5d of it passed into the treasurers' hands. Had this not been so the total of £31,305 0s 9d paid out by them and the £29 6s 8d which remained with them 'ad voluntatem regis' after payments would not have been possible. Excluding Hermesthorpe's transactions, therefore, the 1385 lay subsidy yielded £44,653 5s 11¼d.[64]

If we turn to the Issue Rolls, we can try to find out where this money went. During the 1385–6 Michaelmas term, excluding the assignments of December 1385, there are no further charges against the subsidy, though some £3,500 spent on the East March, Berwick, Roxburgh and Carlisle might properly have been debited within the terms of the parliamentary appropriation.[65] After Easter 1386 the Issue Roll concludes with a schedule of 'soluciones ffacte' from the lay subsidy in two parts, those paid by the Exchequer and those paid by the war treasurers.[66] In the lists of 'soluciones ffacte' £9,742 was paid out by the Exchequer and £31,305 0s 9d by the treasurers. The former were contrary to the arrangement of 30 January, based, as this had been, on the agreement conceded in parliament at the Commons' demand in 1385. All sums passed by the Exchequer were in conformity with the parliamentary grant – £5,033 6s 8d in part repayment of loans made in April (a small proportion) and May by

Walter Bardi and Matthew Cheyney for the expeditions of Lancaster and
of Darcy and Trivet, £1,233 6s 8d to John Hatfield, Lancaster's naval
paymaster, and £3,475 6s 8d on Berwick, Roxburgh and Carlisle. The
charges borne by Hadley and Exton were also war expenses, the largest
being the £26,666 13s 4d for Lancaster's army. The treasurers each
received a fee of £20 and a futher £46 for their expenses which included
boatage. Perhaps they were personally engaged in supervising the payment
of the admirals' crews. The total of all 'soluciones ffacte', the Exchequer's
and the treasurers', was £41,027 0s 9d, some £3,600 less than the £44,650
received from the lay subsidy. This sum had been absorbed into the
unappropriated revenues of the Exchequer.

At first sight it might appear that with the exception of this substantial
sum all the proceeds of the lay subsidy had been spent in accordance with
the parliamentary appropriation. But closer examination of the 'soluciones
ffacte' shows that this was not so. Herein lies a point of substance. In fact
the 'soluciones ffacte' charge the sum of £5,033 6s 8d against the lay
subsidy twice. It was paid (i) *by the Exchequer* as repayment of loans made
by Bardi and Cheyney for the finances of Lancaster and of Darcy and
Trivet, and (ii) it was included among the payments made *by the war
treasurers* to the duke and to the admirals. There is thus a double charge
against the receipts of the war subsidy, whereas the money involved was
received only once among the appropriated receipts. The money does
appear a second time in the Receipt Roll but, quite separately from the
subsidy receipts, among the unappropriated revenues of the Exchequer. In
these circumstances it was unmethodical to charge the loan repayments
against the appropriated funds. By this double charge upon the appropriated revenues some £5,000 became unavailable for the purpose for
which it was intended and the second voyage of Darcy and Trivet could
not be fully financed. Naturally the resultant failure of the council to
implement a naval strategy promised to the Commons by the king and
lords, a strategy which had been an express condition of their grant,
incensed the Commons. The government had broken its word.

Deliberate financial dissimilation or underhandedness by the
government can be ruled out. The reasons for the failure can be seen in its
own records. What happened was the result of an overall monetary crisis
which first seriously emerged in May 1386 and thereafter sharply deterio-
rated. In May the council had borrowed from Bardi and Cheyney to get
Lancaster and the admirals to sea. These loans were mostly secured against
the yield of the half-subsidy due on 24 June. It was to cover the repayment of these loans that, departing from the principle that the war
treasurers were to 'take, receive and keep' all proceeds of the parliamentary
subsidy, the treasurer and chamberlains side-tracked the proceeds of the
half-subsidy into their general funds. They received, as we have seen,

£15,444 15s 11d. Of this the Exchequer disbursed £9,472 in 'soluciones ffacte' and £2,125 17s 5d passed to Hadley and Exton. These sums leave a shortfall of £3,576 18s 6d on the subsidy receipt, and possibly the £5,033 recorded as repaid to Bardi and Cheyney should be added. It was this sum together with the £3,600 mentioned above which was spent 'en autre manere'. We can but speculate where this money went. What mattered was that it had not been spent on naval defence. However, in mitigation of the government it may be observed that there were some necessary areas of war expenditure, like the £3,700 spent on the defence of Calais in the spring of 1386, which were not covered by appropriated revenues. No doubt it was hard to cover this cost, and others like the wages of the garrisons of Brest and Cherbourg from unappropriated revenue. The Exchequer was suffering an acute cash squeeze and therein lay the undermining of the tax appropriation and of naval policy. Therein, too, it seems, lay the untidiness in the usually meticulous entries on the issue roll of the Lower Exchequer.

For the Commons in October the government had broken its word. It had also disregarded the procedures for the receipt and expenditure of extraordinary revenue which they believed to have been guaranteed by the appointment of the war treasurers. At a heavy price in public confidence and trust a formal undertaking in parliament had been disregarded. This failure could not have come at a more demoralizing time. It exacerbated the distrust in the financial probity of de la Pole which was expressed in several articles of his impeachment.[67] And all this when a bankrupt government, desperately in need of a grant and almost scavenging for loans, was divided as to strategy and it seemed the French might arrive any day.

It has been argued that the accusation that de la Pole 'so neglected to carry out the tax appropriations of 1385 as to jeopardize the safe-keeping of the sea would seem to have been the least reasonable of all the charges preferred' against him.[68] This paper, however, suggests a different conclusion. The issue involved was in fact serious and it is not surprising that at a time of great danger the Commons struck back against the chief minister. There was a case to answer. On the other hand the lords in parliament were correct that the chancellor was not alone to blame. Responsibility had been more widely distributed.[69]

## Notes

1  T.F. Tout, *Chapters in the Administrative History of Medieval England*, 6 vols (Manchester, 1923–33), III. 411; A. Tuck, *Crown and Nobility, 1272–1461* (1985), p.186; J.J.N. Palmer, *England, France and Christendom, 1377–1399* (1972), pp.74, 84; J.S. Roskell, *The Impeachment of Michael De la Pole, Earl of Suffolk, in 1386* (Manchester, 1984), p.44.

2   *Rot. Parl.* III. 204; *CFR 1383–1391*, p.135; Roskell, op. cit. pp.74–5; Tout, op. cit. III. 396 n2; A.B. Steel, *Receipt of the Exchequer, 1377–1485* (Cambridge, 1954), pp.52–3; PRO E401/563, 11 to 15 Dec. 1385; E403/511, 9 to 15 Dec. 1385.

3   PRO E101/40/9; E364/20 mm.5, 7; T. de Loray, *Jean de Vienne, amiral de France, 1341–1396* (Paris, 1877), p.cxxxviii (May 1385).

4   *Foedera*, ed. T. Rymer, 20 vols. (1704–35), VII. 490, 501; PRO C76/71 mm.22, 15, 4, 3.

5   PRO E101/40/19; P.E. Russell, *English Intervention in Spain and Portugal in the time of Edward III and Richard II* (Oxford, 1955), p.403; H. Knighton, *Chronicon*, ed. J.R. Lumby, 2 vols. (RS, 1889–95), II. 205; cf. Roskell, op. cit. p.71. The Anglo-Portuguese treaty of May 1386 demonstrates English appreciation of strength at sea, *Foedera*, VII. 520.

6   PRO E401/563, 7 Feb. to 10 Mar. 1386.

7   *CPR 1385–9*, pp.141, 147; PRO E403/511, 12 Apr. and after.

8   PRO E101/40/19.

9   *Rot. Parl.* III. 313; PRO E403/512, 26 June 1386.

10  PRO E101/40/19; *Westminster Chronicle, 1381–1394*, ed. L.C. Hector and B.F. Harvey (Oxford, 1983), pp.140–3.

11  *Foedera*, VII. 524; PRO E403/512, 26 July 1386.

12  PRO C76/70, 26 Jan. 1386.

13  *Westminster Chronicle*, pp.160–1, 164–7; N. Du Bosc, *Voyage littéraire de deux religieux bénédictins de la congregation de Saint-Maur*, ed. E. Martène and U. Durand (Paris, 1724), pp.349–360; cf. Palmer's analysis in op. cit. p.60.

14  *CCR 1385–9*, p.60.

15  *CPR 1385–9*, pp.123, 134, 174–5, 180; *CCR 1385–9*, p.77.

16  Palmer, op. cit. pp.164–7; T. de Loray, op. cit. p.cxlvii, p.j. no 119; the aid was payable end-May and end-June.

17  *Westminster Chronicle*, pp.164–7; PRO C76/70 mm.18, 16, 13 Mar., 3 and 18 Apr.; E403/512, 3 May and after. In May a Cinque Ports squadron convoyed victuals to Calais, E101/183/10, and nearly £3,500 was spent on Calais defences to which some 300 soldiers were sent. This money was not charged against the lay subsidy.

18  *CPR 1385–9*, pp.160, 175–7, 181, 190, 196; PRO E403/512, 26 June; *Calendar of Letter-Books of the City of London, Letter-Book H*, ed. R.R. Sharpe (1907), p.283. On 22 July a chaplain, an 'expert in guns and the management of artillery', was appointed to the new tower at Southampton.

19  PRO E403/511, 16 Apr.; E403/512, 12 May.

20  PRO C76/70 m.27; E403/511, 25 Jan.

21  BL, Harley Charter 49 D 3.

22  PRO C76/70, 28 Mar.; *Foedera*, VII. 507.

23  PRO E101 42/21. An issue of 30 May (E403/512) for crews arrested 'pro certis secretis ordinacionibus . . . pro custodia maris et costerarum' shows that the sailing of the 'grande armee' was still intended.

24  PRO E101 40/22, 42/21; E364/24 m.34.

25  PRO E364/25 m.41d; *CPR 1385–9*, pp.236, 255, 266; *CCR 1385–9*, pp.165–6, 239; J.F. Baldwin, *King's Council in England during the Middle Ages* (Oxford, 1913), p.508.

26  T. Walsingham, *Historia Anglicana*, ed. H.T. Riley, 2 vols. (RS, 1863–4), II. 146; *Chronicon*, II. 211.

27  *CCR 1385–9*, p.170; Baldwin, op. cit. pp.507–10; *Diplomatic Correspondence of Richard II*, ed. E. Perroy, Camden Society, 3rd ser., XLVIII (1933), no. 65, pp.198–200.

28  PRO E101 40/22, 42/21; E364/24 m.34; E403/512, 26 July (charged to Hadley and Exton with the assent of Exeter and Cobham), 26 July (not so charged).

29  *Journal de Jean le Fèvre*, ed. H. Moranvillé (Paris, 1887), p.275; cf. Palmer, op. cit. pp.73, 78.

30 T. de Loray, op. cit. pp.cl–cli, p.j. no.120; L. Mirot, 'Une tentative d'invasion en Angleterre pendant la guerre de Cent Ans', *Revue des études historiques*, LXXXI (1915), p.273; F. Lehoux, *Jean de France, duc de Berry, son action politique, 1340–1416*, 3 vols. (Paris, 1966–8), II. 182 n2.

31 *CPR 1385–9*, p.196; PRO 403/512, 28 July; C76/71 m.23.

32 PRO E403/512, 2, 3 Aug.; *Letter-Book H*, p.311; CCR 1385–9, pp.253–4; PRO C76/71 m.23. On 3 Sept. doggers and other vessels from Lynn to Blakeney were licensed to sail at their own cost, taking all profit, to defend their coast and the realm, *CCR 1385–9*, p.209.

33 *Rot. Parl.* III. 215; PRO E101 42/21; *CPR 1385–9*, p.208 (20 Aug.); PRO E403/512, 25 Aug., £50 spent on body armour for the king.

34 PRO E403/512, 2, 25 Aug. 6, 17 Sept.; E403/515, 2 Oct. (messengers bringing news from Calais), 5, 23, 28 Nov.; E101 40/21; C76/71, 8, 18 Sept.

35 PRO E403/512, 5, 6, Sept; E401/564, 15 Sept.; E101 40/21; *CPR 1385–9*, pp.226–7.

36 PRO E403/512, 5, 6 Sept.; *CPR 1385–9*, pp.212, 214, 259–60.

37 PRO E403/512, 2, 30 July, 6 Sept.; E403/515, 5 Oct., 22 Nov.; on 30 July Burley received £594 13s 4d for garrisons at Rye and Sandwich. Dover castle was ruinous at this time, *CPR 1385–9*, p.225.

38 Ibid., pp.259–60, see also pp.169, 174–5, 186–7; PRO E403/512, 6 Sept.

39 *Letter-Book H*, pp.285–6; *Hist. Ang.* II. 145–6. Destruction of houses near walls was in fact a sensible measure, cf. *CPR 1381–5* p.467 for rasing of houses within 100 feet of Chichester walls in May 1385.

40 *Chronicon*, II. 212; *Hist. Ang.* II. 147; Froissart, *Chroniques*, ed. L. and A. Mirot, Société de l'histoire de France (Paris, 1957), XIII. 92–3; *Chronique du religieux de Saint Denys*, ed. M.L. Bellaguet (Paris, 1839), pp.430–1.

41 PRO E403/512 6 Sept.; E403/515, 2 Oct. and after. The size of several retinues, including those of Gloucester, Nottingham, Warwick, Sir Henry and Sir Thomas Percy and Sir Gilbert Talbot, is unstated.

42 The positioning of men in the king's retinue is variously stated. CCR 1385–9, p.192 has 'within London and 30 leagues around'; PRO E403/515, 2 Oct. and after has captains swearing that their men 'infra limites sexaginta miliarum a civitate Londin' . . . non traxerunt nec inhabitati fuerunt'; *Chronicon*, II. 212–4 has men placed within a radius of 30 leagues of London and not coming nearer than 10 leagues, and *Hist. Ang.* II. 147–8 has within a 20 mile circuit of the city.

43 PRO E403/515, 2 Oct. and after; captains received some £4,500 between 2 Oct. and 15 Jan. 1387. The bulk of the money was paid in cash or assignments after 31 Oct.; more than £1,000 was disbursed in December; CCR 1385–9, p.190.

44 Froissart, XIII. 16–18, 86 has a description, often grossly inaccurate, of English coastal defences, which happen to be better documented for 1385 than 1386, cf. G. Templeman, 'Two French attempts to invade England during the Hundred Years' War', in *Studies in French language, literature and history presented to R.L.G. Richie* (Cambridge, 1949), pp.228–9.

45 CCR 1385–9, pp.264–5, CPR 1385–9, p.217.

46 CCR 1385–9, pp.193–4. Archers from 23 shires had not reached London by 2 Oct. Writs of this date show that except for Wiltshire, the government's summons had omitted to say that the men should travel at the cost of the shire, ibid. p.187. In fact the Wiltshire archers never came and money raised for their costs and expenses went astray (CPR 1385–9, p.315) as did money raised in Bucks., ibid. p.322. cf. P. Morgan, *War and Society, 1277–1403* (Manchester, 1987), p.187 for six days' wages paid by the chamberlain of Chester to 43 esquires and 818 archers.

47 PRO E403/515, 16, 19, 27 Oct.

48 CPR 1385–9, pp.217, 242.

49 Ibid., p.322; CCR 1385–9, pp.193–4.

50 *Chronicon*, II. 212–4; *Hist. Ang.* II. 147–8.

51 *CPR 1385–9*, p.216. Loans during Oct. from Bristol (£200), Chichester (£50) and Oxford (£10) may or may not be relevant, PRO E401/566.

52 PRO E101 42/21; *CCR 1385–9*, p.169. A writ of 24 Sept. (PRO C76/71 m.19) refers to 'the fleet ordained for the defence of the realm.' 26 shipmasters of vessels under arrest since June or earlier were commissioned to arrest and bring to London crews necessary for their vessels. At Great Yarmouth impressments of sailors were resisted and 'other men' were to be taken in their place, *CCR 1385–9*, p.169 (26 Sept.).

53 Mirot, loc. cit. p.267 n15.

54 *Séjours de Charles VI*, ed. E. Petit, *Bulletin historique et philologique de comité des travaux historiques et scientifiques*, XI (1893), p.433.

55 Froissart, XIII, p.xxi n3.; *Chronique du religieux de Saint-Denys*, p.458; Lehoux, op. cit. II. 185–6 has a helpful discussion of the likely date of Berry's meeting with Charles VI.

56 *Sejours*, p.433; *Chroniques de Franche, d'Engleterre, de Flandres, de Lile et especialement de Tournai*, ed. A. Hocquet (Mons, 1938), pp.287–8, 359–60.

57 Mirot, loc. cit. p.268 n4; *Chroniques de Tournai*, p.286; Froissart says (XIII. 78) there are too many French lords to be able to name them.

58 Lehoux, op. cit. p.182 n3; Froissart, XIII. 2–4; *Chroniques de Tournai*, p.286 has the ships collecting since June.

59 The Tournai chronicler (p.292) has Charles VI leaving Sluys for Bruges on 16 Nov.; Froissart, XIII. 97–9; Palmer, op. cit. pp.77–81 has an important, if debatable, examination of the causes of the cancellation of the French expedition.

60 *Hist. Ang.* II. 148; *Rot. Parl.* III. 215; *Chronicon*, II. 215.

61 *Eulogium historiarum sive temporis*, ed. F.S. Haydon 3 vols., (RS, 1858–63), III. 359. For the dating of this continuation of the *Eulogium* see J.I. Catto, 'An alleged great council in 1374' in *EHR*, LXXXII (1967), 764–7.

62 *Chronicon*, II. 216–9; *Diplomatic Correspondence*, no.66, pp.42–3.

63 *Rot. Parl.* III. 216.

64 PRO E401/563, 11 to 15 Dec. 1385, 7 Feb. to 10 Mar. 1385; E401/564, 5 May to 23 July 1386.

65 PRO E403/511, 9 to 15 Dec. 1385, 8 Feb. 1386 and after.

66 PRO E401/564, 1 May; E403/512, 5 May 1386 and after.

67 *Rot. Parl.* III. 216–20; Roskell, op. cit. pp.59–66, 113–196.

68 Ibid., pp.188, 67–8.

69 I am grateful to Dr Anthony Tuck who kindly read this paper and made helpful suggestions.

# 7

# Richard II and the Hundred Years War[1]

Anthony Tuck
*University of Bristol*

The starting-point for this discussion is the series of negotiations which took place between envoys of France and England from 1389 to 1394 with the object of securing a final peace between the two countries. The attempt to find a negotiated solution to the Anglo-French conflict was not, of course, unique to Richard II's reign: peace-making was a contrapuntal theme during the years of war-making under Edward III, though even in the face of French defeat at Poitiers and the capture of their king no lasting settlement acceptable to both sides could be achieved. Perhaps the most significant feature of the peace negotiations between 1389 and 1396, however, was the lengths to which the English were now prepared to go to accommodate the French. In this respect these negotiations differ significantly from those which had taken place earlier in the century, and an examination of the peace process may serve to illuminate not only the intractable nature of the issues underlying the Anglo-French conflict, but also the political and financial difficulties in England which impelled Richard II to seek a way out of the war.

From the French point of view, the advantages of a negotiated end to the war were obvious. Despite the setbacks suffered by the English in Aquitaine immediately after the resumption of the war in 1369, English commanders had shown in the 1370s that they were still able to mount chevauchéces in France with impunity, and Charles V had preferred to allow them to do so rather than risk giving battle. When John of Gaunt took his army on its 'long march' from Calais to Bordeaux in 1373–4 Charles and his councillors had debated whether to engage the English forces but had decided against doing so, having lost none of their belief in English superiority on the battlefield.[2] The French still regarded England as a formidable military power, supported by a bellicose community: in 1399 the Duke of Berrry was to observe that 'the Commons of England want nothing but war'.[3] A settlement which put an end to the threat of English invasion and resolved the problem of Aquitaine was very much in

French interests; and so too, from the point of view of the Duke of Burgundy, whose ascendancy in French politics was scarcely interrupted between 1392 and 1399, was a settlement which ensured stability in Anglo-Flemish commercial relations.[4] It is not necessary to resort to hypotheses such as an interest in Italian affairs or a renewed enthusiasm for the crusade to explain the willingness of the French to seek a settlement with the English: these were opportunities which could be exploited if the war ended, rather than reasons in themselves for seeking peace.[5]

Although, as we shall see, the king had powerful financial reasons for seeking a negotiated end to the war, not everyone in England was necessarily so eager for peace.[6] It was an unknown quantity; it might be particularly unwelcome in parts of the country where military service had traditionally been an important occupation, as the rising in Cheshire in 1393 perhaps implied;[7] and it had no obvious rationale in purely military terms. Although the English had lost ground in Aquitaine in the early 1370s, they still had the will to deploy sufficient resources to defend the coastal region from the Gironde to the Pyrenees, and they still controlled three important ports of entry into France, Calais, Cherbourg and Brest.[8] Furthermore, the Castilian naval threat had receded after the Lancastrian settlement with Castile in 1388, when Juan of Castile apparently gave an assurance to Gaunt that naval assistance to France would not in future exceed sixteen galleys. The government of Charles VI viewed the agreement between Gaunt and Juan with some concern, for although the Franco-Castilian alliance remained in being, Juan had little inclination to continue the war, and Castilian interests were best served by a *de facto* neutrality, with Castile making only a limited naval contribution to the alliance. Indeed, it seems that France had to exert some pressure on Castile in 1388 to ensure that the alliance remained in being at all.[9]

The peace negotiations of the 1390s ended, of course, in failure. But, in face of the evident good will on both sides, there has been much disagreement over why it proved impossible to agree on a treaty of peace. In 1889 H. Moranvillé argued that the responsibility for the breakdown 'doit retomber uniquement sur l'Angleterre, ou mieux sur la nation anglaise', for public opinion in England made an agreement impossible.[10] Edouard Perroy laid more emphasis on the intractability of the problem of sovereignty over Aquitaine, and the English king's demand for greater territorial concessions than the French were prepared to offer.[11] In the only substantial reassessment of the problem this century, John Palmer has argued that it was 'Bordeaux, rather than London or Paris, that stood in the way of the final peace', and that the negotiations foundered on the rock of the Gascons' objection to the alienation of their duchy to the House of Lancaster.[12] Dr Palmer's thesis was criticized in certain respects by Dr Vale, who expressed scepticism about the reality of the English king's intention to transfer Gascony to the House of Lancaster,[13] but Palmer successfully disposed of the idea, derived from Perroy, that the crucial issue was the extent of the territory that was to compose the reconstituted Duchy of Aquitaine. Dr Palmer showed convincingly that the French were prepared to make generous territorial concessions, and he argued that the nub of the problem was not the extent but the status of the duchy, which was to be separated from the English crown as a fief for the House of Lancaster.[14] Yet an examination of the draft articles for peace that were agreed in 1393, and of the English parliament's reaction when these articles were reported to it in January 1394, suggests that the crucial issue was not a proposed alienation of the duchy to the House of Lancaster but the willingness of Richard II to do liege homage for the duchy.

From the outset of the negotiations, the French appear to have been willing to make substantial territorial concessions, provided the English offered concessions on the question of homage, and provided the interests of the Duke of Berry as Count of Poitou were somehow accommodated. In the negotiations at Leulinghem in July 1390, the French insisted that whatever territories the English king were to hold in France should be held 'en foy et hommage lige, ressort et souveraineté de la couronne de France'.[15] The English envoys responded by saying that liege homage had not previously been discussed, and that the French should offer territorial concessions to the English before discussing on what terms the territory should be held. Even at this stage, however, the English appear to have abandoned their insistence on holding at least some territory in Aquitaine in sovereignty, and this represented a major change of policy.[16] During the negotiations at Bruges between 1375 and 1377 the English had held out for some sovereign territory in Aquitaine.[17] Yet by 1390 Richard II had evidently decided to abandon a principle which had been central to his grandfather's negotiating position since the outbreak of the Hundred Years War.

One possible explanation for this change of policy is that Richard II had already decided that Aquitaine should be separated from the English crown and granted in perpetuity to the House of Lancaster, to hold of the King of France.[18] Such a plan was not new: it had been discussed during the negotiations at Bruges in 1375, when the French had suggested that Gaunt should become duke of a greater Aquitaine, including Poitou, and that he should do homage to the French king for his duchy. In return, he was to resign to his father all his English lands, to compensate Edward III for the loss of Aquitaine. The English had rejected this proposal out of hand, for, as Edouard Perroy observed, it is very difficult to see why such a proposal should appeal either to Edward III or to John of Gaunt. It would certainly have solved the problem of Aquitaine, but in a manner which would have been much more to the advantage of the French than the

English. The French suggested as an alternative, in the spring of 1375, that a much smaller Aquitaine, without Poitou and other territories, might remain to Edward III in sovereignty, but they were evidently not prepared to allow Poitou to become part of the lands held directly by the English king.[19]

It is not surprising, therefore, that the French chose to revive the proposal that Aquitaine should be granted to John of Gaunt when negotiations between the two countries resumed in the 1390s. At Amiens in 1392 the French proposed that the lands still under English control in Gascony should be granted to Lancaster and his heirs in perpetuity, and that to these lands should be added those held by the Duke of Berry in Aquitaine when the duke died; only under such terms, it seemed, would the French agree to the inclusion of Poitou in a revived Duchy of Aquitaine. In all probability no other arrangement would have been acceptable to the Duke of Berry himself. In the following year the French offered Richard a substantial cash sum in return for abandoning his claims in Poitou, and in the draft peace terms on 1393 the two sides agreed that Richard should receive 1,200,000 francs, though there is no specific indication that any of this was in respect of Poitou.[20]

The suggestion that the duchy of Aquitaine might be separated from the English crown now met the same fate as the earlier proposal in 1375. The proposal, it should be stressed, emanated from the French; there is no evidence in any of the surviving documents that either Edward III in 1375 or Richard II and John of Gaunt in 1392–3 had any intention of accepting it, and there is no mention of it in the draft articles of 1393 which both sides hoped would form the basis for a final peace. When John of Gaunt put the French proposal for Aquitaine to the council at Stamford in 1392, it was rejected out of hand, according to the monk of Westminster.[21] Richard also went out of his way to reassure Gascon opinion that no such proposal was in his mind: in his public statements to the Gascons, he insisted that his grant of the Duchy of Aquitaine to John of Gaunt was for life only, and was not to be taken as prejudicial to the Gascons. He did so in March 1390, at the time the life-grant was made; in November 1390, and again July 1392, when in response to representations made by the Gascons and to rumours that he had not made the grant of his own free will he reiterated his assurance that the grant was for life only.[22] The suspicions of the Gascons are understandable, but their hostility to Gaunt is explicable in terms of his life-grant of the duchy, and it is not necessary to postulate an intention on Richard's part to alienate the duchy to Gaunt *and his heirs*. Even the alienation of the duchy to Gaunt for his life only was a breach of the charter of the duchy, and of repeated undertakings by English kings that Gascony would remain integrated with the English crown, and would be alienated only to the king's eldest son. In the event of Richard dying before Gaunt, however unlikely a prospect this may have been, the duchy would not pass with the crown of England, and the alienation *for life* of the duchy to someone other than the king's eldest son and heir was not only unprecedented, but offered the possibility, as the Gascons pointed out in 1394, that 'lodeyt dugat poyre estre de tot en tot separat foras de la corona danglaterra'. The Gascons also argued that neither the proprietary right nor the usufruct of the duchy should be transferred from the king of England to anyone except his eldest son.[23] Furthermore the phrase 'the king of England and those having cause of him (aians cause de lui)', which has been taken as evidence of a covert intention on Richard's part to alienate Aquitaine to Gaunt and his heirs, is again explicable in terms of the life grant. The expression is not used in respect of Calais and its march, which did not form part of the life-grant to Gaunt, and it could be taken to mean either the king's representative in Gascony for the time being, or someone other than the direct heir to whom the king's rights had been assigned, as they had been in the life-grant to Gaunt. The essence of the problem, therefore, was the grant of the duchy to one who was not the king's heir, rather than any supposed intention to make the grant hereditary in the House of Lancaster.[24]

Although we cannot know the secrets of Richard's mind, there is reason to doubt whether he intended to alienate the duchy to Gaunt *and his heirs*, and therefore to doubt whether such a proposal played a significant part in the collapse of the peace negotiations. Yet if this interpretation is rejected, it is necessary to offer an alternative explanation for Richard's readiness to agree, in 1393, that Aquitaine should be held by liege homage. For the French, liege homage was the *sine qua non* of a peace settlement; for the English, its concession represented a fundamental change of policy and an abandonment of the principle on which Edward III had negotiated. But if the war was to be ended, if there really was to be a final peace, the French insistence on liege homage would have to be accepted, and Richard's eventual willingness to meet the French demand for liege homage is indicative of his overriding concern that the war should be ended. But this was not his initial negotiating position. In 1390 the English envoys had been instructed to agree only to simple homage for the duchy, if simple homage could be so construed that it did not become a cause for war or the confiscation of the duchy,[25] and only with the draft agreement of 1393 did the English concede liege homage. Even then, the draft treaty contained a proviso that a commission of legal experts should be set up to see how liege homage could be modified so as to prevent it leading to war or to the confiscation of the duchy. These attempts to have it both ways, to concede the principle of homage for Aquitaine while at the same time mitigating its worst effects, from the English point of view, are interesting as earnest, if ultimately futile, attempts to reconcile two fundamentally opposed points of view. But it is difficult to see how such modifications could have worked in practice. As English diplomats must have realized, the crucial problem was the appellate jurisdiction of the French king, and it is hard to see how, in the end, this issue could have been fudged.[26] Liege homage entailed an acknowledgement of *sovereineté* and *ressort*, and in the last analysis confiscation was the only means by which *sovereineté* could be enforced. However understandable the efforts of both sides to mitigate the effects of the French king's sovereignty over Aquitaine they were probably doomed to failure, and indeed it is possible that they might have brought the whole agreement down with them.

The essence of the draft agreement in 1393, therefore, was that Richard would perform liege homage for Aquitaine, and it is necessary therefore to explain why war had become such an unattractive option for Richard that he was prepared to make peace with France without the unequivocal gains that Edward III had achieved in 1360. It has sometimes been suggested that Richard lacked both the physique and the inclination to display prowess on the battlefield.[27] There is little evidence by which to judge such a hypothesis; but in more general terms he does not seem to have shown either an aversion to war in principle or a reluctance to lead campaigns. Richard's conduct of his first Irish expedition in 1394 does not suggest either a distaste for war or any great incompetence in planning and executing a campaign,[28] though both his Irish campaign and his Scottish expedition in 1385 suggest a certain caution in strategy, a preference for the successful achievement of a limited objective rather than a riskier and bolder strategy which might over-extend and endanger his troops. Nor is it easy to demonstrate that the nobility had lost interest in the war. The Earl of Arundel had been prepared to offer himself as Bishop Despenser's lieutenant on the crusade to Flanders in 1383, and his naval expedition in the summer of 1387 had won him wide popularity.[29] Thomas of Woodstock had taken an expedition to Brittany in 1380, and when he and his fellow Appellants came to power in 1388 he was evidently prepared to continue the war. His reluctance to go to Ireland in 1394 sprang, if Froissart is to be believed, from a sense that the land offered no opportunities for profit or conquest, and that campaigning there was futile; but in the event he did serve in Ireland, together with many other nobles, and neither in 1385 nor in 1394 did Richard have much difficulty in persuading his nobles to serve on his campaigns.[30]

In seeking an explanation for Richard's determination to bring the war to an end, it seems likely that the problem of resources is crucial. Several scholars have drawn attention to the unprecedentedly high cost of waging war in the last quarter of the fourteenth century. James Sherborne has calculated that over a million pounds was spent on the war between 1369–81, with little to show for it. The war at sea in these years comsumed nearly a quarter of these resources, and the expenses of the garrisons of Calais, Brest and Cherbourg another quarter, while little more than a third of the total expenditure went on campaigns in northern France.[31] The high cost of the garrisons was one of the most significant sources of financial strain, and if English forces had succeeded in capturing other strongholds such as St Malo and Harfleur, besieged in 1378, or Sluys, which the Earl of Arundel attempted to seize in 1387, it is very hard to see where the money to finance the garrisons of these ports would have come from. The will to conquer substantially outran the government's ability to finance its hoped-for conquests.

Between 1376 and 1386 the burden of taxation provoked unprecedented resistance from the Commons in parliament.[32] In 1378, for instance, they were prepared to make a grant only of the wool tax, and they had to be persuaded that the maintenance of the garrisons of Calais, Cherbourg and Brest was essential to England's own security. The Peasants' Revolt brought home to the Commons the dangers that lurked in any attempt to extend the burden of taxation more widely through the population, and three out of the four parliaments which met between November 1381 and February 1383 refused to grant a subsidy. The regular yield of the customs revenue went some way towards funding the garrisons of Calais, Cherbourg and Brest, and the garrison of Aquitaine, but the organization and despatch of expeditions to France depended crucially on the willingness of the Commons to vote funds; and in the early 1380s that willingness was often just not there.[33]

The government was therefore placed in the invidious position of having to seek alternative sources of income to supplement the meagre sums voted by the Commons for the expeditions undertaken after 1381. The subsidy voted in October 1382 was earmarked for the Bishop of Norwich's crusade in the following year, but the crusade was to be financed in part by the sale of indulgences, authorized under papal bulls which arrived in England in September 1382. The Scottish expedition of 1385 was intended to be financed in part by the levy of scutage, but parliamentary pressure forced the cancellation of the levy, and, as Dr Palmer remarked, the Commons then emphasized 'their own control over the most important single item in the royal revenue' by withholding the subsidy on wool for six weeks in the summer of 1385. Even when the Commons were prepared to grant a subsidy, they went to some lengths to ensure that the money they voted was properly spent. In the parliament of January 1377 they petitioned for the appointment of four 'Treasurers of the Subsidy' who would ensure that the proceeds of the poll tax were entirely devoted to the war. The Commons eventually withdrew this petition, but in the next parliament, in October of the same year, they succeeded in having two treasurers of war, the London merchants Walworth and

Philpot, appointed to see that the subsidy of two-tenths and fifteenths was applied exclusively to the war.[34] These measures may be seen as part of the legacy of mistrust about the integrity of the king's ministers which was evident in the Good Parliament; but in the September parliament of 1388 parliament turned its critical gaze not upon the king's ministers but upon the Earl of Arundel. His naval expedition in the summer of 1388 had been financed out of the subsidy granted during the Merciless Parliament, but although its departure had been delayed, Arundel had still been paid for the full term specified in his indenture. The financial implications of the delay aroused the concern of parliament, and two of Arundel's servants, Sir William Heron and John Stephens, were required to appear before parliament and explain why the expedition's departure had been delayed. There is no evidence that Arundel was thought guilty of financial malpractice, and he was exonerated of responsibility for the delay; but the critical attitude of parliament towards a noble who had won the acclaim of the public a year earlier for his exploits at sea shows a significant widening of the range of its critical scrutiny.[35] It is worth noting in passing that Arundel never served again on any military expedition. He was the most notable absentee from Richard's Irish expedition in 1394, and he did not again hold military office in any overseas garrison.

The parsimony and the critical attitude of the Commons necessarily had its effect upon the willingness of the nobility to engage their retinues for the king's wars. The contract army was still the essential means of fighting in France, yet the financial stringency of the 1380s could not but inhibit the effectiveness of the military system which had underpinned England's war effort since the 1340s. Anthony Goodman has shown that in the 1370s John of Gaunt was owed large sums of money by the Crown for his expenses in war.[36] Thomas of Woodstock found great difficulty in obtaining payment from the Exchequer of debts due to him for his expedition to Brittany in 1380, and the decision to proceed with the Bishop of Norwich's crusade in 1383 arose from the unwillingness of the Commons to provide sufficient funds for a contract army raised in the traditional way. According to the monk of Westminster, the Earl of Arundel offered 'to find at his own cost a specified number of armed men' and join the bishop as his secular lieutenant, but the offer was rejected.[37] It is hard to believe that Arundel, wealthy though he was, would have been prepared to lay out his own money on a substantial force which the Commons were in effect unwilling to finance, and in all probability he intended to take only a small contingent, perhaps just a token force, under his own command. It is true that Gaunt had used his own resources to supplement the funds made available by the Crown to finance his expeditions in the early 1370s, but Gaunt's resources were exceptional, and in any case he still expected repayment from the Crown.[38] The private resources of the nobility were not an acceptable alternative to money voted by the Commons, even when the object of an expedition could be represented as personal gain for its leader. Thus in 1385, when Gaunt was preparing his expedition to Castile, the Commons agreed that part of the one-and-a-half fifteenths and tenths voted in November 1385 should go towards the costs of the expedition, but the total yield of the subsidy was slightly less than £50,000, and the king had to make a personal loan to Gaunt to cover his initial outlay. The expedition was organized by officials of the Duchy of Lancaster, but it is not clear to what extent Gaunt contributed to the costs of the expedition out of his own pocket, nor, according to Professor Russell, is it known exactly how large an army he recruited. It seems unlikely, however, that he could have expected to cover his costs out of the portion of the subsidy allocated to him, and only the Castilian pension he eventually received prevented the expedition becoming a long-term liability for him.[39]

There is no reason to suppose, however, that the nobility were averse to taking expeditions to France provided they were adequately and securely funded. The criticism of the Earl of Arundel in 1388 demonstrated that a nobleman ran political risks if he appeared to be making profits for himself out of money voted for the war; but the political consequences of the financial crisis were, of course, much more serious for the Crown than for the individual noblemen who engaged to serve. The parliamentary crises of 1385 and 1386 both have their origins in the financial pressures engendered by war. The largesse tactlessly handed out by the king at the opening of the Scottish campaign and the promise of finance for de Vere's supposed expedition to Ireland, combined with the proposal to levy scutage for the Scottish campaign, brought about a proposal from the lords to restrict the king's power to make grants and to implement other reforms in royal finances, proposals which the chancellor, Michael de la Pole, failed to carry through. The attack on the chancellor and the treasurer in 1386 was precipitated by a demand from the chancellor for a tax of four-fifteenths and tenths, a levy of unprecedented size, to cover the costs of defending the realm against the threatened French invasion. Even the Appellant regime was not spared: the hostility which the Commons showed towards the government in September 1388 arose in part from the chancellor's request for a subsidy when they believed that the revenue from the forfeited lands of the victims of the Merciless Parliament should have augmented royal finances sufficiently to avoid the need for further taxation so soon after the subsidy granted by the Merciless Parliament.[40]

It is not surprising, therefore, that Richard regarded a settlement of the war with France as the essential means of relieving the fiscal burden on his subjects and removing the opportunities which the Crown's financial weakness offered to its political opponents. In 1387, according to the monk of Westminster, Richard had concluded that 'if he was going to have to maintain a ceaseless state of war against the king of the French, he would inevitably be compelled to be forever burdening his people with new imposts, with damaging results for himself'.[41] In a proclamation to his subjects on 16 May 1389, shortly after he had resumed responsibility for government, he recalled the numerous heavy subsidies which had been levied during his tender years, and in respiting half the subsidy granted in the Cambridge parliament he expressed his hope that henceforward his subjects would be burdened with fewer and lighter taxes.[42] The financial benefits of the series of truces which were agreed in the early 1390s were soon apparent, and over the years from 1389 to 1397 the pressure of taxation eased. Royal finances ceased for a time to be the highly contentious issue they had been in the 1380s.[43]

It would, however, be unwise to overestimate the extent to which the Crown solved its financial problems by ending the war. The customs revenues fluctuated considerably between 1389 and 1399, reaching a peak of over £60,000 in 1392–3, but little more than half that (£35,000) in 1396–7, and the Crown could not entirely dispense with parliamentary subsidies.[44] In the November parliament of 1391 the Commons voted a half subsidy to be levied at Easter 1392, and authorized the levying of a whole subsidy two months later if the war were renewed and the king were to lead an expedition in person. In 1393 parliament granted three half subsidies, but two of these were conditional upon the war being renewed or the king undertaking an expedition to Scotland or Ireland, and in January 1395 the Commons voted one-fifteenth and tenth for the king's Irish expedition. These grants were made in a form which would have allowed the king to resume the war if he wished,[45] but their conditional nature made the connection between light taxation and the maintenance of peace obvious to public opinion. Rather than face the political consequences of asking parliament for regular taxation in time of truce, there is evidence that the king preferred to exploit other sources of revenue. In 1390 he raised a subsidy of 1000 marks from his north Wales lands, and in the autumn of 1391 he raised 2000 marks from Cheshire, both regions of course being outside the scope of parliamentary representation; in 1392 the council tried to raise money by distraint of knighthood, and of course the Londoners turned down requests from the king to lend him money, thereby provoking the quarrel which ended with the king better off by £10,000.[46]

Thus in the face of the financial difficulties which the Crown experienced in the 1380s, and the political dissension to which its financial difficulties gave rise, Richard perhaps had little alternative but to seek a negotiated end to the war, though there were political risks at home in appearing to go along with terms for a settlement which were essentially set by the French and which appeared to offer little to the English except some relief from financial pressure. In the event, of course, the draft articles of 1393 were never embodied in a final treaty, and the two sides agreed in 1396 to a twenty-eight years truce.

The reasons for the 'failure' of the peace negotiations have been much debated, and Dr Palmer has emphasized the hostility of the Gascons to the proposal that their duchy should pass to Gaunt and his heirs.[47] Yet there is ample evidence that the draft proposals of 1393 were unacceptable to a substantial body of opinion in England. When the draft agreement of 1393 was presented to parliament in January 1394, the knights in parliament argued, according to the monk of Westminster, that it would be 'ludicrous for the king of England to do homage and fealty to the French king for Aquitaine and other overseas territories and in fine become his liegeman, with the corollary that every single Englishman having the king of England as his lord would pass under the heel of the French king and be kept for the future under the yoke of slavery'. In the event, the monk tells us, both Lords and Commons refused their consent to the draft terms, saying that 'if it had been men of modest station who had propounded them, they would have been immediately, and deservedly, branded as traitors on the spot'. The monk suggests that is was Gaunt who put the draft agreement before parliament: in his account of the parliament the monk may have been anxious to present Gaunt in as bad a light as possible, and he may have exaggerated the vehemence of the Commons' reaction.[48]

The parliament roll indicates that the Commons accepted the draft terms, subject to conditions laid down by the Lords. These conditions, it seems, included the crucial proviso that the king should not do liege homage for Aquitaine.[49] The Commons took the view that homage for Aquitaine should not have any adverse implications for the king's English lieges, a point the monk of Westminster echoed when he wrote of Englishmen passing 'under the heel of the French king'. The implication of parliament's response to the draft peace was that simple homage might be acceptable, but that liege homage, with its supposed implications for the status of all Englishmen, was unacceptable. Yet the essence of the draft agreement with the French was that the English king should do liege homage for Aquitaine, and without liege homage the negotiations would collapse. Perhaps, therefore, it is unnecessary to look beyond Westminster for an explanation of the failure of the peace negotiations. For the French, liege homage for Aquitaine was an indispensible condition of an agreement; and both Richard II himself and John of Gaunt were willing to accept that liege homage was owed for the duchy, albeit perhaps with some modifications; yet the wider political community in England, expressing its opinion in parliament, was prepared only to agree that the

king should do simple homage for Aquitaine. It does not seem unreasonable to conclude that, faced with the rejection by parliament of a crucial
part of the draft agreement, Richard and John of Gaunt now abandoned
the attempt to conclude a final peace with France.

The twenty-eight years truce which was concluded in 1396 has often
been presented as a failure, as the best that could be salvaged from the
wreck of the negotiations that had gone forward with such apparent ease
between 1390 and 1393. In one sense, of course, the truce was an
admission of failure, for it left unsolved the fundamental issues in
contention between the two kingdoms. But the problem of Aquitaine was
probably insoluble, and negotiators both before and after the 1390s
confronted the same issues and found equal, if not greater, difficulty in
trying to resolve them. From Richard's point of view, however, if final
peace proved impossible to achieve, a twenty-eight years truce offered a
number of advantages as long as it could be made to stick. The war was
over for his lifetime, even at a much more generous estimate of his lifetime
than he was actually to enjoy; yet no concessions limiting his *de facto*
freedom of action in Aquitaine had been made, even though that freedom
was exercised over a much less substantial area than the French had been
prepared to offer in the draft agreement of 1393. At home, the benefits
which the Crown could hope to derive from an end to the war were well
apparent by 1396. In 1393 Cherbourg had been handed back to the king of
Navarre, perhaps in anticipation that the draft agreement would be
ratified, and in 1396 Brest was returned to the Duke of Brittany. The
abandonment of these two ports ended an outlay on their garrisons which
had amounted to over £40,000 between 1378 and 1381. Even without the
dowry of Queen Isabella, which was eventually set at a down payment of
300,000 crowns and 100,000 crowns a year for five years (in total, in
sterling, £133,333 6s 8d) the truce was in the financial interests of the
Crown.[50]

The political consequences of the truce with France, however, were less
clear-cut. The diminution of financial pressure was advantageous to the
Crown politically, but both Froissart and the author of the *Traison* suggests
that the terms of the truce were unpopular, particularly with Thomas of
Woodstock.[51] Indeed, there were circumstances surrounding the 1396
agreement which might almost have been calculated to raise political
tension in England. In the draft instructions given to the envoys who
negotiated the dowry agreement, the king of France was to be asked to 'aid
and sustain his son-in-law against any of his subjects'.[52] Although no such
clause was included in the dowry treaty itself, the mere suggestion that
Richard might invoke the aid of the King of France against his own
subjects was enough to arouse suspicion and to reawaken memory of
Richard's impetuous retort to Woodstock and Bishop Arundel in 1386,

when he had threatened to seek help from the French king against his rebellious subjects.[53] Another, more public, sign of a political understanding between the two kings was given in October 1396 when, in an agreement at Ardres near Calais, Richard undertook to aid his father-in-law of France against all men.[54] This agreement bore fruit the following winter, when Richard sought a subsidy from the Commons for a proposed Anglo-French expedition to Milan. The Commons asked not to be party to the expedition, and accepted an assurance from the king that it would not be a charge on the community.[55] In such an atmosphere of apparent cordiality between the two courts, and after the return of Cherbourg and Brest, it is not surprising that rumours began to circulate about the fate of Calais. In 1397 Froissart reported that the Count of St Pol had come over to England to negotiate the return of Calais, and Walsingham maintained that in 1398 Richard was contemplating selling Calais to the French king. The rumours seem to have been entirely baseless; but their circulation perhaps indicated the degree of suspicion in England that had been aroused by the king's apparently cordial relationship with Charles VI.[56]

The author of the *Traïson* believed that the final crisis of Richard's reign had its origin in Thomas of Woodstock's hostility to the *rapprochement* with France; Walsingham, on the other hand, believed that in a time of peace and prosperity Richard began to contemplate the destruction of his enemies.[57] The one author probably over-emphasized, the other minimized the significance of the negotiations with France in precipitating the events of the summer and autumn of 1397. Recent work has emphasized the importance Richard attached to placing members of his affinity in key positions in the shires in the 1390s,[58] and we cannot go all the way with the French authorities in arguing that the king's attack on his old enemies originated in the ill-feeling aroused by the twenty-eight years truce. On the other hand, contemporary French writers, and such well-informed noblemen as the Duke of Burgundy and the Duke of Berry were surely not wholly misled when they believed that the Anglo-French negotiations of the 1390s had exposed divisions between Richard and Gaunt on the one hand, and other influential members of the higher nobility together with the Commons on the other. In the end, for Richard, neither war nor peace seemed certain to promote political stability.

## Notes

1 An earlier draft of this paper was given to a postgraduate seminar at the University of Edinburgh. I have benefited greatly from the observations made then by Professor Kenneth Fowler, and I should also like to thank James Sherborne for commenting on a later draft of the paper.

2    R. Delachenal, *Histoire de Charles V* (Paris, 1928), IV. 494.
3    F. Lehoux, *Jean de France, duc de Berry* (Paris, 1966), II. 420–1.
4    See, for instance, R. Vaughan, *Philip the Bold* (1962), pp.182–3.
5    See, for example, A. Steel, *Richard II* (Cambridge, 1941), pp.188–9.
6    See for this A. Tuck, *Richard II and the English Nobility* (1973), p.159.
7    J. *de Trokelowe et H. de Blaneforde Chronica et Annales*, ed. H.T. Riley (RS, 1866), p.159. See now on this question P. Morgan, *War and Society in Late Medieval Cheshire 1272–1403* (Manchester, 1987).
8    J.J.N. Palmer, *England, France and Christendom* (1972), pp.6–8.
9    P.E. Russell, *English Intervention in Spain and Portugal in the Time of Edward III and Richard II* (Oxford, 1955), pp.500–1.
10   H. Moranvillé, 'Conférences entre la France et l'Angleterre, 1388–1393', *Bibliothèque de l'Ecole des Chartes*, L (1889), 366.
11   E. Perroy, *The Hundred Years War* (English translation, 1951), pp.196–7.
12   J.J.N. Palmer, 'The Anglo-French Peace Negotiations, 1390–1396', *TRHS*, 5th series, 16 (1966), 94.
13   M.G.A. Vale, *English Gascony* (Oxford, 1970), pp.28–9; also his review of J.J.N. Palmer, *England, France and Christendom*, in *EHR*, LXXXVIII (1973), 848–53.
14   Palmer, 'Anglo-French Peace Negotiations', pp.82–3, 85–9; idem, *England, France and Christendom*, pp.36–40.
15   Moranvillé, 'Conférences', p.367.
16   Ibid., p.368; *Proceedings and Ordinances of the Privy Council of England*, ed. Sir N.H. Nicolas, 7 vols. (1834–7), I. 19–23.
17   E. Perroy, *The Anglo-French Negotiations at Bruges 1374–1377*, Camden Miscellany, XIX (1952), xvi–xix, 9–11, 14–20.
18   Palmer, *England, France and Christendom*, p.148.
19   Ibid., pp.33–6; Perroy, *Anglo-French Negotiations*, pp.xvii, 11.
20   Moranvillé, 'Conférences', pp.371–5; *The Westminster Chronicle 1381–1394*, ed. and trans. L.C. Hector and Barbara F. Harvey, (Oxford, 1982), pp.488–92; Lehoux, *Berry*, II. 284; J.J.N. Palmer, 'Articles for a Final Peace between England and France, 16 June 1393', *BIHR*, XXXIX (1966), 185.
21   Palmer, 'Articles for a Final Peace', pp.180–5; *Westminster*, ed. Hector and Harvey, p.490.
22   *Foedera, Conventiones, etc.*, ed. T. Rymer, 20 vols (1704–35), VII. 662, 687–8, 731–2.
23   PRO E30/1232 mm. 3, 5; see also Vale, *English Gascony*, p.28.
24   Palmer, 'Articles for a Final Peace', pp.181, 183; idem, 'Anglo-French Peace Negotiations', pp.88–9.
25   *Proceedings and Ordinances of the Privy Council*, I. 19–23.
26   I owe this point to Professor Kenneth Fowler.
27   See, for example, Steel, *Richard II*, p.41.
28   J.F. Lydon, 'Richard II's expeditions to Ireland', *Journal of the Royal Society of Antiquaries of Ireland*, XCIII (1963), 146–7.
29   M. Aston, 'The Impeachment of Bishop Despenser', *BIHR*, XXXVIII (1965), 129; Tuck, *Richard II and the English Nobility*, pp.113–4.
30   Palmer, *England, France and Christendom*, p.122; Froissart, *Chroniques*, ed. Kervyn de Lettenhove, 25 vols, (Brussels, 1867–77), XVI. 5.
31   J. Sherborne, 'The Costs of English Warfare with France in the later Fourteenth Century', *BIHR*, L (1977), esp. p.149.
32   Palmer, *England, France and Christendom*, p.10.
33   *Rot. Parl.* III. 35–6; for some discussion of this topic, see Palmer, *England, France and Christendom*, pp.9–11 and J.A. Tuck, 'Nobles, Commons and the Great Revolt of 1381', in *The English Rising of 1381*, ed. R.H. Hilton and T.H. Aston (Cambridge, 1984), pp.208–9.

34  *Rot. Parl.* II. 364; III. 7; J.J.N. Palmer, 'The Last Summons of the Feudal Army in England', *EHR*, LXXXIII (1968), 771–5.
35  Tuck, *Richard II and the English Nobility*, p.135.
36  A.E. Goodman, 'John of Gaunt', in *England in the Fourteenth Century*, ed. W.M. Ormrod (Woodbridge, Suffolk, 1986), pp.78–80.
37  *Westminster*, ed. Hector and Harvey, p.40; Sherborne, 'Costs of English Warfare', pp.148–50.
38  Goodman, loc. cit.
39  Russell, *English Intervention*, p.408; Goodman, 'John of Gaunt', pp.80–1.
40  J.S. Roskell, *The Impeachment of Michael de la Pole in 1386*, (Manchester, 1984), passim; A. Tuck, 'The Cambridge Parliament, 1388', *EHR*, LXXXIV (1969), 225–43; see also James Sherborne's paper in this volume.
41  *Westminster*, ed. Hector and Harvey, p.205.
42  *Foedera*, VII. 620–1.
43  Tuck, *Richard II and the English Nobility*, p.144–5.
44  J.H. Ramsay, *Revenues of the Kings of England*, (Oxford, 1925), II. 372–387; A. Steel, *The Receipt of the Exchequer, 1377–1485*, (Cambridge, 1954), pp.60–80.
45  *Rot. Parl.* III. 285–6, 301–2.
46  Tuck, *Richard II and the English Nobility*, pp.144–5; Caroline Barron, 'The Quarrel of Richard II with London 1392–97', in *The Reign of Richard II: Essays in Honour of May McKisack*, pp.173–201.
47  Palmer, 'Anglo-French Peace Negotiations', pp.92–4; idem, *England, France and Christendom*, pp.159–63.
48  *Westminster*, ed. Hector and Harvey, pp.lxii–lxiii, 516–8.
49  *Rot. Parl.* III. 315–6. See also *Westminster*, ed. Hector and Harvey, p.518 footnote 3, where this interpretation of the text in the Parliament Roll is supported.
50  *Foedera*, VII. 756–7, 820–32, 852–3; Sherborne, 'Costs of English Warfare', p.147.
51  *Chronicque de la Traison et Mort de Richart II*, ed. B. Williams, (English Historical Society, 1846), pp.1–2; Froissart, XVI. 1–6.
52  *Foedera*, VII. 811.
53  *Chronicon Henrici Knighton*, ed. J.R. Lumby (RS, 1895), II. 217–8.
54  Froissart, XVIII. 582–3.
55  *Rot. Parl.* III. 338.
56  Froissart, XVI. 15.
57  *J. de Trokelowe et H. de Blaneforde Cronica et Annales*, p.201.
58  C. Given-Wilson, *The Royal Household and the King's Affinity* (New Haven, 1986), pp.212–26; see also Nigel Saul's paper in this volume.

# 8

# The Deposition of Richard II[1]

Caroline Barron
*Royal Holloway and Bedford New College*
*University of London*

It is almost fifty years since K.B. McFarlane first exploded the myth of
Lancastrian 'constitutionalism'.[2] In a famous essay he laid bare the
opportunism of Henry Bolingbroke in seizing the Crown in 1399, and of
those – in particular the Percys – who supported him. Moreover there was
no cooperation between Crown and parliament in the fifteenth century
that was not, McFarlane argued, born out of necessity. But although
Henry Bolingbroke has been effectively stripped of his hero clothing,
Richard II retains still the popular reputation of a tyrant.[3] In consequence
his deposition is seen to be, in some way, predictable, deserved and, even,
necessary. The time is ripe, perhaps, to sweep away the last vestiges of
Lancastrian propaganda, and to take another look at contemporary
attitudes to Richard's government in the late 1390s, and at the events of
1399.

There are three widely-held views about Richard's rule which need to be
challenged: first the view that Richard's government in the late 1390s was
widely unpopular and so contributed in an important way to his deposition; second the view that Richard had few supporters and none of them
rallied to his cause in the summer of 1399; third the view that there was
widespread enthusiasm for Henry Bolingbroke's 'challenge' of the Crown.
These three views, none of them very well grounded, have served as a
mutual support group in which each has been used to prop up the others.

Historians have almost universally condemned Richard II's government
as unsuccessful, unpopular and doomed. Bishop Stubbs who saw Henry
Bolingbroke as a constitutional monarch, characterized Richard as an
'absolute monarch' a 'royal tyrant' and a king who 'without subterfuge or
palliative, challenged the constitution'.[4] Much more recently Professor
May McKisack in her exemplary *Oxford History of England* volume
summarized the moderate Whig view of Richard II. She admitted that he
was a man of personal charm and 'good character' but yet 'he rode

roughshod over common right: and the nation at last repudiated him for the tyrant that he was'.[5] The articles of deposition embodied in the official 'record and process' and copied into the rolls of parliament, it is true, repeatedly accused Richard of violating his Coronation oath. Doubtless he did do so on occasion, but whether he did so more often than, say, Edward I before him or Edward IV after him, is a moot point. But while it may well be true that some of the accusations against Richard in the deposition articles may have been contrived and embroidered, yet there is no doubt that several of Richard's actions in the years following 1397 were innovative and capricious.[6] But this does not necessarily mean that his government was unpopular, or that his subjects found the level of Richard's capriciousness and innovation unacceptable. It was, however, the purpose of Henry Bolingbroke's supporters, who drafted the articles, to make a connection between Richard's uncustomary style of government and widespread unpopularity. But is it true that Richard's government was unpopular? Historians have tended to see support for the claims of the deposition articles in the testimony of the chroniclers of the time. Dr Tuck is not alone when he writes that 'the chronicles make it clear that Richard's rule was widely unpopular'.[7] It is indeed from the chronicles, and not from any surviving documentary material, that we have inherited the pervasive view that Richard's government was widely resented and that, in the 1390s, he ruled over a restless and discontented people, eagerly awaiting the chance to rebel.

Since the chronicles bear such a weight of testimony they need to be carefully considered. Some of the accounts are blatantly hostile and critical; others are fawning and hagiographic, but all of them, it should be remembered, were written *after* Richard's deposition.[8] We have no accounts for the years 1395–9 which were written without benefit of hindsight. We have no way of knowing, therefore, whether Richard's government seemed tyrannical and oppressive to those who were living under it. By 1396 the excitable Henry Knighton was dead and the judicious Westminster chronicler had stopped writing. The most influential chronicle of the time, Thomas Walsingham's *Annales Ricardi Secundi* was written after Henry had become king and from a careful Lancastrian point of view.[9] Walsingham used the account of the deposition, the 'record and process' which was enrolled on the parliament rolls and which seems to have been circulated widely. Dr Gransden has written of this part of Walsingham's history that 'The text from the end of the annal for 1396 is a highly coloured narrative of Richard's arbitrary rule, apparently written as an historical introduction to the account of the deposition itself. Some passages are copied word for word from the articles accusing Richard of misgovernment, which were included in the "record and process".' Other passages, she points out, 'have such an exaggerated, romantic tone that their melodramatic details are hard to believe'.[10]

Walsingham was not the only chronicler to write during the early years of Lancastrian rule with a copy of the 'record and process' in front of him and hindsight guiding his pen. The monk of Evesham, who wrote the *Historia Vitae et Regni Ricardi Secundi* also used the 'record and process' as the basis of his account of these years but 'synthesized it with other sources and with his own rhetorical moralizations'.[11] The continuator of the *Eulogium* (possibly a Franciscan attached to the Greyfriars house at Canterbury)[12] also wrote after 1399 and used a copy of the 'record and process'.[13] Not surprisingly neither the Evesham monk nor the Canterbury friar offers a particularly flattering picture of Richard, or his government.[14]

Of a rather different kind is the account of the events of 1399 written by Adam of Usk: this is full of interest since Usk joined Henry's invading entourage in July 1399 (perhaps as a result of his attachment to Thomas Arundel, the deposed Archbishop of Canterbury who came from France with Henry) and later helped in September to draft the articles of deposition.[15] On 17 November Usk's support of the Lancastrian cause was rewarded with the grant of a living in Kent.[16] His chronicle provides a personal and vivid account of events in the second half of 1399 but it cannot be considered – nor was it intended – as an impartial account of Richard's government.

To serve as a counterbalance to the weighty pro-Lancastrian chronicles, written after the deposition of 1399 had made clear on whom Fortune had smiled, there survive three very slight, but important, chronicles written in northern Cistercian houses (not normally noted for chronicles), Kirkstall in Yorkshire,[17] Dieulacres in Staffordshire[18] and Whalley in Lancashire.[19] The Kirkstall chronicler writes glowingly of Richard's achievements in ridding himself of his treacherous enemies in 1397–8. He writes that Richard is like the sun lately concealed by cloud 'but now in arms he bounds on the mountains and leaps over the hills, and tossing the clouds on his horns he shows more brightly the light of his sun'.[20] This, apparently contemporary narrative breaks off in 1398, and is later resumed after the events of 1399–1400 when the tone has changed. In the words of Maude Clarke, 'There is no marked change in style. The same writer was at work, but now he knew the end of the story and walked delicately in fear of those in high places.'[21] In the same way the first part of the Dieulacres chronicle was written by an author who was sympathetic to Richard II: the second part, which covers the years 1400–1403 was compiled by a monk of the house who had been a supporter of Henry IV.[22] Here again there is a notable change of tone in 1400. These northern Cistercian chronicles, slight as they are, were used with devastating effect by Clarke and Galbraith in the 1930s to discredit the bland account of Richard's willing deposition to be found in the official Lancastrian 'record and process'. In short, they concluded, that Richard had been tricked into leaving Conway by promises which were subsequently broken; he did not give up his crown 'hilari vultu' in September and he may well have made a protestation at that time which was swept aside.[23] But beyond discrediting the official account of the events of 1399, these northern chroniclers, and in particular the Kirkstall chronicle, suggest that Richard's government was not necessarily widely unpopular and there may have been some among Richard's subjects who admired his assertion of the regality and prerogatives of the Crown.

Recently Dr John Palmer has re-examined the historical value of the French chronicles of the Lancastrian revolution.[24] Several accounts were compiled at the French court in the years immediately following Richard's deposition. They are not of equal value, as Dr Palmer has demonstrated and some, like Froissart, have no value at all. The two most important accounts were made available to the English public in the first half of the nineteenth century when they found little favour amid the prevailing Whig constitutionalism of the time. The *Histoire du roy d'Angleterre Richard*, attributed to Jean Creton, was translated and published as 'The Metrical History of the Deposition of King Richard II' in *Archaeologia* in 1824.[25] The second account, the *Chronicque de la traison et mort Richart Deux* was printed with an English translation in 1846.[26] These two French chronicles had, however, been known to Tudor antiquaries. Holinshed certainly knew Creton's work and Stow had a copy of part at least of the *Traison*.[27] Shakespeare seems to have known both chronicles and his sympathetic portrait of Richard in his last months is clearly derived from these French accounts.[28] Indeed Shakespeare's play is a neat, but obvious, fusion of the Lancastrian view of Richard to be found in Acts One and Two, followed by the French interpretation of Richard as a tragic hero derived from the French chronicles in Acts Three to Five. What may appear as a somewhat capricious change in Richard's character between his departure and return from Ireland reflects, quite simply, a change in Shakespeare's source material.

It is important to know what reliance may be placed on the accounts of the events of 1399 to be found in these French chronicles. Dr Palmer's work is of great help here. He believes that the *Traison* was written by an apprentice herald, living in the house of John Holland, Earl of Huntingdon and later Duke of Exeter, who was the king's half-brother.[29] The author was in England from April 1398 (he may have come to England with Richard's bride, the French Princess Isobel) and he may have left England with Isobel when she was sent back to France in 1400.[30] The author did not go to Ireland with Richard's expedition in 1399, but he stayed in, or near, London and provides an account of events in the south of England during 1399.[31] The *Metrical History* was probably written by Jean Creton, a valet de chambre of Charles VI. He arrived in England in

May 1399 and accompanied Richard's expedition to Ireland. He returned with the advance party led by the Earl of Salisbury, joined Richard at Conway, accompanied him to London and then left for France before Richard's deposition on 29 September.[32] Both the author of the *Traison* and Jean Creton wrote their accounts after Richard had been deposed, probably in 1401–2. They too, like the compilers of the Lancastrian 'record and process', wrote with hindsight and for propaganda purposes. Their accounts are as much vitiated by their pro-Richard bias as the Lancastrian chroniclers are by their pro-Henry bias.[33] The purpose of the French writers was to glorify and sanctify Richard (for whom they seem to have had a measure of personal affection) and to demonstrate the perfidity of the English. They may also have been writing to justify the possibility of French intervention in English domestic affairs.

This brief survey of the surviving chronicle accounts of the years 1395 to 1400 has demonstrated that, with the possible exception of the first account in the Kirkstall chronicle, there survive no accounts of these years which were not written *after* the deposition of Richard II and the accession of Henry IV. The French and the Cistercian chroniclers revealed the duplicity of the official Lancastrian account of the events of August and September 1399. Insofar as the Lancastrian accounts have anything to say about Richard's government in the preceding years they are likely to be equally unreliable and to base their information on the official 'record and process' which was deliberately circulated for propaganda purposes. There is no doubt that Richard did introduce innovations in government, and that there were aspects of his rule which were arbitrary, uncustomary and bore heavily on certain individuals. But it seems unlikely that these injustices, which formed the normal small change of English medieval kingship, were widely resented, or were so unpopular as seriously to undermine Richard's government. There was certainly material out of which Lancastrian apologists could fashion a case against Richard, and they did this effectively in the 'articles of deposition'. But it is necessary to distinguish between the likely impact of Richard's government at the time, and the significance which lawyers for the prosecution chose later to give to those uncustomary acts.

The government of Richard II has been condemned because there seems to have been so little support for the king in the summer of 1399. The rapidity with which the opposition to Henry Bolingbroke melted away has been taken to indicate the general unpopularity of Richard's rule. But this explanation may well be too facile. There may be good reasons for the failure of the armed resistance to Henry in 1399 which have more to do with logistics than with loyalty.

The only armed resistance which could be offered to an invader would be that provided by the king's retinue or by the retinues of those loyal to the king. To raise men meant to summon retainers. Since the early 1390s Richard had been developing the range and size of his retinue: from 1397 he had particularly focussed on Cheshire and he began to recruit specifically for military, as opposed to general, service to the Crown.[34] In 1399 Richard took the greater part of his retinue with him to Ireland, and so seriously weakened the resistance which might be offered to an invader.[35] It had also been Richard's intention to make Chester into a secure 'inner citadel' from which he could hold his realm, but he left the castles of the principality, for example Chester itself, and Holt, too thinly garrisoned to be able to offer effective resistance. As Dr Philip Morgan has written, 'Richard's principality could guarantee his personal security, but not that of his realm and, stripped of its military strength for the campaign in Ireland, it could offer little resistance to Henry of Bolingbroke's campaign'.[36] Retinues do not rally easily in the absence of their leaders and Richard, who took such trouble to bind his retinue to him personally, seems to have failed to appreciate how important it was for the king, the retinue leader, to be present.

It is clear that Henry Bolingbroke's invasion took everyone by surprise (unlike the long-planned invasion of Henry Tudor nearly a hundred years later). Richard left for Ireland believing that Bolingbroke was safely under house arrest in Paris, supervised by the Duke of Burgundy.[37] On 28 June the Duke of York, left by Richard as guardian of his realm, and a man who, throughout his life was found to be unequal to the tasks entrusted to him, learnt that the 'king's enemies' were gathering at Calais. He sent writs to the sheriffs to summon men to defend the realm.[38] At this point York may have underestimated the danger for he appears not to have sent messengers to Richard in Ireland until 4 July, at least two days after Bolingbroke had taken Pevensey castle in Sussex, but failed to establish there a bridgehead for his invasion.[39]

Dr Dorothy Johnston has effectively described the difficulties which Richard faced on learning of Bolingbroke's movements from the Duke of York.[40] It appears that Richard did not leave Waterford until 24 July, or thereabouts, that is three weeks after Bolingbroke was first sighted off Sussex.[41] This delay in leaving Ireland was seen by contemporaries, and has been judged by historians, as the crucial error which cost Richard his crown. So serious was this mistake that Jean Creton attributed it to treacherous counsel on the part of Aumerle who deliberately argued in favour of a delayed return.[42] Creton, however, only wrote this after he knew of Aumerle's later treachery. But Dr Johnston has demonstrated how acute were the difficulties which faced Richard in trying to get his household, and his treasure, an army of some 5,000 men, their horses and equipment, back to England.[43] By the time Richard learnt of Bolingbroke's arrival, the ships which had brought the royal army to Ireland had been dispersed. Rather than the king return with a few men in disarray, it was decided to send the Earl of Salisbury at once to north Wales to hold the situation for the king until Richard himself could gather up his army, and a fleet, and return. It is extremely difficult to achieve a secure chronology for these events in July 1399, but Dr Johnston argues that Salisbury may have left Ireland on 17 July, and Richard himself a week later, sailing from Waterford. The returning fleet seems not to have had a common destination. Whereas Richard himself appears to have landed in south Wales, either at Haverfordwest or Milford Haven, other vessels in his fleet turned up at Plymouth, Dartmouth, and at Bristol; unfortunately, in this last case, after the town had capitulated to Bolingbroke on 29 July.[44] Later goods from Richard's household were found in Devon, Somerset, Dorset, Wiltshire, Bristol, and Southampton.[45] Much was also left behind in Ireland, including £6,500 in the castle of Trim in the custody of the Duchess of Surrey, wife of the king's nephew, Thomas Holland.[46] The disorder which accompanied Richard's final return makes the decision to delay that return even less justifiable. Meanwhile Salisbury had been unable to raise troops in north Wales because men believed that the king was dead.[47]

There is no doubt that the crisis of the summer of 1399 revealed flaws in Richard's character and errors in his judgement. It was a mistake to take the heart of his household and the bulk of his retinue to Ireland and he showed lack of judgement in leaving a vacillating incompetent in charge of his realm. Moreover Richard placed too much reliance on the ability of the Duke of Burgundy to control Henry Bolingbroke's movements. But his most crucial mistake was his failure to return immediately from Ireland and so to hold together the forces of resistance. By the time that Richard finally returned to England, about 27 July, Bolingbroke had already been three weeks on English soil. This was too long to expect men to rally to a dream or shadow, or a 'king over the water'. Medieval monarchy was essentially personal monarchy; medieval armies marched for leaders whom they knew and beheld. In the final analysis it was Richard's absence, not his unpopularity, which led men to desert him. As Dr Morgan has argued, 'the collapse of Richard's cause was really due to gross military incompetence and an absence of political will, not to treachery.'[48] Dr Given-Wilson has recently written that 'one might speculate that, had the king's supporters been more effectively organized and directed at that time, they were sufficiently numerous to provide Bolingbroke with a real trial of strength. Unfortunately for Richard, they were never given a chance to do so.'[49]

There are signs, moreover, that Bolingbroke encountered pockets of resistance: his march through England in July and August 1399 may not have been quite the triumphal progress that has often been described.[50]

Some of Henry's advance forces had taken Pevensey castle, held for life by the Lancastrian retainer Sir John Pelham, on 3 July. But the local *posse comitatus*, commanded by some of the Sussex gentry, besieged the Lancastrian troops in the castle and were still doing so three weeks later when Lady Pelham wrote in some desperation to her husband in the north with Bolingbroke.[51] It may have been the hostility of the men of the shires of Sussex, Surrey and Kent which dissuaded Henry from landing in the south of England. The Duke of York was able to raise a force of some 2,000 men in July by summoning the remaining members of the king's retinue, the sheriffs and several magnates.[52] Within Cheshire and Wales there were sporadic attempts to ambush Bolingbroke's troops.[53] But York seems to have been incapable, or unwilling, to lead Richard's supporters against Bolingbroke and as Dr Given-Wilson concluded, 'the affinity came to be led, but nobody was capable of leading it'.[54]

If the response of the city of London to the news of Bolingbroke's invasion is considered, it is possible to detect a reaction which fell some way short of an enthusiastic welcome. There were good reasons why Richard might not have been greatly loved in London. The city may have been in need of a sharp rebuke but Richard's treatment of London in 1392 had certainly lightened the pockets of the citizens.[55] Moreover the Londoners, together with the inhabitants of sixteen other southern counties, had been required in 1398 to seal 'blank charters' in which they submitted in abject terms to the king's grace.[56] Certainly Richard seems to have believed that the city was hostile to him and he avoided going there: he may not have been in London after the prorogation of the Autumn Parliament in 1397 until he was brought to the Tower as a prisoner in September 1399. Moreover Richard and his advisors feared that the Londoners would attempt to rescue the Earl of Arundel as he was led to execution in September 1397.[57] But, in the event, the citizens did not rush forward to save Arundel.[58] There were, in fact, many Londoners who had a vested interest in supporting Richard's regime. Much of what the king saved by refraining from war with France he spent among the merchants and craftsmen of London. The tomb for Richard and Queen Anne which had recently been completed had cost over £900 which had been paid to two London masons, Henry Yevele and Stephen Lote and to two London coppersmiths, Nicholas Broker and Godfrey Prest.[59] In May 1397 William Fitzhugh, a London goldsmith, had supplied various precious objects, including a gold cup, for Queen Isobel.[60] Christopher Tyldesley, another Londoner, was appointed as the king's goldsmith in 1398 and, together with at least ten other London craftsmen, had joined the royal retinue travelling to Ireland in the following year.[61] Many Londoners benefited from Richard's style of monarchy. It was not in the interests of the merchant aldermen who ran the city government to quarrel with a king like Richard, let alone to depose him. Richard was sufficiently astute to realize that neither the English nobility, nor the merchants of London, comprised homogeneous groups. In both cases, therefore, Richard attempted to build up a nucleus of supporters and in London this 'royalist' party may have been led by the mercer, Richard Whittington.[62] But the success of such a policy will depend not only upon the loyalty of the chosen men, but also upon the influence which they can exert over their peers. The Ricardian group among the nobility failed because men of too great influence, for example the Percys, remained aloof, but in London the policy was much more successful. The mayor and aldermen remained loyal to Richard for several weeks.

When Henry found that he could not command sufficient local support to land safely in Sussex, he played safe and sailed to Ravenspur in Lancastrian territory. Whatever Henry's original intentions may have been,(and it is possible that his aim was simply to be acknowledged as Duke of Lancaster) those intentions were, perhaps, transformed by a visit from Henry Percy, Earl of Northumberland. It would appear that Percy offered the support of the ready-armed Percy retinue in return for the promise of the Wardenship of the West March which had been taken from the control of the Percys in 1396. Only the king could grant the Wardenship of the March, so it was in Percy's interest to assist Henry to royal powers. In fulfilment of this promise, on 2 August 1399 Henry granted the Wardenship of the West March to Henry Percy under the seal of the Duchy of Lancaster. As Professor Bean pointed out Henry 'was employing the prerogatives of the English Crown under the seal of the Duchy of Lancaster a fortnight before he met Richard'.[63] Henry Percy and Henry Bolingbroke must, by this date, have shared their intention to make Henry Bolingbroke King of England.

The author of the *Traison* recorded that while Henry was still at Pontefract Castle in Yorkshire, he sent out letters to several English towns and to bishops and nobles of the realm. In the letter addressed to the towns Henry warned Englishmen of Richard's intention of using foreign help to force his subjects into bondage and subjection greater than they had ever known. It was also the king's intention, Henry assured his readers, to arrest all the governors of those towns which had at any point since 1377 supported the views of the Commons against those of the king and his council. All these town governors were to be rounded up at a great festival to be held after the king's return from Ireland. 'Wherefore my friends and good people, when the aforesaid matters came to my knowledge, I came over, as soon as I could, to inform, succour, and comfort you to the utmost of my power, for I am one of the nearest to the Crown of England and am beholden to love and support the realm as much, or more, than any man alive . . . Be well advised and ponder well that which I write to you, your good and faithful friend Henry of Lancaster.'[64] Is it possible to believe that the author of the *Traison* has preserved a verbatim copy of a letter written by Henry at this time? Was the letter, now preserved in French, originally written in English? The *Traison* author was certainly in England at this time, and he may well have been in London. Moreover the author of the *Eulogium* also noted that Henry sent letters to the Londoners in which he styled himself Duke of Lancaster and promised to reform what was amiss in the realm.[65] It is very likely that Henry would have sent out support-seeking letters soon after his arrival, to justify his return and to test the response to a possible bid for the Crown. But if he sent one hundred and fifty of these letters, as the author of the *Traison* alleges, it is, perhaps, curious that not one of them has survived. If such a letter was written to the mayor and aldermen of London, and if they had agreed to receive it, then it might have been copied into the city's Letter Book. As it happens the last two folios of the city's Letter Book H which covers the reign of Richard II have been cut out: what was once recorded on them and the reason for their removal may only be guessed at.[66] But if Henry wrote a letter of the kind that the *Traison* author has recorded, then it would seem that Henry felt in need of wider political support than he currently enjoyed.

Whether such a letter was ever sent by Henry, or ever received in London, it is nevertheless clear that the Londoners did not quickly abandon Richard and offer their support to Henry. While York summoned the remnants of the king's retinue to meet him at Ware,[67] prayers were offered publicly in London for the peace of the realm and the success of the king in Ireland.[68] On 18 July the Duke of York, by now in Oxford, ordered Dru Barentyn, the mayor of London, to ensure that armourers in London sold their goods only to true lieges of the king.[69] There is, in fact, no evidence of any support, either official or unofficial, for Henry in London, in marked contrast to the city of York which lent Henry 500 marks before his accession.[70] The Duke of York, meanwhile, moved westwards in the hope of meeting up with Richard's army returning from Ireland. But on the very day when Richard may finally have reached England, 27 July, the Duke of York capitulated to Henry Bolingbroke at Berkeley Castle.[71] Together they marched to Bristol which, two days later, opened its gates to them. It may have been from Bristol that Henry wrote a second letter to the Londoners: on this occasion the letter was addressed specifically to them and the tone is much more confident, and less insinuating, than his earlier letter. Again for the text of this letter we have to reply on the author of the *Traison* who honestly notes that he has recorded only the beginning of the letter:

I, Henry of Lancaster, Duke of Hereford and Earl of Derby, commend myself to all the people of London, high and low. My good friends, I send you my salutations and I acquaint you that I have come over to take my rightful inheritance. I beg of you to let me know, if you will be on my side or not; and I care not which for I have people enough to fight all the world for one day. Thank God. [72]

The author of the *Traison* may well have seen such a letter posted up in London, or heard it read out. He records that the Londoners, on hearing the letter, decided unanimously to support Henry.

Other evidence, however, suggests that the Londoners did not act quite so precipitately, or else that Henry's letter took a long time to arrive in the city. After the fall of Bristol to the combined forces of the Duke of York and Henry on 29 July, the Lancastrian army moved north to try to take Chester before the king could reach his 'inner citadel'. Meanwhile Richard, with a very small retinue, made his way across Wales to Conway castle. Early in August, (it is impossible to be certain of exact dates), Richard was persuaded by Henry Percy to leave the security of Conway Castle. He was brought to meet Bolingbroke at Flint where the two men came to some sort of agreement, and then Richard was brought as a virtual prisoner to Chester by 16 August. It was not until Richard's fortunes had sunk this low that the Londoners finally decided to renounce their allegiance to him. The Duke of York had defected, Bristol had fallen, and Richard himself was a prisoner before the Londoners brought themselves to take the fateful step of sending a deputation to Henry. No official record of the sending of this embassy survives but it is noted by several chroniclers. The author of the *Traison* records that six or seven of the most notable burgesses were sent, although Usk believed that three aldermen came with fifty commoners. [73] Such a large delegation seems rather unlikely. Usk also records that the delegation came to meet Richard and Henry at Chester (where they were from 16 to 20 August), whereas Jean Creton says that the meeting place was Lichfield (24 August) and the author of the *Traison* records that it was Coventry (26 August). [74] According to Adam of Usk the Londoners in the deputation recommended the city to Henry and, under the common seal of London, renounced their fealty to King Richard. This decisive action by the Londoners may have come late but it was crucial, for the deputation in this way sanctioned Henry's seizure of the Crown before Richard had been officially deposed. But it is worth remembering how long Henry had had to wait for this important mark of approval. Henry was on English soil by 4 July and yet the city of London did not announce its support of him until 16 August at Chester. It had taken the mayor and aldermen of London six weeks to make up their minds to desert Richard and offer their allegiance to Henry. Indeed Bolingbroke had been wise in not landing in the south of England and marching straight on London, for it was only after Richard had become Henry's prisoner and his cause was clearly lost, that the rulers of London were prepared to take the fateful step of renouncing their legitimate ruler.

But in spite of the Londoners' reluctance to accept Henry, once they had done so they supported him whole-heartedly and there are signs, apparent in the first parliament of Henry's reign, that they were able to strike some sort of bargain with the future king. Richard was brought to London and lodged in the Tower to await his walk-off role in Henry's play.[75] On the last day of September 1399 the estates were summoned to Westminster to depose Richard II and endorse Henry's claim to the English crown. There is little doubt that the crowd which provided the 'vox populi' necessary to endorse Henry's seizure of the Crown was composed largely of Londoners. Later the prior of St Botolph's Abbey at Colchester was to claim that the Northerners had risen against Henry in rebellion because he had only been elected king by the rabble of London.[76] At Henry's coronation on St Edward's day, 13 October, the mayor, recorder, and aldermen took their accustomed places at the coronation feast and some of the city companies provided minstrels.[77]

The first parliament of Henry's reign met on 14 October. Several of the general measures, for example the restrictions on the wearing of liveries, would have been welcome to the Londoners.[78] But there were other measures which were directly instigated by the Londoners and these reflect, perhaps, the bargaining of the previous two months. Not only were all the city's charters confirmed but the citizens were granted the additional right of keeping the city's gates and collecting tolls in the markets of Cheap, Billingsgate, and Smithfield.[79] The statute of 1354 which had laid down the procedure for taking away the city's liberties was modified and the Fishmongers' monopoly on the sale of fish by retail within the city was once more abolished.[80] Letters patent appointing a royal clothpacker in the city were declared null and void and the London sheriffs were to be empowered to hold inquests in the absence of the king's coroner, or his deputy, if necessary.[81] The Londoners did not get everything for which they petitioned, for example they would have like to see more stringent measures against foreign merchants introduced, but what they had secured constituted a decent 'package' and would have reassured them that they had backed the right horse at Chester.[82]

Individual Londoners were also rewarded. Dru Barentyn, the mayor in 1398–9, and Thomas Knolles, his successor in office, were given tenements which were in the king's hand.[83] Other Londoners received goods or lucrative offices. Most unusually, Richard Whittington and the two aldermen who had acted as MPs in Henry's first parliament, John Shadworth and William Bampton, were appointed as members of the royal council for the first year of Henry's reign.[84] It was extremely unusual for

London merchants to serve on the king's council and suggests, perhaps, the extent to which Henry was anxious to secure the continued support of the city.

This support was to be soon tested. At the Christmas season following the parliament, a group of supporters, still loyal to Richard, attempted to organize an armed rising to restore Richard to the throne. It has been customary to dismiss this as a minor disturbance and a matter of very little concern to Henry.[85] Aumerle seems to have betrayed the plot to Henry who rode to London and there, with the help and support of the mayor, Thomas Knolles, raised an army with which to defend himself against Richard's supporters.[86] But the element of surprise had been lost, the rebels were scattered and many of them were summarily executed. Others survived to be brought to trial before Henry and then condemned to traitors' deaths.[87] But it is worth remembering that this rising took place *after* Richard was deposed and imprisoned. The leaders, the two Hollands, uncle and nephew, Thomas Despenser, Earl of Gloucester, and John Montague, Earl of Salisbury, had all been treated leniently by Henry IV. They had kept most of their lands and had lost only the most recent of their titles; their lives were safe. Their only motive in conspiring against Henry at this time can have been loyalty to Richard, for they had comparatively little to gain and much to lose by their efforts. Several of Richard's household knights and esquires, men like Sir Bernard Brocas and Sir Thomas Blount, joined the rising and died for it.[88] A number of clergymen were also involved: Roger Walden, the ex-Archbishop of Canterbury, Thomas Merks, Bishop of Carlisle, and William Colchester, the Abbot of Westminster, together with a group of royal clerks.[89] This rising, abortive though it was, serves as a reminder that Richard was able to inspire loyalty which was not so shallowly-rooted as that of his cousin Aumerle.

Inevitably, perhaps, this unsuccessful rising led to Richard's death, probably murder. Had he inspired no loyalty, he would not have been dangerous. As it was he could not be allowed to live.[90] Yet within two years there was a rumour that Richard was alive in Scotland 'wherof moche peple was glad and desirid to have him kynge ayeen'.[91] The friars, who considered Richard as their 'furtherar and promoter' seem to have been behind this optimistic episode. This challenge to Henry's authority was not armed but intellectual. As many as twenty friars drawn from houses at Cambridge, Leicester, Aylesbury, Northampton, and Nottingham challenged the legality of Henry's kingship, on the grounds that Richard's abdication had not been made freely, but was constrained, and that Henry had, therefore, usurped the Crown.[92] Needless to say the friars suffered for having openly voiced what many may have felt.

It is important, if we are to understand how kingship evolved in medieval England, to detach ourselves from the Lancastrian interpretation (and the

French) of Richard's personality and government. Many of his initiatives in the last years of his reign were later taken up and developed in the 'new monarchy' of the Yorkists and Tudors.[93] It is doubtful whether Richard's government in the late 1390s was any more unpopular than most governments in the fourteenth and fifteenth centuries in England. Articles of Deposition might easily have been carved out of all of them. What was fatal to Richard's rule was his failure to be where he was needed in July 1399, and his prolonged absence in Ireland reveals that lack of a *feel* for the realities of kingship which was to be fatal. Although he may have been personally disliked by some of the nobility, there is considerable evidence that he was a man of considerable charm, and even charisma. Men were prepared to risk their lives for him after his deposition. Hard-headed realists, like the Londoners, did not judge his government to be a self-evident failure and took six weeks to decide to support the 'popular' Henry Bolingbroke. Bishop Stubbs, who found little good to say of Richard's government, yet was able to diagnose the source of his own historical bias. 'Richard II fared ill at the hands of historians who wrote under the influence of the House of Lancaster, and he left no posterity that could desire to rehabilitate him.'[94] Nearly six hundred years after Richard's deposition, it is time, finally, to rid ourselves of the pervasive influence of the propaganda of the House of Lancaster.[95]

# Notes

1   A draft of this paper was read at the conference held at Leeds in March, 1986, and at the seminar in Late Medieval history held at the Institute of Historical Research and organized by Mr Jim Bolton and Dr Paul Brand in December 1988. I am very grateful for all the suggestions made on both those occasions by those who were present and, in particular, to Dr Helen Jewell, and my colleague Dr Nigel Saul, who both took the trouble to provide me with additional information. Mrs Jenny Stratford kindly read the proofs and suggested a number of invaluable improvements.

2   K.B. McFarlane, *Lancastrian Kings and Lollard Knights* (Oxford, 1972), chapter 3. This lecture was first given in Oxford in 1940.

3   For a brief survey of some of the different interpretations of Richard's reign that have been promulgated since the nineteenth century, see John M. Theilmann, 'Stubbs, Shakespeare and Recent Historians of Richard II', *Albion*, VIII (1976), 107–124.

4   W. Stubbs, *The Constitutional History of England in its Origins and Development* (Oxford, 1875) II. 507–9.

5   M. McKisack, *The Fourteenth Century* (Oxford, 1959), pp.496–8.

6   See, for example, my 'Tyranny of Richard II', *BIHR*, XLI (1968), 1–18.

7   A. Tuck, *Crown and Nobility, 1272–1461* (1985), p.213.

8   For extremely useful surveys of the chronicle writing of Richard's reign, see Antonia Gransden, *Historical Writing in England*, II (1982), chapter 6, and John Taylor, *English Historical Literature in the Fourteenth Century* (Oxford, 1987), chapter 9.

9   Walsingham's *Annales* are printed in *Johannis de Trokelowe et Henrici de Blaneford monachorum S. Albani nec non quorundam anonymorum: Chronica et Annales*, ed.

H.T. Riley, (RS, 1866).

10　Gransden, op. cit. p.140.

11　Ibid., p.187; *Historia Vitae et Regni Ricardi Secundi* (Monk of Evesham), ed. George B. Stow (University of Pennsylvania, 1977).

12　See J.I. Catto, 'An alleged Great Council of 1374', *EHR*, LXXXII (1967), 764–771, esp. 765–6.

13　*Eulogium historiarum sive temporis*, ed. F.S. Haydon, 3 volumes (RS, 1858–65), see esp. III. 382–4.

14　Gransden, op. cit. p.183. McFarlane also notes the wide and purposeful dissemination of the 'record and process', op. cit. p.56.

15　*Chronicon Adae de Usk 1377–1421*, ed. E. Maunde Thompson (1904).

16　Ibid., p.xvi; for a detailed account of Usk's career, see the biography in BRUO, III. 1937–8.

17　The attention of historians was first drawn to the Kirkstall chronicle by M.V. Clarke and N. Denholm Young, 'The Kirkstall Chronicle 1355–1400', *Bulletin of the John Rylands Library* (hereafter *BJRL*), XV (1931), 100–137. This was reprinted, in part, in M.V. Clarke, *Fourteenth Century Studies* (Oxford, 1937), pp.99–114. The chronicle has since been edited and translated by John Taylor, *The Kirkstall Abbey Chronicles*, Thoresby Society, (Leeds, 1952).

18　The Dieulacres chronicle was first printed in its entirety by M.V. Clarke and V.H. Galbraith, 'The Deposition of Richard II', *BJRL*, XIV (1930), 125–181; the Latin text of the chronicle occupies pages 164–181. The essay, but not the text of the chronicle was reprinted in Clarke, *Fourteenth Century Studies*, pp.53–98.

19　The brief chronicle from Whalley Abbey (BL Harley Ms 3600) largely corroborates the version of events to be found in the Dieulacres chronicle, see Clarke, *Fourteenth Century Studies*, pp.75–6.

20　Taylor, *Kirkstall Chronicle*, p.75.

21　Clarke, *Fourteenth Century Studies*, p.100.

22　Taylor, *English Historical Literature*, pp.190–2.

23　Clarke, *Fourteenth Century Studies*, p.88.

24　J.J.N. Palmer, 'The authorship, date and historical value of the French Chronicles of the Lancastrian Revolution', *BJRL*, LXI (1978–9), 145–181, 398–421.

25　'Translation of a French Metrical History of the Deposition of King Richard the Second', ed. John Webb, *Archaeologia*, XX (1824), 1–423.

26　*Chronicque de la Traison et Mort Richart Deux roy d'Angleterre*, ed. Benjamin Williams (English Historical Society, 1846).

27　See Peter Ure, 'Shakespeare's play and the French sources of Holinshed's and Stow's account of Richard II', *Notes and Queries*, CXCVIII (1953), 426–9; also M. McKisack, *Medieval History in the Tudor Age* (Oxford, 1971), pp.59–60.

28　Taylor, *English Historical Literature*, pp.179–80.

29　Palmer, op. cit. pp.163–9.

30　Ibid., p.160.

31　Ibid.

32　Ibid., p.179.

33　Palmer argues that only Creton's account may be trusted, but it is possible that he rejects too much of the *Traison* in pointing out some of the obvious borrowings from Creton, see ibid., pp.402–21.

34　C. Given-Wilson, *The Royal Household and the King's Affinity* (1986), pp.222–3 and Philip Morgan, *War and Society in Medieval Cheshire 1277–1403*, Chetham Society, (Manchester, 1987), pp.198–203; see also James L. Gillespie, 'Richard II's archers of the Crown', *Journal of British Studies*, XVIII (1979), 14–29, esp. 19–29.

35　Given-Wilson, op. cit. p.224.

36　Morgan, op. cit. p.203.

37 A. Tuck, *Richard II and the English Nobility* (1973), pp.212–3; and J.L. Kirby, *Henry IV of England* (1970), p.54.

38 Given-Wilson, op. cit. p.224, citing PRO E101/42/12. On 10 July the writ that had been sent to the city of York to send 60 armed men to assist the king at Ware, was superseded on the grounds that the men would be needed to defend the north from the Scots, CCR 1396–9, p.518.

39 3 July 1399 writ from the Duke of York to the local gentry of Sussex to inform them that 'certain enemies' of the king had assembled to invade and had already taken Pevensey castle; they were to besiege the castle with the *posse comitatus* and guard the coasts against invasion, CPR 1396–9, p.596, on this see below p.139. 4 July 1399 a messenger was despatched to Ireland, Dorothy Johnston, 'Richard II's departure from Ireland July 1399', EHR, LXXXXVIII (1983), 758–805, esp. 792, citing PRO E403/562.

40 Johnston, art. cit.

41 Ibid., p.794.

42 Creton, *Archaeologia*, pp.55–9.

43 Johnston, art. cit. pp.793–4.

44 Ibid., p.794.

45 Ibid., p.796.

46 Ibid., pp.797–8.

47 Creton, *Archaeologia*, p.70.

48 Morgan, op. cit. p.224.

49 Given-Wilson, op. cit. p.224.

50 Ibid.

51 Lady Pelham wrote to her husband, in English, on 25 July, printed in Mark Antony Lower, *Historical and Genealogical notices of the Pelham Family* (privately printed, 1873). This letter, lauded by Lower as 'a truer specimen of female bravery or conjugal love and fidelity than this is probably not to be found in the annals of this or any other country', seems now to be lost. See also Taylor, *English Historical Literature*, pp.232–3 and notes there cited. Clearly the *posse comitatus* had maintained the siege of Pevensey Castle for at least three weeks as instructed by the Duke of York, above p.137.

52 Given-Wilson, op. cit. p.225.

53 Morgan, op. cit. pp.204–5 where he records that there were several attempts to rescue Richard as he travelled south with Bolingbroke; and see Given-Wilson, op. cit. p.225.

54 Ibid., p.226.

55 Caroline M. Barron, 'The Quarrel of Richard II with London 1392–97' in *The Reign of Richard II: Essays in honour of May McKisack*, eds. F.R.H. Du Boulay and Caroline M. Barron (1971), pp.173–201.

56 Barron, 'Tyranny' esp. pp.10–14.

57 *An English Chronicle of the Reigns of Richard II, Henry IV, Henry V, and Henry VI*, ed. J.S. Davies, Camden Society (1855), 10. According to an unprinted section of Giles's chronicle Arundel chose to be led along Cheapside in the hope that he would be rescued, BL Royal MS. 13 C. I f.109v.

58 Monk of Evesham, op. cit. pp.143–4. It appears that the earl's son, Thomas, was helped to escape from custody in the Coldharbour house of John Holland, Duke of Exeter, by a London mercer, William Scot, *The Great Chronicle of London*, eds. A.H. Thomas and I.D. Thornley (1938), p.50.

59 *The History of the King's Works*, ed. H.M. Colvin, I. *The Middle Ages* (1963), 487–8.

60 PRO E403/555.

61 CPR 1396–9, pp.319, 333. For the Londoners who went with Richard's retinue to Ireland, see ibid., pp.519, 522, 523, 546, 566, 573; also *Calendar of the Plea and Memoranda Rolls of the City of London, 1381–1412*, ed. A.H. Thomas (Cambridge, 1932), pp.261, 262. Included in the London contingent were Christopher Tyldesley and four other London goldsmiths.

62 Caroline M. Barron, 'Richard Whittington: the man behind the myth' in *Studies in London History presented to P. E. Jones*, eds. A.E.J. Hollaender and William Kellaway (1969), pp.197–248, esp. pp.205–6, 211, 229–30.

63 J.M.W. Bean, 'Henry IV and the Percies', *History*, XLIV (1959), 212–27 esp. 220.

64 *Traison*, pp.180–2; Thomas Gascoigne preserved a list of the promises made by Henry in 1399 and broken by 1406, *Loci e Libro Veritatum*, ed. J.E.T. Rogers, (Oxford, 1881), pp.229–31.

65 *Eulogium*, III. 381. John Taylor accepts that Henry sent out letters from Pontefract, *English Historical Literature*, p.230. In 1326 Queen Isabella and Prince Edward sent letters to the Londoners expounding their policy and asking for support. Copies were posted in Cheapside, ibid., p.122.

66 *Calendar of Letter Books of the City of London: Letter Book H*, ed. R.R. Sharpe (1907).

67 *CCR 1396–9*, p.518; *CPR 1396–9*, pp.587, 592, 597; Given-Wilson, op. cit. p.225 and references there cited.

68 The writ was sent by Archbishop Walden to Robert Braybrook, Bishop of London (who was, in fact, with the king in Ireland) dated 15 July 1399, Register of Robert Braybrook, Guildhall Library MS 9531/3 f.252v.

69 *CCR 1396–9*, p.509.

70 *Foedera*, ed. T. Rymer, 10 volumes (3rd edn. The Hague, 1735–45), III. iv. 187.

71 For a chronology of these events, see James Sherborne, 'Richard II's return to Wales July 1399', *Welsh History Review*, VII (1974–5), 389–402.

72 *Traison*, p.187. A letter in French, rather similar in tone to that recorded by the French chronicler was written by Henry from Burton on Trent to the Council on 17 July 1403, 'que la Dieu mercy nous sumes asses fort encountre tous les malveullantz de nous et de notre roiaume', *Proceedings and Ordinances of the Privy Council of England*, ed, N.H. Nicolas, 6 volumes (1834–7), I. 208.

73 *Traison*, pp.212–3; Creton, op. cit. p.376; Usk, op. cit. p.28.

74 A chronology for Richard and Henry's journey south is provided by the monk of Evesham, op. cit. p.156. The 'official' itinerary, derived from writs, is provided by the editor, ibid., p.208. The 'official' itinerary dates are given here. The only reference to this London delegation to be found in any of the civic records is provided by the accounts of the Merchant Taylors' Company. They paid 61s 4d as the costs of four horses and a man to ride to Leicester with the mayor, Merchant Taylors' Hall, MS A 4 f.4. It seems likely that these payments, recorded under the year 1398–9, were for the mayor's delegation, but the place cannot have been Leicester since there is no evidence that the royal party went through that town which would have been considerably off the direct route from Chester to London.

75 Richard was taken first to Westminster and then transfered by water to the Tower. Henry meanwhile was received in London 'gloriose', and stayed at the palace of the bishop, Robert Braybrook, Monk of Evesham, op. cit. p.157. Braybrook, who returned to south Wales with Richard, seems then to have left the king, perhaps because at 63 he was too old to make the rough journey across Wales to Conway. He finally reached London on 22 August, only ten days ahead of Henry and Richard. As L.H. Butler remarked 'Nothing seems to have been easier than for the Braybrooks to accomplish a politic change of sides in 1399', 'Robert Braybrook, bishop of London and his kinsmen', (unpublished Oxford DPhil, 1951), pp.162–6.

76 J.H. Wylie, *Henry IV* (1884), I. 420.

77 The Taylors paid 33s 4d to the minstrels, and 6s 8d for their drink, Accounts, see note 74, f.7; the Grocers paid 48s 4d to the minstrels, 8s 6d for their hoods and 6s 8d for their victuals, *Facsimile of the First Volume of the Ms Archives of the Worshipful Company of Grocers of the City of London 1345–1463*, ed. J.A. Kingdon 2 volumes (1886) I. 83.

78 *Rot. Parl.* III. 428; writ to mayor to enforce the new regulations, *CCR 1339–1402*, p.182 and see *Rot. Parl.* III. 477.

79  PRO Ancient Petition 6079; *Rot. Parl.* III. 429; *Calendar of Charter Rolls 1341–1417*, III, 399.

80  *SR*, I. 346–7; II. 117–8; *Rot. Parl.* III. 442–3; Ruth Bird, *The Turbulent London of Richard II* (1949), pp.103, 111 and n2. On the fishmongers' monopoly, see *Rot. Parl.* III. 444; *SR*, II. 118. Richard had restored the fishmongers' monopoly in May 1399 before going to Ireland, *CPR 1396–9*, p.575.

81  *Rot. Parl.* III. 443–4; *SR*, II. 118. On Coroners, see PRO Ancient Petition 6075; *Rot. Parl.* III. 429; W. Kellaway, 'The Coroner in Medieval London', in *Studies in London History*, pp.75–91, esp. pp.83–4.

82  PRO Ancient Petition 6080; *Letter Book H*, pp.53, 222. When Henry IV confirmed the charter for the Hanse merchants he attempted to demand reciprocal privileges for English merchants abroad, *CPR 1399–1401*, pp.57, 140; *Calendar of Letter Books of the City of London: Letter Book I*, ed. R.R. Sharpe (1909), pp.5–6.

83  PRO E368/172 f.73; E404/15/462; *CPR 1399–1401*, pp.407–8.

84  Barron, 'Richard Whittington', p.216 and n2.

85  McFarlane, *Lancastrian Kings*, p.69; E.F. Jacob, *The Fifteenth Century* (Oxford, 1961), pp.25–7.

86  The French sources accuse Aumerle of betraying the plot to Henry, but for a different account of how the news reached the king, see *An English Chronicle*, p.20. Thomas Knolles was later paid for his expenses in providing 10 armed men and 20 archers to defend the Tower at this time, PRO E401/604; E403/564 under date 4 February. For the 1400 rising in Cheshire see P. McNiven, 'The Cheshire Rising of 1400', *BJRL*, LII (1970), 375–96.

87  An incomplete account of the trial of some of the conspirators before Thomas Knolles, the mayor, and Matthew Southworth, the recorder, of London is preserved in *Letter Book I*, pp.1–4.

88  For a survey of those who took part in the Epiphany rising see Given-Wilson, op. cit. pp.224–5. Writs pardoning those who took part are to be found in *CPR 1399–1402*, pp.180, 192, 193, 194, 220, 225, 228, 319, 385. On Brocas and Blount see T.F. Tout, *Chapters in the Administrative History of Medieval England* (Manchester, 1920–33), III. 413, n3; IV. 143, n1, 345; V. 307, n3 and references to Blount to be found in Given-Wilson, op. cit. passim.

89  The clerks who supported Richard included three Cambridge graduates, William Feriby, Richard Maudeleyn and Ralph Selby, see *BRUC*, pp.225, 396–7, 517. Feriby and Maudeleyn were both executors of Richard's will. John Bathe, rector of Stapleford Salisbury, revealed Feriby's hiding place to some officers of the city of London and was subsequently granted absolution, *Calendar of Papal Registers 1396–1404*, p.396.

90  By 29 January 1400 the French king knew that Richard was dead, Jacob, *The Fifteenth Century*, p.27.

91  *An English Chronicle*, p.23.

92  Ibid., pp.23–4; for a discussion of this protest against Henry see Jacob, *The Fifteenth Century*, pp.27–8; R.L. Storey, 'Clergy and common law in the reign of Henry IV', *Medieval Legal Records edited in memory of C.A.F. Meekings*, eds. R.F. Hunnisett and J.B. Post (1978), pp.342–408, esp. pp.353–61. See also *CCR 1399–1402*, pp.529, 570, 577.

93  This argument is developed further in Caroline M. Barron, 'The Art of Kingship: Richard II 1377–1399', *History Today*, 35 (June, 1985), 31–7.

94  Stubbs, *Constitutional History*, II. 499.

95  James Sherborne's interesting and convincing article, 'Perjury and the Lancastrian Revolution of 1399', *Welsh History Review*, 14 (1988), 217–41, unfortunately appeared after this article had gone to print. Although the emphasis is different, our conclusions are perfectly compatible.

# Index